THE SENSELESS HANDLING OF FAT PEOPLE

Susanne Brandheim

Copyright © 2023

All Rights Reserved

No part of this publication may be reproduced, stored in a retrieval system, or transmitted in any form or by any means, electronic, mechanical, photocopying, recording, or otherwise, without the written permission of the author or the publisher.

Contents

Dedication i
Acknowledgments ii
About the Author iii
Foreword 1
Introduction 5
The Threat Images 16
The Health Ideologists 41
They Created the Perfect Enemy 65
The Primitive Notions 88
Entrepreneurs' Market 118
The Failed Actions 155
Stigmatization 180
A Distinguishing System 201
To Be Able To See How We Have Participated In Our Own Oppression 224
A Struggle for Knowledge 246
The Health Ideology Must Be Challenged 275
Resistance and Liberating Issues 298
Nine Keys to Resistance 323
Traps on the Way to Knowledge 350
Concluding Thoughts 375
Final Words 382
Sources 387

Dedication

To my son, Felix.

Acknowledgments

I am thankful for all the resistance I faced. It forced me to work harder, to try to understand their fears, their aggressions, and their hurt self-images when I called out the systemic harm. I could do this, however, only because I stood firmly on the shoulders of those who felt unwelcomed in this world by near and dear, caring institutions, media, governments, and the following entrenchment of negative public attitudes towards fat people – even among fat people themselves. I see you. I feel you. I am you.

In expressing my gratitude, I extend appreciation to translator Michelle Mulheron for her efforts in conveying the message across linguistic boundaries.

About the Author

Susanne Brandheim has spent over 25 years excavating obesity management's underlying ideas, implementations, ignorance, and consequences. In a quest to find the drivers behind the senseless handling of fat people in welfare societies, she earned a bachelor's in psychology and a master in sociology and ended up with a doctoral thesis in social work: A Systemic Stigmatization of Fat People (2017).

Susanne has several academic publications on fatness stigma, involving topics such as misrecognition, transformation, psychological distress, risk, and fat hatred. The senseless handling of fat people turns a pointing finger toward the attitudes, entrepreneurs, and ideas behind the counterproductive launching of an obesity epidemic.

Nowadays, Susanne lives a quiet life amid nature outside of Örebro in Sweden. Here, sequels to this book slowly take shape in days divided between passionate dialogues, learning more, deep philosophical thought, and emotional rest from a stressful life.

Foreword

"Diet. Sharpen up. Hide your innermost feelings. These violent cultural edicts make us strangers to our own bodies, ourselves, and others. They charge us with the belief that we are chronic problems in constant need of fixing. Don't fall for it. Believe me: the problem is in the culture, not in you."

- Linda Bacon

One day the obesity epidemic will be behind us. I don't mean that the fat people will be gone. I mean the epidemic - the outrageous idea that fat people pose an epidemic threat to the survival of society. Scientists will, in the future, try to understand the period in our history when body fat was considered a threat to humanity itself. They will try to make this historic era understandable. Eventually, a reasonably coherent moral lesson can be learned. As is often the case when we look back to see from a distance how people have been harmed in insensitive systems, we will realize how wrong it was. In the guise of time, we will reason about how unscrupulous the people who dealt with fat people seemed to be at the time.

Fat people have been treated unspeakably badly. This is evidenced by a number of books in which, for the most part, fat women have described how a contemptuous environment has made them feel and how it made them unable to live fully as welcomed members of society. A couple of examples of such stories are One Is Not Born Fat (Gabrielle Deydiers) and Hunger: A Memoir of My Body (Roxane Gay). These stories bear witness to the struggles that fat people are forced into in their relationships, in their self-image, and in their everyday lives. At the same time, the number of people, mainly women, who have felt fat without ever having been fat has been innumerable.

Another type of literature has been critical of what is being done to fat people for decades. Examples include Paul Campos' The Diet Myth, Michael Gard and Jan Wright's The Obesity Epidemic, Linda Bacon's Body Respect, Harriet Brown's Body of Truth, and Helene A Shugart's Heavy: The Obesity Crisis in Cultural Context. Here, the authors have convincingly shown that the experiences of fat people during this period had an origin - a structural and systemic basis. In line with them, I myself have presented a doctoral thesis - A Systemic Stigmatization of Fat People - which describes the stigmatization to which fat people have been actively subjected for decades. Now, in this book, I take my critique further. How could we allow public health, medical and ideological systems to single out fat people to the point where the fat body became the most despised bodily variety in the West? Who was so obsessed with the idea that every fat person must achieve thinness through simple disciplinary commands? Why were fat people singled out, not just as sick, but as carriers of an epidemic?

For us social scientists, human history is always a tale of order and disorder. History is filled with instances when those who have governed our societies have attempted to remedy, heal or otherwise deal with a perceived disorder. The examples are many. Human variations such as skin color, ethnicity, sexuality, cognitive abilities, disabilities, poverty, and old age have all been treated as something in need of ordering up by more orderly people. Often the measures have been presented as benevolent, even as caring. But in this book, I will show how this so-called benevolence made fat people sick and branded them as immoral deviants.

I will show how contempt for fat people has been maintained and normalized within an extreme ideology of what the concept of health should include. I will show the forces that have worked together to brand into the self-image of fat people that their bodies are not welcome here. I will discuss how the shared belief was formed that the fat body must be expelled, cut away, starved out, and rejected. I think the question should be answered in the present and not in future history books. History otherwise has a tendency to repeat itself. Once it is transformed into a bygone era, it somehow gives us the right to distance ourselves from the actions of people of the past. I think it is more responsible not to distance ourselves, to hold those who do people harm accountable in the present, and to seek ways to stop it today.

For 25 years, I have diligently studied the widespread exploitation of fat people. I earned a bachelor's degree in psychology, a master's degree in sociology, and a doctorate in social work. And it was all about this topic. At the same time, I plowed through the medical research and public health policies published and launched in the fight against the so-called obesity epidemic. The result, alongside my thesis, is this book.

Susanne, Örebro

Introduction

For many, being a fat person means the disapproving eyes of others on a daily basis. The word obesity epidemic has made the public anxious, especially when the carriers of the epidemic are also considered to be culturally unattractive. Many thin people feel that fat people are treated too kindly. They feel that the big fat threat has not been taken seriously enough by our politicians and authorities. They think that's why so many people are still fat. According to them, tougher action is needed. Someone once told me that the more people told him he was too fat, the more grateful he would be. Then he would have the chance to do something about it. For me, this book is partly about trying to understand the people who reason that way. I want to know how the idea that we should tell each other that we're not good enough took hold with so many people. The extent of being despised in the body you wake up in every day is incomprehensible to those who have never experienced it themselves. But the contempt is downright life-changing for those who are exposed.

In May 2015, the Swedish news program Aktuellt showed a feature on fat children. It was about parents who starve and weight-bully their children. Viewers saw and heard the story of a nearly 70-year-old woman talking about her mother. The mother, who did not want a fat girl, who wanted her daughter to become a ballet dancer, compulsively starved her daughter from the age of six. "It's bullying that never ends," the woman said. It was extremely powerful. It made me, as a viewer, feel how body contempt can concretely destroy people's lives through words and actions. However, what followed in the program showed that the producers, like many others, had not really understood anything about fat people, how they are treated, or what the ultimate consequences of body contempt are.

Instead of questioning the pressure that fat children are subjected to, the question was asked how the pressure can be reworded so that children are told in a gentler way that their bodies are not good enough. A traditional obesity researcher - that is, a researcher who seeks solutions to how people can become slimmer - was interviewed here next. He expressed surprise that fat people felt bullied and singled out. Because that's not what healthcare is supposed to be about, he continued. The job of health care was to help these fat kids, not hurt them. Really? I thought. At a time when the media, backed by obesity researchers, paints fat children daily as the worst public health disaster ever, are scientists surprised that mothers are obsessively trying to starve their fat children?

In the next step, a child psychologist was interviewed. The reporter asked how parents can help their fat children without offending them. The psychologist replied that parents should support their children in their weight loss, not insult them. The alarm bells were ringing loudly in my head. So their question remained. How can we tell our children that their bodies are not good enough - in a kinder, more caring way? The answer is simple. It can't be done. You can't approach another person with the attitude that they and their body are not good enough and then try to support them in becoming more fit. People cannot negotiate themselves and their lives in guilt and shame. Instead, they turn inward to protect their existential selves. Or they align themselves outwardly in their desire to be accepted by sacrificing parts of their self-determination. Many end up with eating disorders for life. Others diet themselves fat.

A few years ago, then UK Prime Minister David Cameron wanted fat, poor people who refused to undergo a starvation operation to have their Stipend reduced. A local councilor in Sweden also thought this was a good idea. Because he said, "We have to do everything we can in the fight against the epidemic."[1] The idea crosses all ethical boundaries in the view of human integrity and variations. Racial biology, forced sterilizations, anti-homosexual medication, and lobotomies of people we have considered deviants are historical examples of some of the worst ideas humanity has engineered in a moralizing quest for a clean population. The horrors of abusive treatment of people are only apparent in retrospect. Ideology, especially when

---
[1] DN 2015

practiced by our social institutions, tends to appear right in the present. We must not forget that many people who were sterilized and lobotomized underwent the treatment "voluntarily." They did so because the experts of the time said it was the best option for them. They said it was for their own good.

Fat people are now considered to be dangerously numerous, and they are said to shake the very foundations of society. Fatness is therefore addressed at all levels of society. Everyone should be thin. At the same time, in a civilized society, people should not be bullied or insulted for the way they look and function. We have created codes of ethics, discrimination laws, and a host of formal and informal rules that agree that every person should be treated with respect. But body weight is not yet protected by such laws. The research that has asked fat people directly shows unequivocally that fat people are not treated with respect at all. Instead, they are devalued in a pervasive system. The system extends from ideological currents, political decisions, through the media, further into caring institutions, and into their closest relationships to eventually inevitably end up in the fat people's own self-image.

And the fewer social and cultural resources they have, such as status and power, the more they are damaged.

The art of reducing a person's value

A poor self-image, said plastic surgeon Maxwell Maltz, can easily be created psychologically. All you have to do is set a standard and then convince the person that they don't conform to that standard. Fat people have been convinced for a long time now that they do not conform to the norm.[2] But because we must not offend people, the belittling of fat people requires that they be dehumanized in various ways. For a whole society, with all its institutions, policies, and interventions, to get away with dehumanization, it must happen in several stages so that it is not visible.

The first step is to separate the unwanted fatness from its opposite - thinness. Fatness, on the one hand, is easy to distinguish because it is visible to the eye. On the other hand, it is difficult to draw a line exactly where thinness ends, and fatness begins. But to distinguish these appearances, it doesn't matter if the line is a little blurred. On the contrary, the blurriness helps to create anxiety and worry just about risking being overweight - and suddenly belonging to the fat. Blurred boundaries keep people's tendencies to conform alert. That's why most adults in the Western world invest in a bathroom scale. They can stand on it daily to check they haven't crossed the line. They are thus actively participating in segregation through their attempts not to belong to the other, inferior side.

---

[2] Maltz 1960

The second step is that the unwanted fatness must be symbolized. This means that the group of fat people must be made visible and reinforced as undesirable in addition to their already visible bodies. Because of the beauty industry, the dieting industry, mass media, social media, public health recommendations, health care advice, school health, and countless influential commentators, the fat body has come to symbolize disease, ugliness, dirt, immorality, stupidity, weakness, selfishness, flaccidity, and inability.

In the third step, the management of the unwanted fat must be organized. Anti-fatness measures are organized from the global to the local level. Billions of dollars are spent annually on organizing the management of fatness. Schools, workplaces, health care, politics, the market, and research are organized in the fight. In fact, individuals organize their entire lives, their eating, their routines, and their movement with the primary aim of keeping the fat off or losing the so-called excess weight they already feel they have.

Finally, in a fourth step, the distinction between the unwanted-damaged fat body and a healthy thin body must be further polarized. The opposition between fat and thin must be sharpened even more. The designation of fatness must be based on moral notions of right and wrong, worthy and unworthy, and pure and dangerous. It is not enough that fatness is clearly undesirable in itself. There must be a counter-image that is as clearly morally desirable as the fat is undesirable. The celebration of thinness, therefore, becomes in itself a distinction of that which is healthy, capable, productive, and self-purifying. Thinness and fatness are so polarized today that some women would rather be dead than fat, and some children would rather lose an arm than consider themselves fat. It's not strange at all. No one wants to be one of the undesirables.

Purity and danger - a pair of opposites in all societies

Having a fat child can trigger such social anxiety and despair that parents try to starve their own child. The fat body is so negatively charged that many fat people arrange their entire lives to avoid social contexts, condescending looks, and words. This book, however, is not about the fat, although I do turn directly to them as the book progresses. Instead, my book is about what holds them down and creates contempt for them. People, institutions, and systems have actively identified the fat body as something that needs to be addressed for the sake of society. It is high time to review this large-scale social experiment.

That fatness poses any kind of threat to society is not a scientific discovery. It is an idea. According to the American sociologist Natalie Boero, there are two main reasons for today's alarmist view of the fat body. First, the media, which reaches into everyone's homes and minds, has managed to fit its moral scare stories alongside other pre-existing narratives about what is right and wrong with people. Second, society's drive to label human phenomena as diseases in order to cure them has widened and broken new ground into areas never before considered diseases.[3]

The globally funded war against an obesity epidemic has, despite research and obesity expertise, failed to cure fat people. Instead, many thin people have become even slimmer and almost obsessed with health, while many fat people have become fatter and even more despised. Rather than improving the living conditions of an allegedly sick group, our common society has, thus, openly and legitimately created people who feel like failures. With a damaged self-image and a weakened position, fat people today have to fight the contempt that the whole haunting ring has led to. For people who despise fat people, fat people do not look like they are struggling. They are still fat. That's how ideology works for those who obey it. It simplifies connections and images to fit into the already established division between what is considered good and what is considered bad. That's why we don't have to think when we see a fat person. Ideology has done thinking for us.

Today, more and more researchers are questioning the links that have been established between body weight and ill-health. They criticize not only the veracity of the

---

[3] Boero 2013

correlations but also their lack of usefulness and unethical consequences.[4] However, the critical research never reaches the public, as the media actively participates in and spreading the disaster thinking about the fat body. A deeply problematic process has therefore been allowed to continue undisturbed within the institutions and by the people concerned with health and ill-health. As a result, many still feel that fatness must continue to be combated with the same ineffective measures. They believe that fat people must be blamed and pressured to lose weight because they simply have to get thin. They still believe that the dangers of fatness are scientifically proven.

What a society's inhabitants are led to believe about their fellow human beings can be explained with the help of systems theory. To consider systems is to consider how things work together, consciously or unconsciously, to ultimately lead to a particular outcome. It is about understanding how a particular phenomenon arises through a network of actions and not just one action. Systems analysis has been used, for example, to understand in retrospect why people once measured Sami skulls, why they lobotomized people who seemed incomprehensible to them, why they sterilized people with undesirable appearances and traits, and how slavery, dictatorships, and Nazism could have emerged.

---

[4] Rail et al. 2010

If history has taught us anything, it is that groups of humanity have always been capable of harming other groups of people. And there are always systemic explanations for how this could happen. When no one says they want to hurt fat people, and at the same time, almost all fat people get hurt, then we have to turn to systemic explanations. It's not necessarily about people lying. Rather, it's about each part of a damaging system being blind to how it contributes to the whole. In dealing with fat people, power, ideology, money, careers, professions, politics, and self-images are at stake. The negative consequences for fat people are clear. They testify to a feeling of total failure.

Anthropologist Mary Douglas has described how all primitive societies maintain order through the opposites of purity and danger. In order to preserve a society's order, what is considered pure should be celebrated and rewarded, while what is considered a danger should be driven out and punished. Douglas's main point, however, is not her descriptions of the tribes and indigenous peoples traditionally thought to live in primitive societies far removed from our own. Instead, she argues that this primitive logic of purity and danger is fully active today in what we call advanced societies - like our own welfare democracy. In this book, I will show what this systemic logic behind the senseless handling of fat people looks like.

I will show how a specific health ideology, in its quest for pure citizens, has portrayed fat people as dangerous in the form of failures. I start my explanation with the anxiety-inducing and profoundly misanthropic images of danger.

"Evolution" ©Patrick Boivin (in White 2013)

The Threat Images

The management of fat people in welfare countries both creates and draws on the images of fatness we carry. Therefore, to get to the bottom of how our attitudes to fatness are maintained, let's start at the core of contempt - in the almost apocalyptic image of threat. The British sociologist Francis Ray White investigated how fat people, through images, have been portrayed as signs of evolution gone wrong.[5] The image above is one of the images investigated.

The image illustrates the evolution of a crouching ape-man with a primitive weapon. First, to a more upright-standing anthropomorphic variant with a simple composite weapon. Then to a fully upright man with a technically

---

[5] White 2013

advanced weapon and a spade. In the next stage, a shorter, squat, and fat man with no working tools or weapons at all. Instead, he has fast food and a soda in his hands. He has also lost his hair. The final step shows a pig. In context, the pig appears to be a throwback to something far below the first monkey - to something even more primitive. The fat man, who represents the decay towards becoming a pig, eats instead of hunting or building. It is an image that is radically designed to dehumanize the fat man, regardless of how you feel about pigs.

The British social worker and criminologist Stanley Cohen is known for his descriptions of moral panic.[6] He described that for a threat to work, the threat images need to be filled with so-called symbolic power. You can't just put a fat person next to a thin person to produce the image of a threat. The image must provide a moral narrative. In the evolution image, the fat man is presented as a symbolic step between the top and bottom of humanity - between man and pig. In sharp contrast to the irresponsible fat man, the worker and the soldier in the step ahead is vigorous and determined. Both men are, at the same time, in the same culture. There are both advanced weapons and fast food. They are both exposed to the same temptations, but the image says there is a choice. It says it is possible to manage one's environment and master one's urges so that we do not

---

[6] Cohen 2002

become or remain fat. It is possible to choose a spade and a weapon instead of food. So thus, the image, while threatening, is also a celebration of the efficiency and rational control allegedly required to stay thin today.

Threat images, as I said, are carriers of power. That power can only be understood in relation to the cultural and political tensions in which those images land. I remember the clothing chains that, decades ago, launched their extremely slim models on meter-high pillars around the country of Sweden. This was long before social media pumped out body ideals to every person's mobile phone. However, criticism of the body ideal was strong even then: "That's not what women look like!", "Young girls are influenced to starve themselves!", "Why don't you use regular bodies in advertising instead?" The interesting thing, however, was not the criticism itself. The interesting thing was the criticism of the criticism! There were many (men) who flapped their arms and said those images were nothing to whine about. "Anyone who doesn't like pictures can look away instead," they argued, claiming that pictures are not reality. They are just pictures. This attitude reflects a profound ignorance of the cultural and political tensions that have always surrounded the (female) body as an object. That attitude also testifies to a profound ignorance of how much images actually determine what we think of our fellow human beings. The power that images emit can simply only be perceived by those who are sufficiently attuned to ideological power or are themselves singled out and devalued in these images.

The American sociologist Jeffrey Alexander uses the concept of power in a way that may explain why the public does not see the threat of fatness as the exercise of power. For Alexander, power is not just about traditions, social structures, and material resources. Instead, he says, the targeting of certain groups is done through "aesthetic means of legitimation"[7] In plain language, the targeting of fat people is done through appealing, perhaps even seductive, images and representations. The singling out occurs, quite simply, in images and representations that people like. Not in images they are provoked by.

The veracity of a threat image does not have to be fixed. There are powerful interests that need threat images and can devote a lot of energy and resources to portraying them as dangerous as possible. In fact, threat images can be crucial to the existence of an entire organization. Nazism, ISIS, and the defense and war units of nations are all examples of organizations that need a threat image. Threat images can also be used to allocate more resources to a particular research area. Medical obesity research is a prime example. The threat of an allegedly growing obesity epidemic has generated billions of dollars in research

---

[7] Alexander & Smith 2003

funding for researchers to apply for the solution to the epidemic. The fact that they are not a single step closer to a solution seems irrelevant.[8]

The image of a threat may be clear. But it can also be as vague as you like. Ambiguity can even be an advantage, as it can be taken as evidence of how difficult the alleged threat really is to grasp. At the same time, a basic rule is that the more simplistic the threat image, the greater its impact. What the public often perceives as contradictory knowledge - for example, that one day we should, according to experts, eat potatoes and the next day potatoes are deadly - paradoxically reinforces the threat image. The content may, therefore, not be the most important aspect of a threat picture. What is important is that the threat image itself is kept alive. This flood of dangers opens up all aspects of life to surveillance and control.[9] Unfortunately, this also applies to our desire to control and monitor others.

Threat Images Speak to Our Primitiveness

Threat imagery is the opposite of intellectual nuance. They are meant to open our emotions, not our doubts about the veracity of the images. We already know that we are not part of an evolution of pigs. The imagery in the threat image serves more as an emotional reminder that things are

---

[8] I am aware of the new 'revolutionary' injections that reduce people's appetite. We have yet to see the long-term effects of these drugs.
[9] Crawford 2004

going to hell if we do nothing. Images of threat thus become, on a primitive level, identity-creating for those who are threatened. A clear example is the pro-ana movement, which since the 1990s, has been celebrating the anorexic, self-starved body. Here, young people use discouraging examples of fatness to motivate themselves to starve themselves into a fat-free identity. A thirteen-year-old girl, severely ill with anorexia, told me that she devoured documentaries about fat people. Nothing, she said, could make her more certain about her identity as a fat-free non-eater. While watching these documentaries, she would walk back and forth in front of the TV screen, spitting into a cloth to get rid of as much body weight as possible.

Threat images can also be used to divert attention from something else. For example, nationalist movements may paint one-dimensional negative images of immigrants to reinforce the positive image of themselves as heroes of the nation. At the same time, this means that many images of threat act as a unifying and solidarity-building force for those who are threatened. The phobia of fatness has had the ability to create cohesion and solidarity around body production, health, and thinness. For example, openly dieting in the workplace can create topics of conversation filled with encouragement and solidarity. Social media brings together many health enthusiasts who are happy to use human fatness as a starting point for passionate discussions about how others have not cut themselves as well as they have.

In fact, it is possible to succeed with any threat. All it needs is enough public space to be repeated. However, the more unlikely a threat is, the more force is required for the repetition to work.

It's both about successfully pinpointing a destructive process and presenting suggestions for ways to repair it.[10] For the image to be successful, it needs to evoke, in the recipient, "symbolic extension and psychological identification."[11] In short, enough recipients need to buy the threat image. The threat image must land in beliefs and power relations that are already open to that kind of threat.

Much of the anxiety, worry, and fear that people carry is due to threat images. We live our lives in a flux of permanent threats, ranging from the end of the world, through war and climate change, to the fear of losing parts of our lives we have built up in terms of relationships, status, and wealth. In such a permanent state of threat, we become increasingly fragile in the face of new threats. The more widespread these threats become, the deeper they penetrate our skin. There is no limit to the amount of threat images that can penetrate simultaneously. The increasing

---

[10] Alexander et al. 2004
[11] Ibid., p. 199

proportion of old people, a melting Antarctic, meteor rains, the obesity epidemic, viruses, refugee disasters, police shortages, crime, socio-economic collapse, and endangered animal and plant species have no problem competing to be "one of the most difficult challenges we face." They don't steal energy from each other. Rather, they reinforce each other when the sheer volume of threats stimulates our sense of being in crisis. Each threat image seems to open our vulnerability wide for us to take in more threat images. It is, so to speak, easier to convince someone who already thinks everything is going to hell that one more thing is going to hell.

The hard part of the jungle of threats is sorting out real threats from imagined ones. This has proven to be very difficult. When there are strong vested interests behind amplifying some threats and diminishing others, the desire for more knowledge becomes blurred.

This means that threat images are handed over pre-packaged to the public's emotions and moral opinions. This is a primitive way to go in what should be an enlightened society. An enlightened society would not have allowed the image of fatness as a threat to go unchallenged. Only by trying to understand the forces behind a threat image can we have an honest debate about our view of humanity, our values of others, and our treatment of human variation. Right now, when an ever-growing dieting market is inundating the public with threats about the dangers of fatness, while the dangers are not scientifically proven, the threat must be shattered. It has to be because threat images give some people the right to do things to other people.

Threat Images Give Some the Right To Do Things To Others

Threat images give some people a self-imposed right to take action. Fatness has been pointed out with drama in sensationalist headlines. Headlines such as "Our children are dying of obesity" and "Now more people die of obesity than starvation in the world" create calls for even tougher action against fatness. Institutions, policies, and action programs are being built. Together they have not solved the so-called threat but rather reinforced the seriousness of the threat in the eyes of the public. At the same time, all these organizations against fatness are built around the idea that the solution to the problem lies with the fat people themselves. In this way, the very organization of the threat image is completely free of responsibility. In the eyes of the public, fat people become responsible because they do not become thin despite all these measures. The fact that the measures themselves are not effective due to pervasive ignorance is not highlighted.

Preventive measures have been built into the threat images. Prevention has almost been presented as a new science.

The authorities should not just make sure that those who are already fat fix themselves. Everyone at risk of becoming fat should do so too. And the threat continues to grow larger and more obvious. Eventually, it is so deeply cultivated in entire populations that everyone knows that fatness is dangerous, but no one can answer why. No one asks questions about why fatness is dangerous and when it is not, how dangerous the fatness is, or how harmless it is. The public thinks it is already mapped out. But around the launch of an obesity epidemic, it is useful to reflect on what philosopher Paul Feyerabend said: "When arguments really have an effect, it seems to depend more on how often they are repeated than on their actual content."[12] Consider how often you have heard that an obesity epidemic threatens us and how rarely you have heard anything of real substance on that issue. Consider how often you have heard any nuance whatsoever about the difference between 10 kilos and 75 kilos of so-called excess weight.

In simple terms, threat images make the public feel that the social order is in some way fatally disturbed. Let us return to anthropologist Mary Douglas who described how all societies, modern and traditional, maintain a sense of order by creating images of cultural counter-pairs.[13] By exaggerating, separating, purifying, and classifying good

---

[12] Feyerabend 1975
[13] Douglas 1984

versus evil, pure versus dangerous, and good versus bad, an appearance of order and security is created. Security is created when society addresses the designated bad. The threat image can thus be likened to a moral map of the future, where not only is the threat clear. The map also shows the other way - the possibility. The very purpose of even creating a threat image is to simultaneously launch, in its shadow, the defense that can prevent the threat from being realized. The threat of fatness, for example, can be considered eliminated when we no longer see fat people in our streets and squares. Many hope for that. They think it would make them safe.

In the US, the threat of fatness is linked to pure war rhetoric. American media frequently show images of a fat Uncle Sam as a reminder of how fatness threatens the nation itself. In the 2003 reality show The National Body Challenge, the first season opened with a voiceover announcing that "the war against the nation's obesity begins at one of the world's toughest military training grounds - the naval base at Quantico." In the reality show, the fat contestants undergo rock-hard challenges in mud and low temperatures. In slow motion, viewers witness a bunch of panting, crawling, crying, and collapsing fat Americans as they struggle to become worthy patriots in a country shaken by terrorism and, therefore, in dire need of well-trained soldiers.[14]

Threat images reveal the seriousness with which society views the threat and the force with which the threat should be responded to. The existing power that created the first threat images, that had the language, the arenas, and the strategies, was the emerging field of a new modern public health ideology. Their demanding tone, focusing on the health of the population, was taken as evidence of the seriousness of the obesity problem. It was about the health of both the individual and the nation - a rhetoric cut from 1930s wish lists of strong, healthy, disciplined citizens. How far such authorities can go with their threats without being criticized depends on the moral limit of any threat. The limit is reached when the violation of people becomes more pervasive than the threat itself. At that point, ideas about human rights and whether the threat image is even real begin to be bumped and bruised. I would argue that that line has long been reached when it comes to dealing with fat people. The line was actually reached immediately when fat people were suddenly singled out as the carriers of an epidemic. From the moment healthy people started being called sick in a full-scale global experiment to create a purer population.

---

[14] Biltekoff 2007

Fat People Were Singled Out as Carriers of an Epidemic

To even suggest that perfectly healthy people carry an epidemic because they are fat is an incredible suggestion. The Centers for Disease Control and Prevention (CDC) states that the most well-known epidemics have been yellow fever, smallpox, measles, and polio. In fresh memory, we can perhaps add COVID-19 to these. Others would add more complex epidemics such as Ebola, cholera, dengue fever, influenza, asthmatic conditions, and SARS. But, the CDC adds, even non-communicable diseases like diabetes and obesity exist in epidemic proportions. By epidemic proportions, then, they mean a phenomenon that exceeds in number some kind of abstract expectation. Within the framework of epidemic proportions, there are no limits to what can be included. Everything from violence and mental illness to mobile phone use and business bankruptcies.

In fact, the idea that fatness was an indication of an epidemic outbreak came from the same agency - the CDC. The idea was spread internationally via a PowerPoint presentation in 1997.[15] The man who presented the epidemic was a new employee of the CDC, USA. The ambitious man believed that fatness was a far greater threat to humanity than the media and scientists had previously

---

[15] Oliver 2006, p. 38

recognized. In his slide presentation, he showed the United States depicted as a living organism, where fatness had spread like an infection from state to state, eventually invading the entire country over decades.

The graphics were overwhelming. The visual power of his presentation, showing how "healthy" white states had become increasingly "infected" red states over the years, has laid the groundwork for international attention to the new epidemic. The world's scientists downloaded these images and began disseminating them through their own research, while media outlets across the Western world launched the images into headlines about a looming new obesity epidemic.[16]

As an epidemic, fatness is really special. It is an epidemic that the public has been taught through public health education. The fat didn't suddenly start filling up the world's emergency rooms, sounding the alarm of a new impending danger. Instead, the fat was made to look sick. They were singled out as carriers of something dangerous, but at the same time, they did not infect or harm themselves, society, or other people. No more than the thin ones, anyway.

The European Parliament's White Paper on Nutrition, Overweight, and Obesity identified irresponsible consumption of unhealthy foods and excessive sedentary

---

[16] Ibid., p. 39–42

behavior as the causes of a statistically explosive obesity epidemic. It describes how people's own behaviors and choices are what create and sustain the epidemic.[17] The World Health Organization (WHO) concluded that the obesity epidemic is caused by genetic, environmental, social, behavioral, nutritional, cultural, societal, and lifestyle factors.[18] In doing so, they managed to include everything to do with being human as a possible cause of the obesity epidemic. Exactly everything. One might actually wonder what causes the so-called ill health of thin people with that logic. Yes, they have at least as much ill health as fat people.

The obesity epidemic was portrayed in the media as a "timebomb of public ill health,"[19] as "terrorism from within,"[20] and as something so serious that it was "second only to climate change and war[21] – "an epidemic to declare war on."[22] The enormous risk posed, according to health experts, by an increasingly fat population has since dominated the general public health debate.[23] The message has gone forth and created a people obsessed with thinness and filled with fatphobia. Anxiety-ridden and shame-ridden

---

[17] Europaparlamentet 2007
[18] WHO 2014
[19] Barry et al. 2009
[20] Monaghan 2008
[21] Oliver 2006
[22] Komesaroff & Thomas 2007
[23] Guthman 2016

self-starvation is now mixed with injuries from overtraining and yo-yo dieting. While the man who launched the obesity epidemic at the CDC over the years received scores of awards for his epidemiological knowledge, fat people were not only made fatter by the hype but also sicker and increasingly despised by both themselves and others. Other epidemics were solved with structural measures, hygiene changes, and vaccines. But when it came to fatness, there was never any medicine other than denigration. The fact that so many people continued to be fat despite the huge roll-out of solutions was never blamed on the roll-out. All that was left to blame was the inability, unintelligence, and lack of reason of fat people.

The launch of the epidemic is of unimaginable proportions. The threat of an obesity epidemic was among the first news stories to break the coverage of the terrorist attacks on the twin towers in New York on 11 September 2001.[24] Just months after the attacks, two wars were launched in the US - one against terrorism and one against the growing waistline of the US military. Despite widespread scientific criticism of the claim that obesity killed over 300,000 Americans annually, the media continued to repeat that figure. Between 2002 and 2004 alone, this alleged death toll was repeated over 17,000

---

[24] Oliver 2006

times in the US media.[25] They put a lot of thought and effort behind their words. Meanwhile, no scientific study has shown that fatness kills.

The public health ideology of a threat and of who is responsible for the threat was sucked into the self-image of the fat people as they saw themselves from a whole new perspective. It silenced them. As the designated carrier of a socially disruptive epidemic, it is impossible to protest, especially when the epidemic is alleged to have been caused by motivations within the fat people themselves - by being less knowledgeable. The rapid leap across an ethical boundary - calling healthy people epidemic carriers - probably made us not fully understand the content of it all. The silence and shame of the fat, and the dieting they indulged in, allowed the idea of the epidemic to go on undisturbed for far too long. Instead of backing down when the results failed - fat people didn't get thin - the pharmaceutical companies and health institutions realized they had to further emphasize the seriousness of the issue. They had to step up their game. Epidemic expansion required a scientific establishment of fatness as a disease. Perhaps that would make the fat people understand the seriousness?

---

[25] Biltekoff 2007

The Epidemic Idea Required a Disease

It took the AMA (American Medical Association) sixteen long years after the launch of an obesity epidemic to finally, in 2013 vote and classify obesity as a disease.[26] The decision meant that one-third of the North American population suddenly went from being considered healthy to sick. The sixteen-year road to that decision consisted of many steps in which the idea of fatness as a disease was built up. First, as I said, the epidemic itself was launched. Next, the overweight threshold was lowered by 5 BMI units, making 30 million normal-weight Americans overweight overnight.[27]

In concrete terms, this meant that a man of 180 centimeters would now be considered overweight at 80 kilos (previously 97 kg). If we recalculate the same for a 165 cm tall woman, she is now considered overweight at 68 kg (previously 81 kg).

Action against the epidemic was taken at the international level. The World Health Organization (WHO) recommended a variety of approaches to tackle the so-called obesity problem. The measures consisted of instructions, monitoring, and evaluation. The aim was to warn each individual of the risks of obesity and to point out

---

[26] BBC News 2013
[27] Boero 2012

the immediate need for self-regulation.[28] This neoliberal form of citizenship - where the individual is expected to regulate him or herself for the benefit of society rather than the other way around - was also evident in the UK's National Health Guidelines report. The title of the report – Choosing Health – was clearly chosen to shift the focus from structural measures to individual responsibility.[29] The focus on fatness thus differs from how we have historically approached other public health issues or other epidemics. The creation of a structural epidemic disaster, rather than leading to structural change, has given authorities the right to put pressure on individuals to recover from a disease that these authorities themselves have invented.

Once something is defined as a disease, there is an inherent idea in the concept, namely that the role of the disease should, to some extent, release the sick person from guilt.[30] But this has not happened in the case of obesity. On the contrary, Julie Guthman, a professor of social sciences, finds it ironic that while the obesity epidemic is described as a structural public health problem at the population level, the entire emphasis is on personal responsibility. It is, she says, a reversal of the entire public health and welfare

---

[28] Lewis et al. 2010
[29] Warin 2011
[30] Boero 2012

model that was once created to place the individual in a supportive society rather than the other way around.[31]

While we know that it is not possible to translate epidemiological statistics into action at the individual level, that is precisely what they did when the epidemic was declared an individual disease. Via the National Board of Health and Welfare, epidemiological statistics were transferred straight down to the closed rooms where health professionals sat face-to-face with their fat patients. There, they were free to start instructing their fat (i.e., now sick) clients on basic nutrition. Now that they had the tool of "disease" in their hands, they could air their condescending attitudes towards fat people undisturbed.

Threat Images Preserve a Moralizing Order

That the handling of fat people is a fundamentally moral and disciplinary issue of order is clear in many parts. When the epidemic was launched, a whole new type of human category was created with entirely new characteristics - the fat person. Sure, fatness has always existed, but it had not been categorized as an epidemic outbreak before. Body weight was previously considered to be an individual variation and, therefore, the sole concern of the individual. When fatness was singled out in epidemic language, the characteristics were lined up as an instruction manual for a human type that was broken in its personal

---

[31] Guthman 2009

responsibility. This "instruction manual" of an immoral person in need of discipline is what makes it enough for many people today to see a fat person and feel that they know something about that person. And that this is negative.

When the fat ones look in the mirror, they, too, begin to see the same thing. Shame ridden, they incorporate the negative qualities attributed to them. If they are the least bit socially aware, they also see the brokenness. They feel it clearly. In the new health ideology, the power of fat people's negative self-image is not at all strange. Nikolas Rose explains how the ideology works: it leads citizens to want to be healthy (thin) because society so clearly punishes those who are not.[32]

We are all assigned a place in the moral order.

"Community describes not just what they have as fellow citizens but also what they are, not as a relationship they choose (as in a voluntary association) but an attachment they discover, not merely an attribute but a constituent of their identity." [33]

The quote by Michael Sandel above goes completely against the neoliberal ideologues who claim that we all choose our lives. We don't. Rather, the price of breaking a

---

[32] Rose 1999
[33] Sandel 1982

given order is so high that we are left behind. In his study of crime and shame, criminologist John Braithwaite described how the deep human need to be included can become so overwhelming that individuals may confess to crimes they did not commit.[34] By their silence, fat people are admitting to a crime they never committed. By hiding, by staying away from social venues, by remaining silent when health professionals inform and advise at a low level of intelligence, they are conforming to the social order. Those who are labeled as sick are expected to also behave as if they are sick.

Sociologist Natalie Boero describes the obesity epidemic as a postmodern epidemic. By that, she means an epidemic that does not need a real disease to be called an epidemic. The main thing is that a medical framework is applied and that the condition is medicalized. Moreover, a post-modern epidemic is kept alive by the media, pharmaceutical companies, and the individuals themselves, those who are struggling to get well. But the most important component of a postmodern epidemic is that no medically designed measures need to result in any lasting solutions.[35]

---

[34] Braithwaite 1989, p. 162
[35] Boero 2012

Measures can continue even if they do not work. No one is controlling an epidemic that includes such a large proportion of the world's population.

Psychologist Louise Adams, who runs the blog Untrapped, wrote a furious post comparing the COVID-19 pandemic to the so-called obesity epidemic. She wrote how a real epidemic (like corona) needs no constructs, no set-up, and no ideological proposals. It is enough that the virus is dangerous. In the case of the obesity epidemic, she continued, there are no mass graves, no contagion, and no need for closures and isolation. Unlike a real epidemic, I argue, the obesity epidemic has been built up over the long term in an alliance between market forces, health policy, and the interests of privileged people in super-health. These are two very different kinds of law and order. In viral epidemics, the focus is on saving lives because the virus affects everyone, rich and poor alike. In the obesity epidemic, a certain immoral type of person is singled out as the bearer of an undesirable body. These individuals are then pressured to reform by more moral and desirable people. It is a horrific order.

The strength of social order cannot be overstated. We humans are so sensitive to ideologies of right and wrong that we often harm those who are considered wrong. Artist Stina Wollter was interviewed in the Swedish TV program Min Sanning (My Truth) 2021. Her account of her mother, who eventually died of dementia, was extremely thought-provoking about the power of human social order-making. Stina's sister had died relatively young of self-starvation. The sisters' mother had always believed and pointed out that it was very important to be thin. Her sister's death had left Stina with enormous feelings of guilt for a long time. The guilt was that it was she, the fat one, who had survived and not the thin sister.

All her life, she had seen through her mother's eyes that she was not pretty enough. But at the end of her life, as I said, her mother suffered from dementia. And suddenly, Stina saw love in her mother's eyes. The judgmental look at Stina's body was gone. With dementia, her mother no longer remembered to dislike fat bodies, and for the first time, the two could meet without a moralizing filter. I was taken by this little anecdote from a real relationship. Will it take dementia to be able to rise above the condemnatory order created by the pursuit of thinness? The order created in the launch of an obesity epidemic has apparently become so firmly established that most of us can't break it with sheer thought and intelligence. With all the negative images of fat people we now carry, it takes nothing less than an exorcism to force us to break free from the prevailing order. Otherwise, we will continue to harm fat people until we die or become demented. There is nothing nice about that order. To get out of that order without dying or suffering from dementia, we must, in my view, with knowledge as our goal, turn our attention to those who perpetuate the contempt for the fat body - the health ideologists.

The Health Ideologists

The dislike of fat people manifests itself in everyday life.

"Don't come and tell me that fat people are healthy!" this was written by a very upset, hard-working man on social media. He was reacting to a woman writing that fat people can indeed be healthy and that discrimination must end. The man's post was long and aggressive - almost panicked. He argued that there must be an end to ideas that fat people can be healthy: "Surely the doctors know best!" he continued. He seemed to regard his own outrage as a sign of concern for the group of people he regarded as seriously ill. He actually believed more in the knowledge of doctors than the doctors themselves do in the case of fatness.

Studies of fat people show that the discrimination they face must be understood in relation to prevailing power relations.[36] The very idea of an obesity epidemic ran parallel to three other emerging phenomena: a new moral and appearance-fixated health ideology, a powerful shift from political to personal responsibility, and a widening medicalization of non-medical phenomena. In these power relations, personal thinness became the bearer of a super-value. The philosopher Monica Greco says that speaking in

---

[36] McPhail 2009

the name of health has become one of the most powerful rhetorical devices in the Western world today.[37] The outraged man's words bore clear traces of this imperiousness. Fat people, he said, should not even be allowed to think about being well until they became thin. Robert Crawford, who coined the term healthism, argued that the power grab to be healthy (read thin) should now be understood as a demanding project that has achieved salvation status.[38]

Within the health ideology framework, thinness was portrayed not only as a sign of health but also as a cultural ideal. The fat person was then presented as incapable of doing what is expected of a responsible and healthy citizen.[39] This opposition between cultural ideal and incapacity has perpetuated a totalitarian, culturally embedded negative view of fat people.[40] The dislike of fatness is now cultivated individually through harsh and self-imposed bodily discipline and has become the norm that every citizen should indulge in.[41]

The concept of health shines with a high-gloss veneer that shields it from both moral and intellectual scrutiny.[42] It's hard to be against health. But the fact is that our view of

---

[37] Greco 2004
[38] Crawford 2006
[39] Beausoleil 2009; Burrows 2009; Warin 2011
[40] Boero 2012; Lewis et al. 2010
[41] Meleo-Erwin 2012
[42] Guthman 2007

health has undergone enormous changes from the original idea that health meant not being sick. Today, the idea of elevated super-health gives people the power to value and try to discipline other people by the way they look, with purposes that appear to be good.

Disciplining citizens into so-called health is not really a new way of thinking in the emerging civilization. Rather, the ideology has been resurrected from the ashes of other totalitarian episodes. In 1921, the National Socialist German Workers' Party (NSDAP) drew up a 25-point program for the future survival of a healthy nation. In 1921, the so-called obesity epidemic did not exist, but the horror of the idea of a flaccid, non-Aryan worker and soldier had seen the light of day. In addition to the fear propaganda against Jews, the celebration of German blood, and the proposal to immediately expel all immigrants from the country, public health was in a couple of clear points.

Point 10: The first duty of every citizen must be to preserve himself in body and soul.

Point 21: The state must be responsible for improving public health through compulsory physical education and sport.

Today, a century later, the same logic is floating to the surface again. Human fatness poses a threat to all those who again want society to generate a thin population. The British sociologist Nikolas Rose explains that fatness, in its lack of immediate signs of disease, began to be treated as a warning bell for all the diseases that might follow in its wake. Thickness risked becoming an obstacle to maintaining the economic system through productive work.[43] Therefore, the population would be taught to strive for optimal health.[44] No government-launched public health appeal has been so clear, so costly, and so orchestrated as the launch of thinness as society's salvation. In place of a social-nationalist legal requirement to diet, today's individuals are marinated in moralism about desirable health (i.e., thinness).

But since thinness in no way implies the absence of disease, how could the idea of equating thinness with health have such an impact? In the free, enlightened world, without either force or coercion? How could morality and ideology displace both knowledge and reason in this way? In short, how could they make us all want to strive for thinness, both through self-starvation and through condemnation of all those who did not slim down?

The Health Ideology Emerged in And Contributed to The Widening Class Divide in Welfare Society

In the self-producing part of the world, the thin ideal emerged as class and market interests merged and marketed

---

[43] Rose 2009
[44] Dew 2012

the thin body as a desirable end product.[45] Health consciousness became an ideological, obscure force born out of the beliefs, behaviors, and expectations of an articulate, well-informed middle class.[46] It was about a new class-marking consumption. Like how you live, what clothes you wear, and what culture you live in, the new health ideology reinforced the idea of thinness as a sociocultural ideal. Health ideology caused people to make a large-scale historical division between the controlled, ordered, and moral and the others.[47]

Health ideology today is not about what health is but about how class-marking forces have been able to shape how health as an idea is marketed. Rather than being a state to rest in, health today is a choice, an activity, consumption, a body production, and a weapon in a field of competing, self-realizing people. Health is something to be conquered[48] in the same way as other efforts we make to, as Michel Foucault described it, "transform ourselves in order to achieve happiness, purity, wisdom, perfection or immortality."[49]

Fatness has always been a sign of lower value. At least when it has appeared in lower-class people. John Coveney,

---

[45] Gracia-Arnaiz 2010
[46] Greenhalgh & Wessely 2004
[47] Burrows 2009
[48] Ayo 2012
[49] Foucault 1988, p. 18

a professor of public health, identifies three prominent historical periods when images of fatness carried a moralizing stamp:

- a classical period in which self-control and restraint in relation to food revolved around man's actual needs (about 400 BC)

- an early Christian period in which food was associated with carnal desires and the pure Christians were exhorted to fasting and the denial of pleasure (about 200 years after Christ)

- a modern period that, through nutritional norms, prioritized rationality over pleasure in the creation of self-regulating citizens (the Middle Ages). This latter period has been described in terms of the rationalization of eating, which also included the health of the body, the elimination of disease, and the purification of the soul.[50]

The historical contempt for fatness has always been directed against the so-called "people." Long after the periods Coveney describes, in 17th century Europe, for example, the idea flourished that exotic peoples such as Spaniards, Indians, Africans, and Tahitians could not become fat. Their counterparts, the learned and civilized, were thought to have more malleable bodies, which could be worked on, and above all improved, through various

---

[50] Coveney 2000

rules of nutritional intake.[51] History professor Ken Albala describes a growing interest in class differences in 18th-century food literature. During this time, there was a two-tier system that separated the hard-working class from the more withdrawn upper class. The distinction was based mainly on the physiological reasoning that the digestive system requires more food when working hard than when resting. Therefore, there were two different ways of eating.[52] The people's and the power's. The social significance of how we ate eventually became more important than the physiological logic. Albala explains that the widening gap between rich and poor was accompanied by a growing need for the rich to distinguish themselves as more refined than the rustic coarseness of the working class.

The 1900s saw the return of the historical moralizing of fatness. But in entirely new clothes. Public health ideology was originally a social engineering that emerged in a society that claimed it no longer wanted class divisions. It claimed to work for the health of the people. It was supposed to lift people out of poverty and disease. And at first, they did, when they implemented structural measures that led to a welfare society for all. It simply raised the bar on people's basic needs.

---

[51] Gilman 2008, p. 168
[52] Albala 2002

But when they had refurbished living environments and eradicated certain diseases, improved hygiene, and guaranteed a certain financial compensation for everyone through social policy, they turned against the individual himself. They would make all individuals improve their lives, their health, and their citizenship. They began to see the body as an arena for improvement. Now that everyone had access to food, eating itself was once again linked to various techniques for creating a better, more moral self. Everyone could do it in the new public health era. By focusing on health rather than class, fatness became naturally linked to immorality, ignorance, and emotionally driven, mindless gluttony. The inability to regulate one's desires represented enslavement. Not enslavement to a higher class but to one's own desires.

This sweeping survey of historical attitudes to the fat body tells the story of how our bodies have always represented deeper attitudes about who we are considered to be in relation to others. Not being fat has expressed restraint, self-control, purity, rationality, elevated morality, and discipline.[53] Not being fat has also - since the poor could also become fat - separated a worthier person from others, a capable citizen from others. Michel Foucault described the phenomenon as biopower. He explained how

---

[53] Foucault 2007, p. 1

the more privileged individual, in response to people's bodies becoming the object of political strategies, began to rework their own bodies in order to express such elevated morality and discipline.

Now, in the 21st century, a more chronic moral panic has grown out of the medicalization of the fat body. In the wake of a launched global obesity epidemic, fatness quickly evolved into an increasingly profound moral issue. Focusing on the individual, the visibility of fatness became fundamental to moral imperatives. In the idea of the people in public health, the lower classes are now singled out as the fattest. This has made today's privileged middle class desire the slim, self-produced body even more. In addition, the idea was launched that fat people are carriers of an epidemic. Such cultural degradation is not something the privileged want to be associated with, which further fuels the desire. What Foucault called biopower, therefore, mostly affects the disciplined middle class who, by being thin, by not being subject to intervention, are also the ones who get to "reap" society's rewards in terms of success, status, and esteem.

Responsibility for one's own and the nation's health is now instilled in citizens.[54] The concept of epidemic reinforced the symbolism of fatness for the lazy worker. Both those who were already fat and anyone at risk of

---

[54] Forrest 2009

becoming fat would be urged to manage their bodies so that they would not find themselves in a burdensome sick role in the future.[55] One tactic is to point out how much fat costs those who are not fat.

The Fat Ones Are Considered Immoral and Costly

The public is constantly told that fat people cost society huge sums of money and that costs will skyrocket if nothing is done. Here the media, with its specific dramaturgy, provides alarmism. The picture is painted quite openly that fat people are ruining the rest of us. At the same time, it is true that all health, care, and welfare costs. Old people cost money, mentally distressed young people cost money, and all the torn tendons, bruised knees, and muscle fractures in sports cost money. It is costly to hire doctors, its costly to employ doctors and nurses. Every new hospital bed costs a lot to buy, all the bedding, all the laundry, all the materials, the window cleaning, and the replacement of doors. The governmentally provided health service in Sweden does not earn a single penny for its citizens. It just costs money. So costing money does not really say anything alarming in itself.

Moralism shows when we believe that certain people and groups do not deserve to cost money. That we even think about how much different groups cost society is no accident. We have been brought up and encouraged to think

---
[55] Rose 2009

that way. Individuals in the middle class learn early on to think of themselves as people who calculate over themselves, who create value or diminish in value, who are more or less productive, and who should always strive to produce better.[56] Traditional obesity research - that which seeks solutions to the obesity epidemic - is made up of the same middle class. It constantly reinforces the idea of a link between fatness and a range of medical, economic, and social costs to other individuals and societies.[57] The notion that fat people cost money is persistently promoted and obviously influences the way the public views fat people.

When figures are presented about the billions of pounds that fatness allegedly costs, while the idea that the fat not only chose to be fat but could even easily stop being fat, the public's ability to think humanely about fat people is diminished. Research has shown that the more the public believes that fat people's plight is due to internal, flabby characteristics, the more negative they become, the less empathy they feel, and the more they think that fat people should be pressured to be thin.

Having read through a hundred or so published scientific studies on the costs of fatness, I can conclude the following. The data is cloudy. The studies do not conclude

---

[56] Ball 2003, p. 217
[57] Edwards & Roberts 2009

that fat people cost money. Instead, the studies begin with "obesity costs society enormous amounts of money," ... and only then does their specific research question come in. In a compilation of thirty-two studies that examined the costs of obesity, researchers found that the common feature of the studies was that they never described how much fat people cost compared to thin people.[58] At the same time, for every cost presented, another study showed that the calculations were wrong. Some, including myself, argue that the costs presented are misleading and have had more to do with poor treatment decisions and assessments than with fat people being costly on their own.

The cost of obesity was estimated in the studies to be between 0.7 and 2.8 percent of the total healthcare budget. That range in itself shows how difficult it is to calculate this.

The costs are mostly about treating the so-called consequences of obesity.[59] It is called obesity-related disease and is said to include diabetes, cardiovascular disease, bowel cancer, gallstones, high blood pressure, kidney disease, stroke, osteoarthritis, and high cholesterol, among others.[60] In other studies, obesity-related disease was estimated to absorb anywhere from six to ten percent

---

[58] Withrow & Alter 2011
[59] Lobstein 2014
[60] Kim & Basu 2016; Lobstein 2014

of health care budgets.[61] In short, obesity-related disease means that when a fat person has a disease, the disease is obesity-related.

There are different views on which diseases should be associated with fatness, which has a major impact on how the cost is calculated in a case of heart failure, for example. Moreover, heart failure usually affects thin people, and in fairness should be more expensive than when fewer, fatter people get heart failure. The studies also exclude many groups of people, such as the elderly or the seriously ill. In addition, studies have rarely taken into account factors such as gender, ethnicity, and class. People live in widely different circumstances and experience widely different life chances, all of which affect the cost of their treatment. Studies have shown, for example, that health services spend far more money on women's weight loss than men's, regardless of health status.

The studies also highlighted the problem of using the BMI tool to measure the cost of obesity. Most studies have calculated the cost to people with a BMI above 27. But using that measure, they ring in anything from 10 kilos overweight to 400 kilos overweight, with the costs of the latter so far exceeding the former that the total is seriously misleading. Twenty kilos of excess weight probably do not cost a penny more than the so-called normal weight.

---

[61] Lobstein 2014

Perhaps it costs less. We do not know. As long as it cannot be specified better than that, studies are needed on why we even ask the question of how much fat people cost.

For every ethically conscious person, it is obviously problematic to clamp down on health care costs for certain groups of people. In another systematic meta-analysis, the annual estimate of costs for fat people ranged from 193 USD to 5920 USD, depending on the study design. The analysts argued that the true cost of obesity is impossible to determine without also comparing it to the so-called obesity-related diseases that thin people also suffer from[62], such as diabetes, cardiovascular disease, cancers, strokes ... and so on. Therefore, the reasonable conclusion is that cost estimates should be used with extreme caution and consideration.

When the very serious disease of AIDS was discovered, AIDS sufferers were initially subjected to a powerful and degrading moralism. The attitude was that there seemed to be a relatively broad and self-centered individual choice behind contracting AIDS and thus costing society money. Before learning more about the HIV virus, which could develop into AIDS, the epidemiological findings concerning the spread of the disease were presented as belonging to specific social groups with specific

---

[62] Kim & Basu 2016

lifestyles.[63] These were homosexual men who were enjoying themselves. In the case of obesity, there is much the same underlying attitude. The morality is that fat people have willingly put themselves in the situation and then expected others to pay.

Those who have estimated the costs of fatness have ignored the costs caused by the disdain for fatness itself. Fat people are more likely to avoid seeking medical care in time. They are more likely to drop out of medical treatment because it is substandard or degrading. In addition, the direct adverse physical and mental health effects of dieting have not yet been investigated,[64] perhaps because these are costs that the healthcare system itself has helped to create.

Taken together, the repeated threats of fat people's cost to society have further cemented a moral distinction between two different appearances. The fat one and the thin one.

The Health Ideology's Focus on Appearance Creates Flow or Stress

"A vulgar hierarchy of diseases exist, based on the extent to which symptoms can – or cannot – be readily localized." [65]

---

[63] Epstein 1996
[64] Singh et al. 2018
[65] Canguilhem 1989, p. 39

What the philosopher Georges Canguilhem describes above as a vulgar hierarchy of disease is an important factor in the senseless harassment of fat people. A study of how Canadian youth responded to health messages about body weight showed that young people became more focused on body appearance than on health.[66] However, while mocking the contemporary obsession with thinness, they felt so trapped by it that they still pursued the ideal body in secret. For those young people who were already so-called overweight, the constant attempts led to an ever-increasing sense of insecurity, shame, and guilt because they never achieved the ideal body. The results show the problem of linking an appearance to the idea of health. Paradoxically, this leads to unhealthy starvation behaviors linked to doubts about one's own appearance. As if it wasn't enough that a thin appearance was linked to health, a fat appearance was linked to one of the most powerful expressions we have of the unwanted - epidemic disease.

Increased health awareness, and its value, have been integrated into every part of society. Robert Crawford shows that the individual's improvement of his or her health has become one of the most distinctive practices of so-called modern society.[67] But it is a genuinely distinguishing health consciousness. While health ideology presents a

---

[66] Rail et al. 2010
[67] Crawford 2004

great opportunity to flow for the slim health-conscious middle and upper classes, it breaks down fat people because of the way they look.

More and more people in the Western world are living fantastically privileged lives. They travel, invest in housing and future pensions, and produce their future and that of their children. They have such non-physical jobs that they enjoy working out. They also enjoy eating healthily. Health (thinness) is their interest, their path, and their project. Their children are born into the same lifestyle. Parents are interested in self-production, success, and self-fulfillment and how to maintain such from an early age. And it is extremely important that this self-production is visible.

A friend who grew up with parents who were both senior doctors said she would never have had a chance to even get fat growing up, not even if she'd had the genetic opportunity. Everything was, of course, geared towards health and thinness from the very beginning through careful food choices, physical activity, education, and success. This kind of self-producer has access to the financial, but above all, the cultural and social resources to devote themselves wholeheartedly to body and soul production. It's all about positive flow, upwards and onwards.

Success is thus visible in pure appearance. And because the standards of the privileged become the standards of everyone, everyone wants to look successful. And they want their children to look successful. The woman I told you about in the introduction was actively starved because her mother wanted her to be a successful and glamorous ballet dancer. She thought she was too fat. The focus on a slim appearance becomes, in privileged contexts, being active, creative, and productive. The same focus in a context where a child without the same resources is denied food to be pretty is to be pushed downwards and to be denied the opportunity to develop a strong self-image.

The production and preservation of a slim body become a testament to the success that the privileged already enjoy. But for those who struggle to keep the most basic parts of life intact, the pursuit of thinness becomes an imposition without the same obvious rewards. As the new health ideology merged with the obesity epidemic, appearance became a resource. The bad bodies become threatening and downright "monstrous"[68] in their difference from the slimmer, more chiseled bodies. It, therefore, becomes even more important not to resemble or even come close to the fat ones. It becomes a self-protective separation not to become fat, not to fall for someone who is fat, not to risk having a fat child. Or to help the fat to become thin so that they no longer pose a threat.

---

[68] Shildrick 2002

Pressuring fat people to be thin has proven totally ineffective.[69] Rather, research shows that fat people have absorbed the message that they are failures, leading to deeply problematic self-images.[70] This has concretely made fat people sick and less creative as they have lost self-esteem, hope for the future, and trust in a society that is hostile to them at the mere sight of them.

Here, I am reminded of the angry and very hardworking man who panicked when a woman claimed that fat people should not be discriminated against because of how they look and that they can be just as healthy as thin people. He is not alone. There are many like him out there in the vocal debate. They demand that thinness should count. They feel that they themselves have made an effort while others have been lazy. They thus experience not only a threat but an outright injustice. In a world that for decades has unequivocally identified fatness as the most dangerous and visible enemy of public health, they cannot sit silent when the enemy suddenly comes forward and claims to be treated with respect. This puts even more stress on the fat. And makes them feel increasingly unwanted.

---

[69] Lewis et al. 2010
[70] Tsenkova et al. 2011

The Rituals of the Health Ideology Determine Who Is Undesirable

Although the welfare and public health idea was started as a structural equality project, today, the individualistic desire for a slim body has been implanted as a core of our political welfare model. Psychologists, dieticians, nutritionists, medical specialists, nurses, school nurses, general practitioners, pediatricians, counselors, parents, publicists, journalists, personal trainers, influencers, and carers have all increased that desire.

Twenty years ago, the Bermuda Sun featured the article Gluttony as a Deadly Sin. The article made a religious argument about the explosive spread of fatness that the author believed had occurred in Bermuda in recent decades. To conclude, they had a local sociologist, Geoffrey Rothwell, give his take on the matter. Rothwell compared the efforts an individual in society should make to become dignified (read thin) with religious salvation from sin. I contacted Rothwell to hear more about his reasoning. Rothwell argued that with bulimia and anorexia as evidence, the privileged world had incorporated gluttony and fatness as mortal sin. As something today's modern society deeply despises. The individual seeks the ultimate body, where thinness becomes a symbol of inner salvation. Before the individual should even think of participating in the great scheme of things, of exerting influence over his own life and that of others, he should be purified and made thin.

I don't really see a problem with privileged people with health ideology beliefs exercising a lot or eating extremely controlled and restrained diets. Of course, they can do that if it fills their lives with meaning and vitality. In fact, all people should be given the right to fill their lives with meaning. The problem is all the rituals that perpetuate the idea of the good citizen and the bad citizen. These rituals constantly reinforce the difference between thin and fat people. It is the idea of the health of the privileged that is promoted and celebrated. In the doctor's office, in social forums, by influencers, on TV, in the coffee room's diet tips, and also deep inside, most people suddenly discover that they are the carriers of an epidemic. The undesirable fellow citizen is crystallized in the same process where the desirable citizen is celebrated. And it is the latter group that takes it upon itself to reverse the former. To do something about them.

Exhortations such as "get up off the couch," "keep the pounds off," and "get moving" symbolize important values in society, such as discipline, hard work, and willpower. It signals the need for preparedness and action to keep the fat off. It takes an inner restraining power to resist one's own body's desires,[71] as if fat people do not work hard and are disciplined, as if the thin upper middle class works hard and disciplined. As if. This devaluation is an important tool in the image of fat people. Many of those who lead the health-focused fight against fatness believe that an underlying disdain for fatness is useful and even necessary to influence people to take responsibility for staying thin.[72]

Authorities invoke the individual responsibility as a good citizen to eat right, exercise and stay within certain standards of how one should live one's life.[73] It sounds like such blaming is directed at everyone and therefore hides the dividing dimension linked to the desirable and undesirable citizens. No matter how neutral the health information seems, fatness becomes associated with an unhealthy character with a lack of self-control and discipline.[74] In a time of abundant nutrition, moral character is characterized by abstinence, while the immoral (unhealthy) ones appear wild and unregulated. The basic idea that is trumpeted is that everyone has a choice. Everyone can choose health. Health campaigns give the appearance of being sufficient information for everyone to make that choice. Anyone who then, despite the information, chooses unhealthiness (being fat) is simply

---

[71] Shugart 2016, p. 136
[72] Callahan 2013
[73] Beausoleil & Ward 2009
[74] Shugart 2016

making an immoral choice. To make matters worse, there is no undesirable characteristic more visible to the eye than fatness.

All these health ideological rituals are completely normalized today. They are there all the time. In eating rituals, exercise rituals, at family reunions, in groups of friends playfully teasing each other, in the media, at work, and in direct encounters between the wanted and the undesirables - such as in healthcare. Even between people who genuinely like each other. These are relatively soft but constant transfers of an ideology that values people by appearance. It is these soft transfers that allow contempt for fat people to continue without a single person claiming to harbor such contempt. It is only visible to the analytical eye and to fat people when they are constantly experiencing what others should think of fat people. For much of the public, all this goes under the radar. They think they are witnessing experts exercising care over fat people. And they think it's good that the experts care because the fat people so obviously need help. Everyone can see that.

With all these components, the new health ideology has managed to stir up a so-called perfect storm with the launch of an obesity epidemic. A combination of powerful processes at all levels of society is now automatically sustaining the war on fatness. In the eye of the storm, the visible fat body is becoming increasingly visible. We no longer see all the processes that have stirred up the storm. We see only that it is around the thick body that the storm is raging. That this is where the danger lies, that this is where action must be taken.

They Created the Perfect Enemy

People trying to bring order have always produced threatening images of the undesirable. As stated earlier, to understand why fat people are considered undesirable, we need to understand what kind of policies and ideologies have converged around that decision. The epidemiological measurements of fatness are not evidence of any objective natural disaster. Instead, we must understand why we are measuring this body variation right now and for whose benefit. Professor Kathleen LeBesco argues that history paints a picture of fatness as a "fluid" anomaly that has often been exploited by dominant economic and cultural interests.[75] What we "know and think" about fat people simply follows the same pattern as what we "know and think" about minorities, the poor, and other groups deemed to deviate from cultural ideas of moral citizenship.[76] Within a religion, for example, the enemy can be identified as those who violate the edicts of that particular religion. I am not the first to equate health ideology with religion. In this new health ideology, ideas certainly revolve around virtues such as self-control and abstinence.[77] Salvation is the slender body.

---

[75] LeBesco 2004, p. 17
[76] Boero 2012
[77] Oliver 2006

The sociologist Nils Christie coined the concept of "the suitable enemy."[78] He showed how social problems do not arise of their own accord. They are something a society simply decides on. It is always privileged people who point out such problems. Crime, as he himself studied, never exists of its own accord, he argued. Instead, society chooses to criminalize certain behaviors in order to bring about order and point out what is undesirable. That's why different countries have different criminalization choices.

In order to criminalize, we as a society must identify an enemy suitable for criminalization. It must therefore be a type of crime that can be dealt with in some legal form. Social anthropologist Loïc Wacquant gives examples of how suitable enemies have been criminalized during periods of social insecurity. He describes, for example, how blacks in the United States became the main clients of the prison system. Not because they were more dangerous but because they were arrested more often and sentenced more harshly. They were thus made into dark symbols of social insecurity. Wacquant explains how high unemployment, low-wage jobs, structural racism, and the withdrawal of welfare for the poor instead increased police presence in black areas with many black people. This criminalization of

---

[78] Christie 1986

poverty reinforced the alienated status many blacks already had.[79]

In the EU, Wacquant continues, the same thing is happening as free movement across borders revives xenophobia. Prisons in Europe are being filled with non-Europeans while immigration is linked to terrorism, prompting public pressure for security and increased border protection. Statistics are being requested showing how many crimes are committed by non-Europeans, and overall, the enemy, its victims, and the solution are being identified. "We" are threatened by such enemies, and therefore we want to close the door, either on us or on them. What happens when a specific group at the societal level is designated as an enemy is that the public emotionally associates with danger when they see a member of that group. This is not an intellectual judgment. It is a social defense mechanism.

As a system, I consider medicalization to be a law enforcer in the same way as criminalization. Here, people are not to be dealt with legally but medically, and in the case of fatness, also with shame and guilt. In our extremely health-ideological age, the fat person is not only convenient but the perfect enemy against which to rally remedial forces. The image of undesirable-damaged body variation has been fully established in the public mind. Fat, as a

---

[79] Wacquant 2009

certain type of person, can easily be paired with other undesirable behaviors. They are an enemy that can be visualized, explained, and corrected. As in the case of black prison clients, fatness is linked to structural poverty and low education. The threat of fatness makes us understand what kind of citizens the current order wants to get rid of. We can deal with the enemy that lurks within us. We can fight our inner enemy to become more welcome. We can do anything to stay slim or get slim. At the same time, we can help others fight their inner enemy so that order can be restored. Fatness is considered one of the so-called preventable diseases. It is considered easy to remedy. After all, the slim experts say, it's just simple arithmetic. Eating a little less and moving a little more.

While the management of fatness in the West seems to concern us all, the lower classes are the main problem with their fatness. This is linked to the shift in focus from structural, political responsibility to individual responsibility, especially among groups already considered irresponsible. Numerous studies have been published on how the obesity epidemic is most threatening among underprivileged groups in the welfare society - the low-educated and the socio-economically disadvantaged. However, the link between low status and high weight was not something they discovered during the campaigns but rather was something that helped them get off the ground in the first place.[80] It was because the underclass was getting fatter that fatness under the obesity label became the perfect enemy in the new middle-class-oriented health ideology.

Abruptly, Something Had to Be Done About the Perceived Threat

After decades of research, I know that fat people, by many, are assumed to be unintelligent. Fat people are in the news all the time, and usually as deplorable characters. If they are on film, it is in various types of fat roles - either as clown-like characters or as just fat and therefore automatically filled with problems. In the media, they flourish in reports of the obesity epidemic, often in the form of images of "headless fatties."[81] These are images of fat, headless bodies holding hamburgers, sweets, or ice cream, sitting on a park bench, or walking outside a supermarket. "We can't have that," one doctor told me. He continued, "We can't have it like the US, with a lot of obesity all over the streets."

When something has to be done about the undesirable, and in order to do anything at all, interest in doing something about that particular group must be increased. The development of a moral panic about the fat body requires that the public, both fat and thin, must be

---

[80] Biltekoff 2007
[81] Cooper 2007

sensitized. And they have done so. For decades, the threat picture has been filled with factors that we would never have considered threatening before. Eating itself, for example, can begin to be related to death rather than life. "Our children are eating themselves to death" is a headline that reaches deep into people's concerns and anxieties. Although fatness is not even mentioned in such messages, the threat image becomes more potent. Without such sensitization, fatness would remain on the periphery, among other anomalies that are not considered to threaten the existence of all of us.

Painting the worst possible future scenario is a common strategy in public health campaigns. It is a risk management approach in which future possibilities are considered on the basis of a fear hypothesis.[82] The fear hypothesis concerning fatness can be explained in five steps:

- Fatness as deviation occurs. Someone raises the alarm. The media inform the masses with dark undertones: "Humanity is getting fatter."

- The fat man type is defined and reinforced. Fat people are said to be sick, uninformed, lazy, uncontrolled, unintelligent, emotionally driven, selfish, and unhappy. In this way, the danger inherent in the fat person is portrayed.

---

[82] Diprose 2008, p. 142

- Sensitization produces chronic trauma around the thick body. Not only is fatness itself dangerous. They say eating itself is dangerous. Not staying informed is dangerous. Sitting too long is dangerous. Correlations are sought, with fatness allegedly causing a never-ending series of diseases, problems, and costs.

- Fatness as a danger is overestimated. They give the impression that humanity will perish if nothing is done about the epidemic.

- The cultural control increases. We must do something, and anything we do is better than nothing.

Public health researcher Deborah McPhail has shown how interest in tackling fat people is closely linked to a society's political and cultural tensions. She describes a specific dieting method designed for men - the "Tubby Hubby diet" - which was launched in Canada in the early 1950s. Although it was created to reduce the waist size of Canadian men, the advice itself was aimed at women: 'Reduce his weight in just twelve days,' 'He doesn't even have to notice that he's slimming.'[83] In the study, McPhail asks why the diet came along at all and why it was intended for men but targeted at women. She also asks what it might say about contemporary (nearly seventy years later) power relations and dieting ideals.

---

[83] McPhail 2009

Post-war Canada was marked by a crisis of masculinity linked to the alleged decline of the white middle-class man. White middle-class men had begun to gain weight, take sedentary jobs, and become increasingly tied to the home. The Canadian nuclear family norm had been built around the separation of public and private life. While the man had been a worker/soldier in the public sector, the woman had stayed at home and done the groundskeeping. That order was now under threat, and by targeting the fatter, flabbier, and feminine bodies men suddenly exhibited, an order might be restored. By launching the diet as a women's responsibility, the norm of the man as breadwinner and the woman as a homemaker was emphasized, and Canada might once again position itself as a healthy nation of white, middle-class nuclear families.[84]

The capitalist system has long rested on the division of public and private life. Some parts should be visible, and some should remain hidden. The working body must be kept in motion while the flabby, softer body must be relegated out of the public sphere into the private.[85] As women stepped out into the public sphere while men became a little rounder, the masculine hard suddenly merged with the feminine soft.[86] The "Tubby Hubby diet" therefore aimed not only to remove the feminine fat from

---

[84] Ibid.
[85] Longhurst 2001
[86] Monaghan 2008

the individual but from the entire public sphere. Men would still be men, women would still be women, and the nation would still be safe.[87] Fatness became an enemy of the masculine construction project. Now, seventy years later, the idea of universal public health has taken over the role of the idea of a warlike nation. Now, when everyone is a working individual in the public sphere, unwanted fatness is no longer to be dealt with by housewives. It is now classified as an individually irresponsible disease. The "Tubby Hubby diet" has been replaced by a medicalization of the unwanted.

They Medicalized the Unwanted People

A number of years ago, I attended an international conference on social work. The conference had several thousand participants from all corners of the world. All the meetings and discussions dealt with social work as a profession and science and the future challenges of both. Many hundreds of lectures were given, dealing with poverty, addiction, mental illness, street children, rape victims, torture, migration, war, the Third World, racism, the slave trade, the climate threat, sexual and intimate violence against women, human rights, cultural, ethnic and religious persecution and so on.

I was one of only two to talk about fatness as a social vulnerability. I presented the research I was doing at the

---

[87] McPhail 2009

time. It was to investigate how fat people react not only to patronizing treatment but also to positive treatment. My results showed that fat people were significantly more sensitive to both types of treatment. Being patronized was more devastating for fat people than for thin people. Being treated positively was more beneficial for fat people than for thin people. The results were also most pronounced for women. The results suggested, I said, that fatness was primarily a despised appearance and not a disease.

After some more general questions from the audience, a nurse from Australia raised her hand and said: "How can you say that obesity should not be considered a disease? Do you know how fat people suffer?" She continued indignantly, "I had a patient who just died, twenty-nine years old, from obesity! He was bedridden. The health service refused to treat him. He had diabetes, high blood pressure, and asthma. He had chronic pain and was deeply depressed! Tell him he wasn't sick!" There and then, I was surprised by the outburst. I reeled out, "That sounds absolutely horrible, especially since he wasn't getting treatment. But I never said that fat people can't be sick." She didn't look happy with that answer, and I didn't feel happy either. So after the session, I went up to her and asked her why she had been so provoked by what I had said. She apologized a little wearily and said: "I felt like you were diminishing my patient's suffering when you said it wasn't a disease."

I often think about that meeting. There are many different interpretations behind concepts like illness, suffering, contempt, and obesity. Both she and I really felt the same way - that fat people are treated in a very degrading way by the health service. But while she believed that the suffering was due to the fatness of the disease, I believe that the suffering was due to the fact that the man, despite being demonstrably very ill, was not getting help. And that he was not helped because he was fat.

I argue that the medicalization of fatness was only possible because the cultural class bias against fat people was already there. Moralizing segregation has been ongoing towards lower classes, where privileged people have spent time avoiding, teaching, and trying to fix those who are disruptive. Public health authorities throughout history have talked about nutritional intake in campaigns designed solely to educate the troublesome underclass.[88] At the same time, these same authorities have consistently failed to deal sensibly with disease conditions that are primarily associated with already disordered social groups.[89] Most often, this has been a matter of informing

---

[88] Biltekoff 2007
[89] Puhl & Heuer 2010

people who are, in one way or another, considered to be uninformed. The campaigns themselves separate responsible citizens from the others - those in need of monitoring, management, reform, and action of various kinds. Rather than being about caring for the fat, therefore, contemporary ideas about the fat body resemble earlier attempts to regulate deviant populations.[90] The pejorative concept of epidemic calls for immediate surveillance of those who carry the epidemic itself.[91]

Doctors Became Moral Guardians Protecting Society Against Fatness

The enormous impact of the obesity epidemic threat was helped by the fact that it could be anchored in one of the most powerful institutions in the West - the medical one. The medical field had a ready-made framework for curing abnormalities in the form of ill health. They had the facilities and resources to immediately put the idea of epidemiology into practice. And when obesity took on epidemiological overtones, it could be treated relatively painlessly. Whatever the treatment.

In Sweden, the National Board of Health and Welfare formulated recommendations for health care. All health plans should include an obesity perspective when working with patients. The brief counseling would consist of ten

---

[90] Evans et al. 2008
[91] LeBesco 2010

minutes, where the patient would be encouraged to move more and eat less. The longer consultation would last up to thirty minutes and act more as a personal dialogue. For example, the patient could receive a list of nearby fitness centers and a leaflet with healthy recipes. Advice could also be followed up via telephone contact, for example. According to the National Board of Health and Welfare, this form of advice should be offered to patients who appear to be at least ten kilos overweight.

The highest level of counseling was recommended to be qualified therapy. It should be patient-centered, theory-based, and structured. One example was cognitive behavioral therapy (CBT).[92] However, in the 25 years I have been researching how fat people are managed, I have never come across a single fat person who was offered such a higher level of care for their socially and life-threatening condition. Instead, encouraging the fat person to move more and eat less has subsequently been replaced by motivating the fat person to want to become thin themselves. As if anyone, at any time, in our slimming age, has wanted to get fat.

Behind the advice the fat still receives from the healthcare profession are policy decisions, recommendations from the National Board of Health, the region's responsibility for the health of the population, and

---

[92] Socialstyrelsen 2010

allegedly scientific evidence-based studies and medical experience. In their profession, doctors have conquered the right to categorize, diagnose and treat suffering. But since there were, then or now, no medicines for obesity, the health service instead informs the fat patients that they themselves should change and become thin.

So the cure for the epidemic was for a professionally trained doctor to advise fat adults to move more and eat less. So that's the solution to the obesity epidemic painted by the health experts themselves. Here a profession has slipped into moralizing at the lowest possible intellectual level under the guise of medical knowledge. If there is any science behind such advice, it is unequivocal. Unsolicited simplified advice does not work. In a study of patients with rheumatoid arthritis, those who received information in addition to medical treatment were significantly worse off than those who received medical treatment alone.[93]

The authors of the comprehensive The Oxford Handbook of the Social Science of Obesity conclude that it may not be medical science that can be expected to provide solutions to the obesity epidemic.[94] Instead, they argue, it is public health and welfare measures that can solve the problem. It openly emphasizes that the solution must be to modify social norms and create the conditions for making

---

[93] Guthman 2015
[94] Cawley 2011

the 'healthy choice,' thereby promoting and reinforcing individual behavioral change.[95] Interestingly, however, in the case of obesity, doctors have already left medical science behind and become the extended arm of public health. After all, in their encounters with their fat patients, they do not cure disease. They moralize about people's lives based on their appearance. And they have numbers to help them keep going.

The Fat People Could Be Measured

As I have already told you, the anthropologist Mary Douglas examined how societies - institutions and people - create order. She used the concepts of purity and danger to explain how moral boundaries are maintained within a group.

> *"It is simply a matter of what is desirable and what is not. What is clean and what is dangerous or dirty varies between cultures, eras, ideologies, nations, and religions."* [96]

Counting and measuring create order. Things are put in order, calculated, separated, and categorized. The world is thus made more understandable. We then know what we have in front of us, how much we have, how much we are missing, and how much we can take away. We can also compare these measures against what we call the normal.

---

[95] McKinnon et al. 2009
[96] Douglas 1984

The first thing we learn about our newborn baby is its weight and height. The body measurements are carefully plotted on a detailed growth curve to make sure that, over time, the baby becomes as normal as possible. The baby is weighed and measured right up to late adolescence. By then, the measurement behavior has become so ingrained that the adult individual takes over control himself. A scale is purchased, and weight control becomes part of the daily routine. If there are signs of weight gain or other abnormalities, the individual tries to correct it himself.

According to Cynthia Coburn, a professor of social policy, the disease-oriented view of fatness is rooted in an epidemiological tradition that believes it is possible to divide the world into measurable categories that say something about the reality of the individual.[97] The disease of fatness came about when we divided people by body mass, determined what body mass was normal, and then counted how many had an abnormal body mass. Previously, everyone was just different weights.

Epidemiology is, according to the National Encyclopedia, a scientific discipline concerned with the study of the distribution, causes, and course of diseases in the population. They seek answers to questions such as who and how many people are affected by a particular disease.[98]

---

[97] Coburn 2003
[98] NE 2017

Epidemiological measurements are interesting because they can provide a basis for shaping government action to combat diseases most effectively. It can work to respond to a viral outbreak, for example. However, the difference between virus and fatness is enormous and, in my opinion, puts the task and consequences of epidemiology to the test. While viruses are treated as an independent threat attacking all humans indiscriminately, fatness is treated as a self-inflicted problem where the individual should be pressured to change in order to fall in line. Epidemiological mapping of fat people, therefore, has very different ethical implications from mapping a virus.

As mentioned above, the Body Mass Index (BMI) is used to diagnose fat people as sick. BMI calculates how many kilograms per square meter of length (kg/m2) a person weighs. A person who is two meters tall and weighs 100 kilos has a BMI of 25 (100/22) and is, therefore, on the borderline between normal weight and overweight. Obesity has been defined as starting at a BMI of 30. To be more specific, this means that a person who is two meters tall weighs 120 kilos or that a person who is 165 centimeters tall weighs about 80 kilos. The fact that so-called overweight starts at a BMI of 25 means that at least two billion people are affected by the disease.

So, BMI measures body mass - not health. Showing that the population's BMI has increased says nothing about health or ill health.⁹⁹ It just sounds like it does. That sounds like ill health because the distinction between body mass and health became blurred when the threat of an obesity epidemic and a newly awakened health ideology merged. Epidemiological estimates of the prevalence of obesity are not and never have been, the medical evidence of an existing disease. Epidemiological measurements are intended to be tools for monitoring trends at the population level but cannot provide any conclusions about risks in individuals.¹⁰⁰ Nevertheless, epidemiological measurements are used as a basis for addressing obesity as an individual disease.

In fact, the BMI measure is notorious for its uselessness in defining a person's health or unhealthiness. Most critical researchers today argue that the use of BMI does more harm than good.¹⁰¹ Epidemiologist Katherine Flegal showed, through her and colleagues' research, that people who are considered overweight (BMI 25-29.9) are less likely to die prematurely than so-called normal-weight people (BMI 18.5-24.9). In addition, they found that people with a BMI of 30-34.5 (so-called obesity 1) are at the same risk of dying prematurely as the normal-weighted.¹⁰² My study of 68,000 Swedes shows that differences in perceived

---

⁹⁹ De Vogli et al. 2014
¹⁰⁰ Nicholls 2013
¹⁰¹ Evans & Colls 2009
¹⁰² Flegal et al. 2013

ill health only become apparent at a BMI above 35. But at the same time, this difference is very small.[103] Such results never reach the media but could, at a stroke, clear hundreds of millions of people from the so-called obesity epidemic.

One of the most important findings that Flegal and colleagues made was that the claim that we are getting fatter is somehow false.[104] It is mainly already fat people who are getting fatter. These are pulling up the average body mass of the population, while the weight gain of individuals in recent decades is relatively small. Many people have become thinner.

One study found how staff at a diet clinic used BMI as a tool to determine that there was a condition in need of treatment. Regardless of the patient's condition, numbers somehow strangely make the suffering real and show that treatment was scientifically about health and not appearance.[105] This is probably the reason why we have not yet abolished the much-criticized BMI tool. If they did, they would lose the most important measure for even medicalizing and calling people sick. But since weighing and measuring a person's body cannot detect suffering, BMI is essentially a purely inhumane tool, which should never really have ended up in politics, in health care, in the media, or with the individual himself.

---

[103] Brandheim et al. 2013
[104] Flegal et al. 2005
[105] Forrest 2009

The Fat People Could Be Dehumanized

Thanks to the fact that the fat could be measured as sick, and thanks to the fact that sickness is always a cultural devaluation, and thanks to the fact that there was never any care or medicine, the fat could be dehumanized for real. Everything was blamed on the fat people themselves. They were both the cause and the solution to the problem painted by slim health ideologists. Once people are dehumanized, they can be handled without much ethical concern. Doctors, for example, would never accept being treated the way they themselves treat fat people as less knowledgeable. Christine Halse, a professor of the sociology of education, has taken an interest in the moralistic features of the dominant health debate. Moralism, she argues, consists of a set of values, beliefs, practices, and behaviors that unethically choose to see certain behaviors and traits as worthy, desirable, and necessary virtues.[106] Those who already believe they have these necessary virtues teach those who have not yet attained them. The degree to which the dehumanized can then aspire to these values is limitless. They can always become a little more orderly - a little less fat. And so action against the thick can continue unchecked. Whatever their inhumane and unethical grounds.

At the Netherlands Centre for Ethics and Health (CEG), a group of researchers evaluated the ethical aspects of 60

---

[106] Halse 2009, p. 47

major interventions and proposed measures to combat the obesity epidemic. The results highlighted a number of problems:

- Effects on physical health were uncertain or undesirable.

- Negative psychosocial consequences included devaluation, discrimination, feelings of insecurity, fear, anxiety, and shame.

- Inequalities were reinforced.

- Inadequate information was shared.

- The social and cultural value of eating was omitted.

- People's integrity was not respected.

- The complexities of responsibility for or causes of obesity were neglected.[107]

It is now over ten years since these results were published. The ethics researchers found that in a rush to do something about the problem, attempts to persuade fat people to change their behavior were not at all in line with science. They regarded this as serious because all lifestyle interventions powerfully affect people's identities and habits. Because they touch on people's emotions and inner beliefs, higher ethical standards of accuracy must be set than the interventions showed. There are several similar studies. None have been highlighted in the media.

---

[107] Ten Have et al. 2011

The dehumanization of fat people is reflected in other studies, which have shown that the degree of discrimination and devaluation has a significant negative impact on the quality of life of individuals.[108] Although there is allegedly a growing interest in ethics related to social, economic, political, and environmental conditions of health,[109] this newly awakened interest has so far not involved fat people.[110] On the contrary, say the researchers, fatness has been portrayed as a fate worse than death - a portrayal totally devoid of ethical concerns.

There are no studies that have shown that the current management of fatness leads to health, but a number of studies have shown the damage it has done. The action programs put forward have based their entire argument on equating obesity with ill health. But they do not address the ill health and dehumanization of fat people that go with the programs themselves. Researchers Lily O'Hara and Jane Gregg found that the explicit messages contained in diet-oriented public health programs managed to violate as many as thirteen articles of the UN Declaration of Human Rights.[111]

The new health ideology's moral contempt for fatness has so far miraculously managed to hide the evidence that

---

[108] Townend 2009
[109] Nixon & Forman 2008
[110] O´Hara & Gregg 2012
[111] Ibid.

the promoted solutions do not work.[112] Fat people are now openly treated as enemies of the entire Western conscience through their visible violations of the ideological norm of thinness.[113] As with all types of enemies of society, primitive notions that reinforce the threat image have not been long in coming.

---

[112] Herman & Polivy 2011
[113] Eller 2014

The Primitive Notions

The doctor: There is a lot of knowledge about obesity in our weight group here at the health center. I will send you there, they are very good.

Me: What kind of knowledge do they use then?

Doctor: They do a group pole walk on Thursdays. It's very much appreciated. And they drink some kind of powder from the pharmacy.

I admit that I smiled derisively at the doctor in the above little discussion. My mocking smile was interpreted by the doctor as me being in complete denial about my own problems. He also believed that I had a negative, almost depressive attitude toward the possibilities of slimness he offered me. He felt that he was presenting something positive to his fat patient, like medicine. And so the patient (me) reciprocated the offer with negativity, unwillingness, and a total lack of motivation. But I could not and still cannot understand how pole walking on Thursdays can fit into the category we call knowledge. I have nothing against people engaging in Nordic walking. I don't mind them doing it on Thursdays, either in groups. But my stubborn legal pathos just refuses to accept pole walking and powder as an evolved knowledge of how to handle fat people.

The pole walking on Thursdays "is very much appreciated," said the doctor. I feel I have no way of arguing with him in that case. Those who walk with poles have presumably expressed themselves in positive terms about these meetings. Perhaps even a survey has been distributed asking participants if they feel they are enjoying life more since signing up for the group. People like to move. Many people like to be with others, to do things together, to experience meaning in life - a meaning that has to do with our social nature. So far, it all makes sense. But the concept of knowledge must reasonably have more substance than that.

A number of years ago, a fitness expert told Land magazine that if you walk ten thousand steps every day, you will lose twenty-six kilos of body weight in a year. We all know what happened. It became a bloody walking with a pedometer, especially among those who have always exercised in some form. But unfortunately, that's nonsense. As if the body were a simple mathematical vessel of some kind - "if you fill up a little at one end and drop out as much at the other, the weight is constant." Nowhere has research shown that ten thousand steps a day results in twenty-six kilograms of weight loss. Unfortunately, by now, the slim would be completely consumed after all that step counting. That said, there's nothing wrong with walking.

In the book The Obesity Epidemic and Its Management, the authors move from describing obesity as associated with certain diseases to later equating "metabolic syndrome" with obesity and finally claiming that obesity causes disease.[114] There is no transition between these different definitions. They just come and go as if they were the same thing. Moreover, their book is no exception.

There is no consensus on how to define obesity as a disease among medical experts. Instead, they have managed to open a way forward where the main thing is that fatness is seen as dangerous, but where the question "in what way?" is avoided, blurred, or widened far beyond public perception. Instead, the visibility of fatness is left to speak its own clear language. Just by seeing the fatness, the public "knows" at a primitive level what they are facing. An epidemic.

The Notions Are Kept Alive at All Costs

Behind what purports to be well-informed advice on the links between food, exercise, and weight, there is an unfathomable lack of knowledge about the human body's fat-storage mechanisms. To explain what I mean by that, we need to get down to the nuts and bolts - the concept of knowledge. What exactly is knowledge? According to the philosopher Michel Foucault, knowledge is a means to help

---

[114] Maguire & Haslam 2010, p. 11–55

us live the best life possible by constantly improving our understanding of the world around us.[115] But at the same time, he argues, the production of knowledge is intimately linked to power. Not everyone's knowledge counts. According to Foucault, power is based on knowledge, power uses knowledge, but power also creates the knowledge it wants in order to maintain itself.[116] The relationship between power and knowledge can be understood as an underlying structure of which we are usually unaware. In simple terms, it can be explained as follows: if a doctor says that walking with a stick is knowledge, it is more likely to be received as knowledge than if a five-year-old says the same thing.

We have created an institution dedicated to the production of higher knowledge - scientific research, colleges, and universities. Here, knowledge should not only be the fruit of the collection of data (information) but also involve a time-extended reflection on this data. Here you think about what the data really show, you gather more information, and you form theories. Researchers are criticized by and also criticize other researchers. The goal is to know a little more about a phenomenon than was known before. Facts and information are, therefore, not science. To be science, facts must be surrounded by theory and

---

[115] Foucault 1988
[116] Ibid.

questions. Facts must be put into perspective to become meaningful, developed, and useful knowledge.

The reason we want to know more, the reason we have an established science at all, is that as human beings, we want to be able to solve the problems we face, respond to challenges, and improve our living conditions with a basis so carefully prepared that we are not at risk of making mistakes. That is why it is not up to priests, kings, fortune-tellers, or gods to guide us today. It should be scientifically produced knowledge that has undergone long processes of scrutiny, criticism, and validation by other scientists.

Unfortunately, scientific knowledge about the causes, solutions, and dangers of obesity is nowhere near such self-examination - not in the results that become public, that is. Some researchers equate obesity with ill-health and, in the same breath, suggest that the solution to ill-health is weight loss. At the same time, other research shows the exact opposite: that losing weight can worsen health.[117] This is just one example. For a profession appointed to cure a designated disease, it should be central that the nature of the disease is scientifically proven, that it is treatable and considered serious enough for treatment to be effective.

A wealth of research shows that knowledge about the dangers of obesity is contradictory, vague, sweeping, and

---

[117] O'Hara & Taylor 2018

sometimes even misleading.[118] The suggestion that fatness is a disease in itself has been challenged from the outset by scientists and doctors alike and by many fat people themselves. In a study of 590 doctors' knowledge of the disease of obesity, only seven percent said they had the skills to help fat patients.[119] Other studies have shown that doctors feel uncomfortable with fat patients and do not feel they have sufficient training in how to get patients to change their behavior.[120] Overall, a host of studies show that doctors have absolutely no knowledge to help fat people become thin.[121]

So-called yo-yo dieting impairs health in a variety of ways. It increases the risk of vascular disease, increases the risk of death, and increases the risk of fractures and gallstones. Loss of muscle, high blood pressure, chronic inflammation, and some forms of cancer are other examples. Emphasizing weight loss in the face of all the evidence to the contrary is neither sustainable nor fair.[122] Fat, otherwise healthy individuals are at lower risk of diabetes, cardiovascular disease, stroke, and death than unhealthy thin ones.[123] There is also debate about how fatty

---

[118] Gard & Wright 2005; Saguy & Riley 2005
[119] Morris et al. 2014
[120] Bocquier et al. 2005
[121] Hartmann-Boyce et al. 2014
[122] Tylka et al. 2014
[123] Guo & Garvey 2016

tissue, in various ways, has protective mechanisms that research simply does not want to find.

Several campaigns to combat obesity have cited the burden that fat individuals place on the rest of society as the reason for the measures. This is done, I repeat, to emphasize the importance that every good citizen should take individual responsibility to eat right, exercise and stay close to the norms considered desirable in society.[124] The tactics may seem harmless but have been proven ineffective, unethical, and downright harmful in improving the health of fat people.[125] Rather, as I recounted earlier, many fat people have incorporated these failures into a deeply damaged self-image.[126] Therefore, the prevailing public knowledge about fat people is not knowledge as Foucault defined it. It does not improve the lives of fat people. Quite the contrary.

In 2016, Sweden's then Minister of Public Health said in a news interview, "We lack knowledge about the link between obesity and ill-health, but the fact remains that obesity is on the rise, and we must do something about it!" This is where the problem of leaning on epidemiological breakdowns into categories becomes clear - when we don't even know what those categories mean. For what the Public Health Minister is saying is that the prevalence of obesity,

---

[124] Beausoleil & Ward 2009
[125] MacLean et al. 2009
[126] Tsenkova et al. 2011

rather than its dangerousness, makes it a subject for public health policy action. That is actually quite unacceptable. In order to cling to systemic ignorance, a series of notions about fat people have been chiseled out in the guise of science.

The Six Great Notions of Fat People

For decades, six great notions have dominated the epidemic threat picture and, with it, the mindless haunting of fat people. Each of these notions literally screams that fat people lack basic abilities to think and act:

• The calorie model. It explains human body weight as a result of the equation calories in/calories out.

• The structural model. It says that fat people live too close to fast food restaurants and too far from walking paths.

• The emotional model. It describes how fat people have an emotional hole that is filled with food to numb pain.

• The motivation model. Fat people, in contrast to thin people, are treated as if they lack motivation, willpower, and self-regulating power.

• The dieting-as-a-remedy model. It says that dieting, as a behavior, is medical knowledge.

• The "cause" model. Fatness is thought to cause all health problems.

Let me criticize these notions individually.

The Calorie Model

Government and market perceptions of fat people have resulted in a host of oppressive campaigns, initiatives, texts, programs, images, products, interventions, projects, and treatments. All have been based on the notion of the caloric imbalance, i.e., that a person's weight is the result of the mathematical equation calories in/calories out.[127] It is an extremely strange idea that fatness is about the art of arithmetic. At the same time, it is by far the most widespread notion of the fat body. The body is equated here with a kind of vessel, where you fill up with calories in a hole at the top, and where the calories then leave the body via a hole further down or are burnt out of the body through so-called physical activity. If you're fat, you've taken in too many calories, burned too few, or, more often than not, done both. According to this model, thin people are considered to be in a state of complete caloric balance. They put in the right number of calories and get rid of the same number of calories. At the same time, there is a considerable body of evidence that exercise is an ineffective mechanism for weight loss.[128]

Science journalist Gary Taubes is convinced that experts in obesity and nutrition are so fixated on this

---

[127] Shugart 2016, p. 19
[128] Malhotra et al. 2015

simplistic calorie-balance idea that they are willing to ignore all existing science in order to stick to it.[129] Researcher Giles Yeo even argues that counting calories is a waste of time. He explains that 100 calories of protein, fat, or carbohydrate provide completely different amounts of energy because they are burned differently once they enter the digestive system. When the three main nutrients - protein, fat, and carbohydrates - are also mixed, dried, ground, heated, pulverized, and built up again in the ultra-processed food we eat today, it takes extremely little energy to burn these calories. Calorie content simply does not reflect how much of these calories the body retains and how little of them it burns. This knowledge has been around for 120 years - ever since chemist Wilbur Atwater made the discovery.[130] Yet our governments, health care providers, and the marketplace are still promoting pure calorie counting as knowledge to combat the obesity epidemic.

Weight loss through calorie restriction and increased activity in people who are already fat is almost never sustained in the long term.[131] Advice to move more and eat fewer calories is doomed to failure because a body exposed to starvation becomes better and better at defending and

---

[129] Taubes 2007
[130] Yeo 2021
[131] Martin et al. 2011

maintaining its excess weight at all costs.[132] The fatter you already are, and the longer you've been fat, the better your body is at defending the excess weight at the slightest sign of starvation. The advice is, therefore, as effective as advising someone who is bleeding heavily to avoid sharp objects.[133]

The body of knowledge behind the calorie model is that obesity is a disease caused by uninformed choices about food and exercise and that it is about choices that individuals make every day. The remedy is to be told that weight loss is desirable and that it will occur if the patient eats a little less and moves a little more. The fact that a lot of research has shown that information does not work is not presented in the media or in the meeting between health professionals and patients. Rather, the opportunities for fat people to lose weight are presented almost aggressively, with health professionals making it clear that this is proven knowledge and that all that is needed is motivation.

Researchers interviewing health professionals have found a profound ignorance about obesity among doctors, nurses, and dieticians. For example, health professionals overestimated the number of calories consumed by the majority of fat people. They were also ignorant of metabolic and other biological processes that influence and

---

[132] Ochner et al. 2015
[133] Ibid.

maintain fat storage in many people.[134] In addition, they carried the notion that body weight is easily controlled through the decision to simply eat less and move more, despite repeated evidence that this is not true.

In May 2016, the New York Times featured a study that investigated why nearly all contestants from one season of the American Biggest Loser gained all the weight they lost during the program. Some of them weighed more than they did before their participation in the program. In the study, the researchers followed the participants for six years after the program. The results showed how strongly the body struggles against weight loss in fat people. As a result of the weight loss, the participant's metabolism had been radically lowered. When the weight started to increase, the metabolism did not follow but became even slower. This made it even easier to gain weight from a smaller amount of food.[135] The notion of the calorie model, when used to cure the disease of obesity, does not take into account the integrated hormonal signals that protect the body against weight loss. Reducing energy intake while burning more energy is accompanied by biological feedback mechanisms that actively prevent long-term weight loss.[136] This is done in a variety of ways: via increasingly strong fat storage capabilities, via improved mechanisms for the body to

---

[134] Fabricatore et al. 2005
[135] Fothergill et al. 2016
[136] Martin et al. 2011

access more nutrients, via cravings for energy-rich food due to starvation and nutrient deprivation, and via signaling systems that cool down, slow down and turn off as many active processes as they can to conserve the body's energy. It also means that any extra intake during a period of starvation is better absorbed by the body than before. And so the weight shift is in full swing. Moreover, all the evidence suggests that weight commuting itself has negative psychological and physiological health consequences that need to be considered more carefully in the future.[137]

The calorie model has gained such status that the self-criticism on which all science should be based has been completely suppressed in the case of obesity.[138] However, criticism of this model is growing steadily outside traditional obesity research. Those who are supposed to help fat people become thin are now aware of this criticism. That is why they do not use the term dieting today when urging clients to eat less. Instead, they use the term balanced eating. It means the same thing but sounds more sensible and insightful. Criticism of dieting has caught up with them, and they are looking for new words so that they don't have to admit that they were wrong and caused harm with their advice.

---

[137] Harrington et al. 2009
[138] McAllister et al. 2009, p. 869

The Structural Model

This performance runs parallel to the calorie model. But while the calorie model is applied to the individual, this notion is, in fact, about societal structures. That does not mean, unfortunately, that it is sane. The main theme is simple. The model says that the obesity epidemic follows as a logical consequence of the increased availability of fast food combined with a decreased availability of opportunities to move. Here, the solution to the obesity epidemic is seen to be for people to live as far away from a fast-food restaurant and as close to an exercise area as possible.

Let me start with the fast-food restaurants. So the idea is that the closer a person is to fast food, the fatter they are likely to get. I don't know what upsets me most about that line of thinking. But to put it as simply as possible, the royal family will not get fat if a fast-food restaurant is built outside the palace. Nor are all people who live near a fast-food restaurant fat.

The facts presented by some demographic studies are that where there are many fat people living at the same time, there seem to be more fast-food restaurants. But that's just one correlation. I just can't believe that those who painted this notion themselves really believe that fat people are fat because of their proximity to the fast-food restaurant. They just can't believe it. Instead, I argue, there is something worse inherent in such simplistic notions. In fact, I think the disdain for fatness has become so normalized that it is sought only for causes that are considered morally objectionable in themselves, like eating fast food, for example. Fast-food and fatness, two morally infected concepts, simply marry well together. The fact that they are in the same places only means that. It's not an explanation. I'll come back to the inherent problems of correlation research later.

Now let's turn to the idea of proximity to exercise facilities. The Norwegian sociologist in public health, Inger Helen Solheim, problematizes the one-track tendency to view fatness as something exclusively negative. In her thesis, she shows how a group of people in what has been called Norway's fattest city reacted to public health interventions aimed at reducing fatness in the municipality. One of the proposals from the public health authority was that no Norwegian should have more than a certain number of meters to the nearest walking path. Therefore, in the fight against obesity, these would be constructed. The proposal was met with outright derision by the population. In this small town, the mountains and nature are right next door to every house. Everyone walks along the mountain - they go on tour, as they say in Norway. Yes, the fat ones too. They already had fantastic and natural walking paths all over the town. Everything was basically already walking paths. The bureaucratic idiocy that followed the pretense of too few walking paths is very telling.[139]

In addition to the common motion, the inhabitants of the small town often gathered together and ate. Food culture was considered to be of enormous importance, as was outdoor life. It was these two airs of life that bound people together in the community. There was joy around food and recipes and talking about food, and this applied to local doctors, teachers, and whole families. In between, most people hiked in the mountains. Overall, the thesis shows that the residents of Norway's fattest city had a very different understanding of food and health than public health experts. Such understandings must, of course, be taken into account before measures are taken against fatness - simply so that measures are not dismissed as pure nonsense. Fat people who walk a lot and who never eat at fast food restaurants will naturally lose confidence in these desk experts and will turn away from their advice.

The Emotional Model

I'll never forget the doctor who put his hand on my knee and paternalistically said: "I like to eat sweets too, you know, but not always"! It was one of those moments that left me speechless and brooding for days afterward. There was so much in those few words. Somehow, he managed to

---
[139] Solheim 2013

show forbearance for characteristics he himself attributed to me! He had no idea whether I liked sweets or not. He hadn't asked me. He also had no idea whether I liked it so much that I ate it all the time! Unlike him, who apparently, like me, wanted to eat all the time but could control himself. What's more, he even managed to look at me with a certain amount of amusement. He seemed to enjoy people who couldn't resist sticking their fists into the candy bag whenever the opportunity arose. A bit cute, as children do. After some pondering, I came to the conclusion that it must be that he, the doctor himself, was the one who wanted to sneak up at night and eat some forbidden candy. That it was he who had an emotional craving for food and sweets, a craving that he felt he was disciplining. When he saw me then, a much fatter human, he drew the simple conclusion that I lacked that capacity for self-control.

In Sweden, several medical researchers and nutrition experts have sat on TV sofas over the years and explained that fatty, sweet, and unhealthy food is addictive because it stimulates the brain's reward system. Because we are rewarded with such feel-good hormones, everyone instinctively wants to eat these unhealthy foods, they claim. So it's a matter of disciplined learning to resist and understand your own bodily impulses. We need to teach the fat ones, they say, that instead of opening the fridge, they fill that empty space with other things that give satisfaction.

For example, they could take a walk instead, as thin people do.

What's problematic about this notion is that it suggests that it's all about thinking. In other words, fat people are explicitly portrayed as non-thinking, while at the same time, the notion claims that thin people, by thinking, have managed to keep the fatness at bay. When thinking, people get, as they say, a craving for something really tasty. Well, they think of that piece of chocolate and go for a refreshing walk instead. Our most famous Swedish brain scientist once excitedly said that he had managed to lose 5 kilos just by using his brain. It was "really exciting," he said, that just by "activating the brain," he could manage to change his lifestyle. Incidentally, he was not fat and probably never has been. If only he knew how many pounds the fat, in decades of dieting, lost by activating the brain. After decades of biological, physical, chemical, social, and psychological research on humans adapting to their immediate environment, the idea of the non-thinking fat human is an insult.

Exercise and nutrition researcher Kholoud Alabduljader and colleagues have investigated how fat people and thin people differ psychologically in relation to food and eating. They found something interesting. They found that fat people experienced less food pleasure than thin people and that they rather showed a lack of reward feelings in relation to food.[140] The researchers concluded by discussing whether fatness might be caused by the lack of reward being compensated by fat people through overeating. Regardless of what I think about that conclusion, the study turns on the common idea that eating has become a reward for emotionally uncontrolled fat people. Instead, in the study, it was the thin people who felt rewarded by eating. This could explain why many thin people believe that since eating is so satisfying to themselves, fat people must find eating even more satisfying - otherwise they wouldn't be fat, would they?

The Motivation Model

One long-time researcher on human genetic weight is Dr Jeffrey Friedman. He stresses that:

"Body weight is genetically determined, as tightly regulated as height. Genes control not only how much you eat but also the metabolic rate at which you burn food. When it comes to eating, free will is an illusion."[141]

The idea that body weight has to do with free will, Friedman says, is harmful to the fat because it claims that the fat would have chosen fatness. No person I've met has chosen to be fat. The idea of free will, Roel Pieterman believes, is useful for demonstrating public health muscle.

---

[140] Alabduljader et al. 2018
[141] Friedman, In Kolata 2004.

Pieterman makes it clear that if genes were considered the main cause of obesity, it would be difficult to launch antiobesity measures. Therefore, from a public health perspective, fatness must be seen as something that can be remedied by the individual.[142]

The idea of motivation and self-regulation is central to most proposed solutions to thickness. The calorie model is imbued with this idea.[143] Here, the measures are presented as if the body's own ability to store fat is possible to regulate through simple, responsible choices in the individual's daily life. But since the idea of self-regulation runs counter to the energy-conserving nature of the living organism, the struggle often becomes impossible. It becomes almost impossible for those whose bodies have conserved energy best - either because of genes or periods of starvation that have maximized the body's hormonal ability to store fat. Those who are then considered to have a higher motivation to fight against the body's natural tendencies are those who are usually already genetically and metabolically thin.

Megan Warin, professor of social anthropology, describes it as follows. By ensuring that all our food choices are informed - that is, that we have been given information about the healthiest foods - it is expected that

---

[142] Pieterman 2015
[143] Shugart 2011

each individual will choose how much they want or do not want to improve their health (i.e., want to get slim).[144] Decades of campaigning against the obesity epidemic have spoken volumes; that it is rare to achieve significant permanent weight loss through information about adjustments in eating and physical activity patterns alone.[145] Therefore, if we continue to perpetuate the myth that everyone can become thin if they try hard enough, we are simultaneously saying that fat people are not trying.

A study of 177 young girls (9-15 years old) examined the impact of parental encouragement of physical activity for weight loss on girls' well-being.[146] It found that the fatter the girls were, and the older they were, the more their parents encouraged physical activity for weight loss. The more the parents encouraged, the more anxiety the girls felt about their weight. Encouragement had no effect at all on how much physical activity the girls engaged in. Their physical activity had completely different reasons.

In conclusion, the study showed that the idea of encouraging young girls to exercise in order to lose weight was an ineffective strategy. Instead, where parents encouraged girls to move regardless of weight, and especially where the whole family moved together in a non-compulsory way, girls moved more.

---

[144] Warin 2011
[145] Thille et al. 2017
[146] Krahnstoever et al. 2010

Self-regulation and motivation are not something that can be instilled in an individual through prompts. In particular, it cannot be instilled by people who consider themselves motivated and self-regulating while perceiving that others lack such powers. It is a primitive idea that some people would be less motivated and self-regulating than others. It is a fantasy that those who deal with fat people need to find an explanation for themselves as to why fat people do not become thin. Much of the fight against fatness in health care has consisted of motivating the individual to want to become thin himself, as if the humiliation of being fat and the rewards of being thin weren't motivating enough. These attempts to motivate fat people to self-regulate into thinness have failed worldwide. That's enough evidence that the idea is wrong.

The Dieting-As-A-Remedy Model

Most of the fat people I've spoken to have shown tremendous motivation and lost many more pounds of body weight than the thin ones ever did. But in reality, dieting doesn't work for the ninety-five percent of fat people who try. The under-reporting, I argue, is even greater. However, those figures are never told on the evening news. Above all, it is not told about all the people who get sick or die from dieting. Back in 1958, psychiatry professor Albert Stunkard found that the advice to eat less doesn't work on fat people simply because most of a person's weight or ability to store fat is genetically and metabolically predetermined:

> *"Most obese persons will not stay in treatment. Of those who stay in treatment, most will not lose weight, and of those who do lose weight, most will regain it."*[147]

Stunkard investigated a number of different weight loss programs. He found that no matter how long these programs lasted, how intense they were, or how food intake was cut, only six percent of participants managed to lose nine kilos in a year of treatment. Since then, research has consistently shown the same thing - that it doesn't work.[148] Many pounds have been lost many times over the decades, but more than two-thirds of those who lose weight weigh more when they stop dieting than they did before.

Over a ten-year period, 176,000 people were followed as they tried to lose their fatness. Only two percent of them ever managed to reach a so-called normal weight. Of these 3,500 people, eight out of ten regained their weight after two years.[149] Another 2019 study of 36,000 Americans found that those who were fat at age forty-seven and dramatically cut their weight were thirty percent more

---

[147] Stunkard 1958, p. 79
[148] Merry & Voigt 2014
[149] Fildes et al. 2015

likely to die than those who maintained their fatness.[150] It is findings like these that are leading an increasing number of critical researchers to argue that prescribing weight loss to the fat ones is deeply unethical:

> *"It is unethical to continue to prescribe weight loss to patients and communities as a pathway to health, knowing the associated outcomes - weight regain (if weight is even lost) and weight cycling - are connected to further stigmatization, poor health, and well-being. The data suggests that a different approach is needed to foster physical health and well-being within our patients and communities."*[151]

After a critical review of the assumptions and evidence surrounding fatness, researchers concluded that a paradigm shift is now required regarding the idea of dieting. The researchers published seven widely accepted assumptions behind the idea that dieting is a healthy behavior for fat people. They countered these assumptions with scientific findings that strongly challenge and even contradict these assumptions. The study reproduces numerous scientific references, and I refer readers to their study for further reading. They are too numerous to list here.

---

[150] Chen et al. 2019
[151] Tylka et al. 2014

ASSUMPTIONS	PROOF
Adiposity poses a significant mortality risk.	Except at extreme weights, neither body mass, nor fat stores, can say anything about longevity.
Adiposity poses a significant morbidity risk.	Obesity, i.e., BMI over 30, has been shown to be associated with certain diseases. However, no research has shown a causal relationship.
Weight loss will prolong life.	Studies have shown that weight loss for fat people appears to reduce the risk of premature death.
Anyone who is determined can lose weight and keep it off through appropriate diet and exercise	Studies where individuals are followed over several years, show that the majority regain the weight lost, or more, regardless of whether they maintain the diet and exercise.
The pursuit of weight loss is a practical and positive goal.	Weight cycling is the most common result of dieting and is known to increase weight, mortality, and risk of disease.
The only way for overweight and obese people to improve their health is to lose weight.	This is a hypothesis that has not yet been scientifically tested.
Obesity-related costs place a large burden on the economy, and this can be corrected by focusing attention on obesity	These costs do not take into account the unintended consequences of a global body weight focus, which includes

treatments and prevention	eating disorders, failed dieting attempts, weight shifting, reduced self-esteem, depression, and discrimination. The cost is not in the fat but in the failed treatments.

Source: Bacon & Aphramor (2011)

The Causality Model

The most comprehensive compilation of social research on obesity – The Oxford Handbook of the Social Science of Obesity[152] – presents obesity as the cause of all the conditions we have identified as welfare diseases. The figure below shows how obesity is thought to be caused by skewed energy-balance behavior (the calorie model) and that obesity then causes the diseases that most people eventually die from.

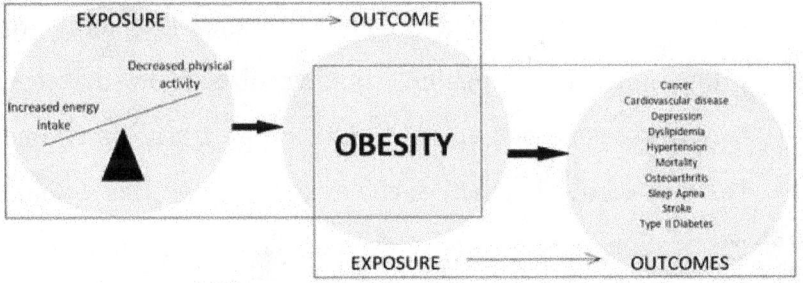

Model designed after Cawley (2011: 19)

---

[152] Cawley 2011

The most striking feature of the model is the status assigned to fatness. Fatness is made absolutely central, both as the main result of a poor lifestyle and as the main cause of fatal welfare diseases. So it seems that if we got rid of fatness, the cause of death would be found. But there is no research to show such a causal link. And that's troublesome for researchers. So they fiddle with words, they leave out important information, and they pretend it's scientifically established. But, as I said, it is not. I've been looking for 30 years for such a causal link.

The worst thing about the idea that fatness causes other diseases is its consequences for the fat. The fat gets blamed for all the ill health that is thought to be caused by lifestyle. They carry the "proof" visibly while the thin become invisible even though they eat fast food and walk around with vascular cramps, high blood pressure, and prediabetes. Fatness is also sweepingly presented as an independent cause of disease and death.[153] There is plenty of information and brochures linking obesity to diabetes, cardiovascular disease, and high blood pressure, but no one has yet proven what such a link looks like. Some speculation is about how fat cells create inflammation, which in turn creates other welfare diseases. But then, shouldn't we be putting inflammation as the cause of disease and not fatness? Thin people get these diseases too,

---

[153] O'Hara & Gregg 2012

and surely a causal explanation is needed there too? Much of the food processed in the West is inflammatory. But by merely emphasizing that fatness is the basic problem of the West, this wider food production problem is obscured.

In 2016, Umeå University presented a study showing that fatness does not increase the risk of heart attack.[154] Another study, among several, has shown that overweight people with heart disease seem to be protected by their extra weight[155] and that overweight people who suffer a heart attack fare better than so-called normal-weight people. This research would have been interesting for debt-ridden fat people to hear. But such research is not presented in the news or in health care.

There is simply no will to do so in the midst of a so-called obesity epidemic. An increasing number of studies show that so-called overweight (BMI 25-30) is of no significance at all and may even be protective. It is worth noting in this context that it was the pharmaceutical industry that financed the proposal to lower the limit for overweight from BMI 27 to BMI 25[156] without any medical justification. Rather, they wanted to raise the profile of a dangerous obesity epidemic in need of weight loss products. I will remind you of this later.

---

[154] Nordström et al. 2016
[155] Angera et al. 2012
[156] Peretti 2013

Katherine Flegal and colleagues questioned how estimates of how fatness causes disease are measured, and they found widely divergent estimates in the research that has been done. Some studies claimed that fatness increases mortality by five percent, while others said fifteen percent. Some studies suggested that 0.2 percent of all cancers could be linked to fatness, while other studies suggested eight percent. The same was true for cardiovascular disease (results ranged from seven to forty-four percent) and diabetes (results ranged from three to eighty-three percent!). The sum of the studies shows that it is impossible to speak of a causal link between obesity and these diseases.[157] No available data can prove that obesity, independently of other conditions, causes these diseases.[158]

Michael Gard calls all these brutal, constant exaggerations about the dangers of fatness "soundbites."[159] He describes these "soundbites" as empty rhetorical shells created to sound scientific. Gard even argues that it is precisely these "soundbites" that are the substance of the obesity epidemic.

"Walking around with an abundance of fat on your body, primarily being seen as big and fat, is perceived as carrying the responsibility of the whole nation's increased prevalence of diabetes 2,

---

[157] Flegal et al. 2015
[158] Tylka et al. 2014
[159] Gard 2022

high blood pressure, stroke, and myocardial infarction, even though you are fat and fit."[160]

It is a terrible notion that it is the fat individuals who are responsible for the nation's ill health.

But because fatness is more visible than the other so-called welfare diseases, the notion fits the market entrepreneurs like a glove. They could start openly exploiting people's insecurities about their bodies. It was possible to make money out of people's guilt about their appearance.

---

[160] Malterud & Ulriksen 2010

Entrepreneurs' Market

There is no money in the cure. The money is in the medicine. /Chris Rock

With the above quote, stand-up comedian Chris Rock strikes at the heart of the logic of the neoliberal market. It goes without saying that if there was a cure for obesity, the dieting market would die. Instead, it flourishes. The idea of launching an obesity epidemic and then diagnosing fatness as a disease has had an unprecedented impact on profit-driven markets.[161] The market has been filled with pharmaceutical companies, weight clubs and programs, diet camps, convenience foods, countless cans of powders and pills, diet books, exercise methods, sweeteners, fat-free products, prescription drugs, prescription physical activity, and exercise equipment that purport to burn fat.

Critical sociologists have shown how the pharmaceutical industry is constantly trying to develop medicines for lifelong consumption. These are medicines that are said to prevent the further development or worsening of certain conditions.[162] I experienced this cynical market when, during lunch, I found myself next to a sales manager from the pharmaceutical company Pfizer. He

---
[161] Jutel 2009
[162] Boero 2012; Rose 2009

was happy to tell us, full of confidence, about his latest assignment. This was over ten years ago, and he told me about the new market in China. There, the public health authorities had just opened the way for new slimming products by pointing to the increasing obesity of the population. As a sales manager, his task here was to quickly catch up with the rhetoric of the public health authorities and sell the products through advertising that referred to what the authorities were already promoting. Not only that, he said but, it was a matter of convincing the consumer that obesity was affecting their entire social life and that Pfizer's product was the savior. The product could then be sold for at least 5 years before the market was saturated (i.e. when no one believed in the product anymore), and by then, it was time to launch the next diet product.

The salesman was a very happy, nice, and privileged young man with the world at his feet. He was slim, fit, and well-educated and showed no empathetic reflection whatsoever on the fact that millions of people would buy deceptive products because of his marketing of them. One wonders here what the chicken is and what the egg is. Are empathy-free people hired to market worthless products, or are they made empathy-free in order to pursue such sales missions? Another word for lack of empathy towards the group to which worthless products are sold is dehumanization. You know, when a specific goal requires setting aside human vulnerability. The blatant goal, in this case, is money, power, and success.

A neoliberal market is shaped in relation to the state and the individual in a way that always favors the market.[163] In neoliberalism, the individual is considered to be rational and self-determining. Directly linked to the market, the individual becomes a citizen linked to society through consumption. All responsibility is placed on the freely choosing individual. Everything the individual displays depends on her own choices. Both the obesity epidemic and the health ideology are perfectly placed at this intersection.

The self-determination that entrepreneurs like to emphasize is largely created by the production market itself. They claim that it is the consumer who demands the products. The individual wants to be thin. The individual wants to strive for health. It is a well-functioning perspective for the market. How much they actually manipulate the psychology of individuals to keep them wanting these things, of course, they say nothing about. Far too few critical journalists seem interested in exposing power structures like these. Presumably, most journalists are also preoccupied with ideology and are themselves striving for the goal of a slim body. The glare of the

---

[163] Shugart 2016

concept of health, as I said, shields it from both moral and intellectual scrutiny.

What we need to realize by now is that the pharmaceutical industry and other weight loss production have become a sales industry in the same way as the shoe industry. What drastically distinguishes selling weight loss from selling shoes is the power of the economy that entire states, and national and global health organizations, have set the stage for with the launch of an obesity epidemic. A smorgasbord was laid out, where a shameless arena could begin to exploit people's feelings of worthlessness for huge profits. They could do so in the name of both health and science.

An Aggressive Exploitation of a Human Variation

The concept of medicalization means that a problem is treated as if it were of a medical nature. It is a specific way of looking at human variation and then putting it into practice. The basic idea is that certain undesirable human variations are seen as something that can be medicated away. The social sciences have been describing medicalization since the 1970s. The American sociologist Peter Conrad argues that the interpretive primacy of medicine over all things human has increased with each decade.[164] Conrad describes how three major changes have led to human variations that were once considered perfectly normal, or at least personal, now being regarded as diseases. In parallel, he argues, there has been a change in biotechnology, a change in the consumer, and a change in our healthcare systems. Together, these changes have woven fatness as the perfect variation to exploit through medicalization. Let's take the changes one by one.

The Biotechnological Change

The pharmaceutical industry has long marketed products for various human problems. In the past, marketing took place only through the doctor. Of course, doctors are still involved in marketing, but today they cannot keep up with the enormous range of medicines now offered directly to the consumer.[165]

The pharmaceutical industry in the US increased its spending on television advertising six-fold between 1996 and 2000 when it spent over $200 billion. Since then, the figure has continued to rise explosively. Promoting new diseases and then offering drugs to treat them is now a common practice following the rise of Prozac (the first "happy pill").[166] It can be described as the pharmaceutical industry constantly making active attempts to blur

---

[164] Conrad 2007
[165] Conrad 2005
[166] Ibid.

traditional boundaries between the normal and the sick in order to gain market share. In the case of obesity, they need to justify drugs and therefore have an invested interest in spinning hysteria around body size to secure their own market.

Consumer Change

As I said, the pharmaceutical industry today can bypass a previously strict control system and focus directly on the consumer. The individual has thus become a co-player in the increasing medicalization process. We are all now considered to be free consumers in a market that, in the absence of real, life-threatening diseases, tries to sell us health-improving and preventive miracle pills and treatments.

A clear example of consumer change is the enormous development of cosmetic surgery and cosmetic treatments.[167] The medicalization of women's breasts, lips, genitals, and skin is driven by enormous consumer demand. There is also still a huge demand for diet pills and other dieting tools. The media constantly point out the need for appearance enhancement and how that enhancement is strongly linked to our well-being and, therefore, our health. The body is a more elaborate project than ever, and the consumer has become the driving force behind it. Those who do not consume themselves thin today do not have the

---
[167] Ibid

same life opportunities as those who actively pursue thinness.

Change In The Health Care System

Healthcare has also become more market-oriented and can now compete for patients in a completely different way than before. If a new drug or treatment comes to market, the pharmaceutical industry can push new disease states to strengthen its products. On the one hand, they can try to change already existing diagnoses; on the other hand, they can broaden the definition and lower the entry threshold for already medicalized problems.[168] When the health sector allows the pharmaceutical industry's sales agents to do this, they become part of the new divide between the normal and the sick. Healthcare gratefully accepts the pharmaceutical companies' new medicines. They do not have to investigate a person's situation because the medicine already exists.

A concrete example is starvation as a treatment for obesity. The previous requirements of severe medical conditions and a very high BMI have been lowered over time, thus including more and more people under the category of fat. Today, a young girl who is sad about her slightly rounded body can be granted an operation on medical grounds and, at the same time, be completely free of disease.

---

[168] Ibid.

Changing body norms are now a cause of medicalization, while medicalization itself reinforces such body norms. Health care is online and accelerates the dissemination and mixing of medical knowledge, commercial advertising, and consumer desires.[169] As soon as a social phenomenon starts to be valued within a medical framework, societal values and ideologies are reflected through the treatments offered.[170] And the desire for new products grows.

Pharmaceutical Companies Clawed at the Fat Body

Pharmaceutical giant Novo Nordisk presented its future market strategy in 2016 at an obesity conference in Australia. In its marketing of products for fatness - or chronic obesity, as it now calls it - it openly outlined its strategic goals for selling its medicine: Goal 1 was to rapidly create legitimacy for the medical treatment of obesity. Goal 2 was to increase and develop medical treatment for obesity. Goal 3 was to include their diet products in high-cost coverage. Obesity, they say, is a severe and chronic disease, but one that their very medicine can alleviate. But, they say at the same time, there are three obstacles in the way of this massive product placement.

---
[169] Ibid.
[170] Canguilhem 1989

The first problem in the launch of new diet products, the pharmaceutical company's salesmen write, is the stigmatization of fat people. Obesity, they continue, must be established as a chronic disease for the stigmatization to end so that fat people will even want to buy their products. Therefore, their ambition is to generate more science on the fact that fatness is a serious disease. I repeat. So they are generating more science that says that fatness is a serious disease. Not whether it is or to what degree.

The second problem they raise is that there is a huge lack of knowledge about the treatment of obesity. More accurately, they write, there is knowledge and remedies (they themselves claim to have both), but they are not fully exploited by the health care system. This, in turn, leads to far too few being treated for their obesity (i.e., far too few buying their product). Their ambition here is, therefore, to support healthcare in diagnosing and treating fat people, i.e., to implement Novo Nordisk's knowledge more widely. They do this through sales conferences, where they invite healthcare professionals to learn about their products while they offer food and refreshments in a relaxed atmosphere as they have always done.

Novo Nordisk identifies the third major problem in the launch of new slimming products as the current HTA use in healthcare. HTA is an abbreviation for Health Technology Assessment. It refers to the systematic evaluation that the health care system makes of existing knowledge for specific treatments. This is where healthcare takes an ethical stance, weighing the pros and cons of one treatment against another. This includes reflecting on desired and undesired effects before decisions are made. Here, Novo Nordisk stresses, they must push for greater acceptance of obesity treatment. They will do this by fighting against the use of HTA and finding possible workarounds through policy and new legislation on obesity treatment.

These people have exciting jobs. They are salespeople and entrepreneurs, they are driven by profits, and they are flowing in their interesting marketing work. They are high-performing people in an upbeat environment where everyone is pulling in the same direction - forward and upward. Pharmaceuticals is a lucrative business. Sales increase every year as more contracts are signed with a healthcare system in need of more treatment products for its fat patients. But because none of these drugs can cure fatness, they are sold with the subtext that they can help people lose weight if they diet and exercise at the same time. When weight loss does not occur, it can therefore be explained by the same bad character as usual. And conversely, if there is a minor weight loss, it will be claimed to be due to the medication.

However, the launch shows that they really have been reading up. Entrepreneurs are not dumb. So they cite both the stigmatization and the lack of knowledge in healthcare as problems. So do I. In fact, those are my main points. The difference between our analyses, however, is that I see the market as one of the fundamental problems in terms of both stigma and ignorance.

They have not yet come up with a medicine that cures fat people. They want science to show that fatness is a disease, not whether it is. The stigmatization of fatness also means that customers are queuing up for new hopeful products. So they don't want to get rid of the stigma. On the contrary, they try to gain the trust of the fat by painting the stigmatization as a problem. They show that they see and care and have products that can help. They say they certainly don't stigmatize the fat people who buy their products.

What the Market Looks Like

In a Swedish study, 960 Swedish children were asked what they thought of their own bodies.[171] As many as 200 children said they were ugly because they were too fat. Among these 200 children, the majority were thin, while a few were slightly overweight. Similar delusions were revealed in a study of how thousands of Spaniards seek medical treatment for fatness each year, despite being only

---

[171] Erling & Hwang 2004

slightly overweight.[172] The growing and widespread fear of fatness means that those who have ever felt dissatisfied with their bodies are ready to act. And the market is inexhaustible.

Sociology professor Lee Monaghan, with colleagues, describes the producers in the dieting market as entrepreneurs. These entrepreneurs all contribute in one way or another to the continued portrayal of obesity as a problem that should be addressed as soon as possible.[173] All of the entrepreneurs help to define obesity as a public health issue that affects everyone. They are all in an arena where solutions to the problem are constantly being produced.[174] Moreover, in their drive, entrepreneurs actively contribute to blurring the line between care and oppression.[175] The following is a description of the different categories:

• Creator. This is where the science is, where facts and statistics are generated, and where epidemiological research is funded and made available to the public through the media.

• Amplifier/Moralizer. Here are media that unabashedly report the creators' results. However, only a fraction of all the knowledge produced is presented. At the same time,

---
[172] Gracia-Arnaiz 2012
[173] Monaghan 2010
[174] Smith 2009
[175] O'Hara & Gregg 2012

they moralize, create opinions, and stir up emotions about and commercialize this knowledge. They report exclusively on a looming epidemic. No nuances, no questioning, no distinctions.

- Legitimator. There are public health authorities, the National Board of Health and Welfare, and international organizations addressing the problem of obesity through government action. The World Health Organization (WHO) and medical powerhouses have been very active here in spreading the threat of a global obesity epidemic.

- Supporter. Here are the campaigns run by pharmaceutical companies, health companies, and global food companies looking for, and constantly claiming to have found, the miracle cure for obesity.

- Enforcer/Administrator. Here are the health professionals, from doctors, nurses, dieticians, and psychologists to gym instructors and life coaches, all acting as if they have the necessary knowledge to make fat people thin.

- Entrepreneurial self. Here are the active dieters, both fat and thin, all those who make a daily effort to become or stay thin in order to achieve a higher moral value. Those who have managed to lose a few kilos condemn the person they were before they became real, thin human beings.

Journalist Jacques Peretti has for many years examined the capitalist market that surrounds the concept of the obesity epidemic. The word epidemic is central to making money from obesity.[176] Once something is medicalized, new cures can always be launched. And everything has gone the way of the market in the widespread launch of an obesity epidemic. Just think of the scale of the epidemic when, with the help of entrepreneurs, the threshold for obesity was lowered from BMI 27 to BMI 25. There was no scientific evidence for the lowering. It was accepted because eager drug salesmen were able to paint a bleak future if nothing was done about obesity. And millions more people were suddenly fat, in need of even more products.

The pharmaceutical industry has survived all the scrutiny of both dangerous and long-term ineffective anti-thickness drugs. When a drug has received strong enough criticism, they have just stopped selling it and started selling new ones instead. Along with the food industry, they have flourished as more and more dieting methods have been developed under the guise of science. The former chief financial officer of Weight Watchers in the US, Richard Samber, openly told journalist Peretti why they have been so successful: "Because the 85% who can't keep the weight off, but gain it back, come back again and again."[177]

---

[176] Peretti 2013
[177] Ibid.

We should not forget that the individual, the consumer, fat or thin, is also, as I said, an entrepreneur. The activity is high, and the stakes are played to achieve as dignified a self as possible. Consumers' daily efforts to avoid fatness, get rid of fatness, get even thinner, or complain about others who are fat constantly glue together the otherwise dubious foundations of the market. Every time the consumer openly berates or makes negative comments about weight, and every time the fat deal with the disparagement in silence, the contempt for fatness is perpetuated ever more strongly.

The diet and health market permeates everyday life and offers so many self-improvement tips that the choices for consumers never end.[178] Many so-called normal-weight people today live their lives between eating unhealthy foods and abstinence, allowing the food industry to reap more economic capital in both areas.[179]

Research Has Sided With the Market

Scientific research is a bigger player in lucrative markets than many would like to admit. Nowhere is this more evident than when the pharmaceutical industry funds the research that will sell its products. Pharmaceutical companies are free to decide what questions to ask. And above all, they can control which ones not to ask. This arrangement has obvious consequences for the knowledge

---

[178] Dixon & Winter 2007
[179] Peretti 2013

that is built up in the current so-called obesity epidemic. An epidemic that the pharmaceutical market has helped to create. Consider Novo Nordisk's strategy, where their goal is to generate - that is, create - knowledge that fatness is a serious chronic disease.

Weight loss surgery, or starvation surgery as I like to call it, is a clear example of the marriage of research and marketing. It has been one of the fastest growing and lucrative medical fields we have had in modern times.[180] Much of the research done on these operations is funded by market players in such surgery. This has had a major impact on the positivity surrounding the idea of surgery for obesity, despite the fact that it is an invasive procedure that cripples people's ability to access nutrition.

Let me give a detailed example of market-driven know-how and present the article Myths, Presumptions, and Facts About Obesity. It was published in the highly ranked scientific journal New England Journal of Medicine and had as many as twenty authors.[181] The aim of the publication was said to be to clarify the state of knowledge about obesity by separating myths from facts. Myths, according to the authors, were beliefs disproved by science. Assumptions were beliefs that had not yet been proven, and

---

[180] Brown 2015
[181] Casazza et al. 2013

facts were knowledge that had been scientifically proven. Here are their examples of myths, assumptions, and facts:

Myths (ideas that, according to the authors of the article, have been disproved by science):

- Small changes in energy balance lead to lasting weight loss.
- Those who do not set realistic goals will not lose weight.
- Fast weight loss leads to worse results than slow weight loss.
- Motivation is the key to success.
- More physical activity at school prevents and/or reduces childhood obesity.
- Breastfeeding protects against obesity.

Assumptions (ideas that, according to the authors of the article, have not yet been scientifically proven):

- Eating breakfast protects against obesity.
- Childhood eating and exercise habits determine our weight as adults.
- Fruit and vegetables help us lose weight.
- Yo-yo dieting is dangerous for your health.
- Eating too little leads to weight gain and obesity.
- The structure of the environment (access to walking paths, parks) influences obesity.

Facts (ideas that, according to the authors of the article, are scientifically proven):

- Genetics plays a big role but can be overcome.
- Reducing energy intake is effective for weight loss, but dieting or recommending dieting usually does not work in the long run.
- Increased physical activity improves health - regardless of weight or weight loss.
- Moderate, regular physical activity helps maintain weight.
- Continuous weight loss methods and products help to keep weight down.
- For overweight children, programs involving parents and the home lead to more weight loss or weight stability.
- Having meals that promote weight loss delivered at home or using meal replacements is beneficial for weight loss.
- Some medications can help patients achieve meaningful weight loss as well as prevent weight gain with continued use of the medication.
- In some (extremely obese) patients, bariatric surgery leads to sustained weight loss.

So far, it may look like simple, straightforward conclusions. But the conclusions change in significance when the article's credits are examined. In scientific publications, so-called conflicts of interest are disclosed in the credits. Conflicts of interest refer to anything that may have influenced or had an impact on the findings. This is an important part of the transparency of scientific research. You can do research on whether surgery for obesity is good or bad, but if, at the same time, you make your living from performing such operations, then it is important that the reader knows that. This is because it can color the results if the researcher gains from some results and loses from others. In this article, there were plenty of disclosed conflicts of interest. It is often quite harmless to actually report them because nobody reads these postscripts anyway. The lead author disclosed conflicts of interest shareholdings in the company Mobile Fitness, as well as patent ownership for three different slimming products. The rest of the twenty researchers were funded to varying degrees by the following producers/organizations:

Food, drinks, and snacks: Archer Daniels Midland, The Coca-Cola Foundation, Danish Brewers' Association, Danish Dairy Association, European Dairy Association, Global Dairy Platform, International Dairy Foundation, Knowledge Institute for Beer, Kraft Foods, Mars, McDonald's, Global Advisory Council, Mead Johnson Nutrition, National Cattlemen's Beef Association, PepsiCo, Red Bull, Weiss chocolate, World Sugar Research Organization, and Wrigley Company.

Pharmaceutical industry: Arena Pharmaceuticals, AstraZeneca, Chandler Chicco, Eli Lilly and Company, GlaxoSmithKline, Jason Pharmaceuticals, McNeil Nutritionals, Merck, Novo Nordisk, Orexigen Therapeutics, and Pfizer.

Other business activities: Jenny Craig (commercial dieting company), Mobile Fitness (preventive lifestyle change app), Pathway Genomics (DNA and health scanning), Ulmer and Berne (lawyers for the largest multi-companies in the US), and Wharton (management, business, technology).

Overall, the final results of the study were as follows: It is possible to lose weight despite genetic predispositions. Small changes, different diets, more walks, more fruit and vegetables, and avoiding petty eating do not help. What does help is physical activity, continuous use of weight loss products in the form of meal replacements, and home delivery of low-calorie foods and medicines.

However sympathetically I choose to read the publication's findings, it is impossible to ignore the fact that they take on a whole new meaning when we see how research is funded. The results, in this case, benefit the very food giants, pharmaceutical companies, and organizations that funded the research. It subtly promotes meal replacements, pharmaceuticals, mobile apps for physical activity, and home delivery of low-calorie diets. At the same time, no negative mention is made of soft drinks, beer, sugar, dairy products, or sweets, the producers of which helped fund the research in question. Note that this is not the same as saying that they are presenting false knowledge. They just choose which myths, which assumptions, and which facts to present.

Particularly salient facts in this publication are that "weight loss products work" and that "the main thing is that the fat person continues with them". Right. In a purely mathematical way - that is, without taking into account the biopsychosocial vulnerability of humans - dieting "works" if you never finish it. If you are imprisoned for ten years with access to a bowl of cabbage soup every day, well, then you are guaranteed to lose weight. But humans don't work that way, so how highly should such facts be valued? People can't handle drinking cabbage soup and sandy powdered drinks for the rest of their lives, so should we say that it works?

This study is not unique. The market is actively looking to obesity research to sell products to those who want to lose weight. The results must show that the solution lies in methods and products that can be sold, not in methods such as abstinence. Abstinence does not make money for the market. What I want to say with this example is that the confusion between marketing and knowledge makes it extremely difficult for ordinary people to find their way around everything that is said. By reading the fine print of the conflicts of interest, we can at least get an idea of the resources behind the results that are presented. It can help us understand why no products or methods have worked for fat people. They are often just marketed products. They try to convince us that they work. Even through advertising masquerading as science. Because people believe in science.

Let me take a Swedish example, where Lund University has become entangled in the market's dieting frenzy. At Lund University, there is a professor who has researched a spinach pill against obesity (she mixed spinach and dried it into a powder). The tests (scientific) were done on a small number of pigs and a few more rats, with one group fed only fat and the other fed fat and spinach. The pigs and rats that were given the spinach did not gain as much weight as those who ate only fat. The pill was marketed in these tests as if it had been scientifically developed at a real university. And yes, it was. Of course, that doesn't mean the pill made fat people thin. Fat people don't live on fat alone. But the spinach pill spread around the world. The dieting craze is a booming industry, even for scientists. Since then, other pills have come along, and one by one, these fall into oblivion so that new pills can emerge. They are advertised as scientifically backed in clinically white jars. To support their marketing, they promote the image of fat people as people in decline, and in need of action, through the media.

The Pure Barbarism of Reality TV

The image of a looming obesity epidemic permeates deeply into the maintenance industry, and today has stepped all the way into the contemporary barbarism we call reality TV. Nowhere is the narrative more morally clear about who fat people are, how they should be managed and by whom, and with what attitude we should approach them. In the 2000s, most reality shows designed to make fat people thin featured a doctor in a white coat. His job is to tell fat people, with medical legitimacy, how unhealthy they are. But above all, reality shows try to present this unhealthiness to the viewer.

I'll never forget when Scottish diet agitator Gillian McKeith asked the fat contestants on You Are What You Eat to poop in a cup. She wanted to sniff how bad their poo smelt and tell the viewer what the stench said about the deeply immoral nature of the fatties. Apparently, fat people's poop smells extra disgusting. Thin people's poo apparently smells good. I felt something hit bottom there and then. Purely existential thoughts intruded about who is human and about who can do what to other people. I was overwhelmed with shame at this terribly intimate distinction between people and people. One person had the right to judge the other person through their poop. The other person, the fat one, would confess his poop, admit his guilt, and promise to do everything to get good poop again.

The fat body is an open game in the cascade of reality shows where "real people fight real problems". Through the educational barbarism of reality TV, we learned how to keep our homes clean, to be sexy, to train our dogs to be obedient, to cook better food, to exercise more, and to stop being fat. In the formal explosion of health-oriented reality shows, the negative image of fat people has been intensified and moved forward for entertainment purposes.[182]

A Moralizing Theatre

So how is it possible that the entertainment industry is allowed to portray fat people as obnoxious, disgusting, offensive, and ridiculous? At a time when equality, human rights, diversity, justice, humanism, and tolerance are the watchwords of all our democratic institutions? Well, the contempt must pass for something else. The production of these reality shows is a kind of craft in which the dieting that fat people have to undergo in front of millions of viewers is painted as a solution based on good intentions and knowledge. In this way, the devaluation of the fat body must be masked.

---

[182] Dutta 2007

The ruins of the Roman amphitheater Colosseum are one of the seven wonders of the world. It was a magnificent creation, almost sixty meters high, and could seat sixty thousand spectators. It was a gift to the people, an arena for the execution of criminals, for battles between animals, between gladiators and animals, and between gladiators themselves. The shows took place at prime time: executions at noon and great bloody battles in the evening. Today, we have left such barbarism behind. We think. Today we get our more distant entertainment via a screen in our homes.

Studies have shown that people who consume many televised crime dramas are more likely to believe that crime, in reality, looks like the media's version of it.[183] Therefore, such moving images also influence people's perceptions of specific groups in society. It is just another expression of the extreme sensitivity of the social human being to impressions.

In the first reality TV series in the early 1970s, Americans simply followed the everyday life and experiences of an ordinary family. From then on, the format developed at a rapid pace across the Western world. Here in Sweden, Expedition Robinson set in motion what can be likened to an explosion of different television formats where "ordinary" people are filmed in more or less

---

[183] Morgan et al. 2009

ordinary situations. It was 1997, in fact, the same year that the obesity epidemic was launched. Today, almost anything, often in the form of various competitions, can be shown on television. Social experiments are mixed with problem-solving, people eat spiders, are locked up in small houses, show off their unkempt homes, are helped with their disobedient children and dogs, are scolded for financial negligence, survive in the jungle and walk around half-naked in luxury paradises with constant access to booze to spark sexual, emotional and relational conflicts. It's all broadcast every day on television and streaming sites across the Western world. And then there are the fat shows.

While reality TV was intended as entertainment to engage viewers' emotions, people's private lives became of interest to public health ideologists. This is where what has been called the pedagogical turn in television, where citizens are to be trained to manage their own well-being through self-modification, took place.[184] The reality show has, in this sense, become an arena for governance and action rather than a representation of reality. Here, viewers are inundated with cultural ideologies. In these relatively simple scripts, the action simultaneously has a moralistic dramaturgy that seemingly naturally separates good people from bad.[185]

---

[184] Oullette & Hay 2008
[185] Warin 2011

These morality plays work by appealing to the viewer's emotions.[186] But no matter how naturally humans appear to act, there is a created narrative. There is a plot in which various codes are laid out in a certain order, which rectifies a moral narrative that fits perfectly into today's power relations and constructed health ideology. This emotional technique is very effective, net you are told scene by scene what to feel. The moral of all dramas is personal responsibility and self-improvement. Such moral edicts probably sound pretty good to many viewers, especially to those who despise fatness. They can then feel that someone is actually trying to do something about the problem. From the negatively presented problem, the morally right can emerge in theatrical overtness. The enemy has been made clear. Fat people have thus become dark symbols in the pervasive ideology of health. In the same way that young black men were made into dark symbols of America's social insecurity.

The TV Drive against Fat People is Unprecedented

We don't put the fat enemy in jail. However, no human variation has been attacked more harshly and more clearly by the media. In You Are What You Eat, the fat person is held accountable for the contents of his fridge. Bad food is

---

[186] Kavka 2008

dramatically thrown in front of the camera. The bad food is colorless, messy, and often in quantities. Often it is piled up or mixed to look even more disgusting. When the fat person sees all this, his/her face splits open in horror. He/she admits to being a sinner and is now ready to repent. Henceforth, discipline and a new focus. Fresh new food in lots of colors is displayed, and wonderful music accompanies the camera as it sweeps over the new table that is supposed to look like a clean paradise for a dirty fat person.[187]

In Biggest Loser, a group of fat people compete against each other, isolated in a castle and surroundings. Here they have constant access to so-called healthy food, trainers, a gym, a sauna, doctors, fantastic surroundings, advanced training equipment, and a TV crew. For a few months, the contestants are weighed and measured as they lose weight. One by one, they are voted out until the Biggest Loser is left standing on the podium to receive cheers and a large sum of money. A white-clad doctor begins by explaining to the contestants that they are in very poor health. The same contestants are told at the end that they now have very good health. This makes *The Biggest Loser* seem to be about serious medicine. I am not questioning here that the biochemical values of individuals with higher body weight improve after three months in a castle with healthy food,

---

[187] Warin 2011

training, and coaches around the clock. Rather, I am questioning the very connection of the theatre to the reality of fat people. The evidence is overwhelming about how participants fare when they leave the sheltered and structured workshop. Unless they embark on a strict diet and cultivate a rabid interest in thinness, they gain weight again after the program.

In some more overtly moralizing reality shows, values other than health are at stake. In the make-over show Bulging Brides, where the goal of the fat girls is to come in a small-size wedding dress, no reference is made to medicine at all.[188] Instead, the slender female body is linked to sexiness, desirability, and the ability to be a proper partner in the heterosexual marriage contract.

The same is true in the show Darling, You've Become a Fatty, which ran on TV3 a number of years ago. Here, ten different couples are on the brink of divorce because one partner has become fat. To prevent divorce, the fat partner has to lose weight. Together with a trainer with a marine aura, the fatty is trained to become the sexy person the thin partner once fell in love with. The fatty has become so ugly and disgusting that he or she is encroaching on the slim's self-image. In all scenes, the fat person is portrayed as lazy, gluttonous, depressed, and disgusting, while the thin person is active, alert, careful, and responsible. The underlying

---

[188] Sukhan 2012

theme is that the thin person deserves better than to live with a fat person and that everything can be fixed with military discipline.[189]

The Saviour and the Sinful Masses

As a TV savior of fat people, no one has been as persistent as English chef Jamie Oliver. He tried his hand at slimming down an entire nation through his TV show. He set his sights on slimming the whole world by teaching people basic cooking skills. In the reality show Jamie's Food Revolution, Oliver is presented as nothing less than a food saint, "descended on earth to save working-class children from British school food by teaching school matrons in 'England's fattest city' how to cook healthy food".[190] Australian researcher Megan Warin asks how it was even possible to orchestrate the idea that a young, rich, white man would come to England's poorest city to save its inhabitants from obesity.

Working with the Public Health Agency of England, Jamie Oliver claimed that obesity in England was caused by a total lack of knowledge about how to cook. Therefore, the population needed education. "Now, all of Rotherham will start cooking," Oliver said. The idea was that if he taught a few people to cook, they would then teach a few others to cook, and eventually, as a snowball effect, all

---

[189] Brandheim 2018
[190] Warin 2011

250,000 inhabitants would be able to cook healthy food. In the series, the threat image of fatness is explicitly built up by military metaphors. There is a "manifesto" and an "arsenal" of strategies with which Oliver arrives in the city to declare war on fatness. By "bombarding the population with health advice" in order to "arm them with knowledge", the population is mobilized to form a "front line" in a concerted attack against junk food.[191]

Similar to the show You Are What You Eat, viewers are taken into the contestants' homes to see what is eaten, what is not eaten, and even where and how it is eaten. The symbolic codes that accompany any story about fat people are repeated through a host of assumptions, such as that fat people are sloppy, uneducated, lazy in need of change. In the show, Jamie Oliver struggles to evoke the participants' sense of responsibility, their obligation to maximize their lives and not to be a burden on society. The experiments are fully in line with the new public health ideology that promotes principles such as personal responsibility, active health consumption, ability, and empowerment.[192] Especially among the least privileged. The residents of Rotherham would choose to improve their health and reduce the risks associated with being fat and thus become

---

[191] Ibid.
[192] Raphael & Bryant 2002

good, ethical citizens.[193] And yes, indeed. The experiment failed, of course.

The Art of Distinguishing Between People and People

In reality TV, it should be said it is not only personal responsibility that is emphasized. There has also been a shift in the narratives presented, where fatness is now presented as a symptom of a particular inability to cope with emotions.[194] In shows such as Oprah, The Biggest Loser, My 600 lb. Life and Big Medicine, the overconsumption of food (which all fat people are assumed to engage in full-time) is portrayed as a sign that there is an emotional void to be filled. Through various dramaturgical constructions, the viewer learns that this emotional void was created in childhood. It involves physical, psychological, sexual, social, and emotional abuse, neglect, abandonment, divorce, shyness, sadness, and loneliness.[195] It was these traumas, the fat people tell us, that led them to start eating.

The story of the imagined emotional void of the fat is brought to a head in the reality show My 600 lb. Life. In that show, we meet the stern surgeon Dr. Nowzaradan who performs starvation operations on people weighing around

---

[193] Warin 2011
[194] Shugart 2011
[195] Ibid.

600 lbs. As viewers, we get to follow the fat individual path to their desired surgery. After the fat people are operated on, a psychologist is brought in to find out how they got fat. They all tell of a childhood trauma when headless comfort eating was allegedly set in motion to fill the emotional void. It's about finding what led them to fatness. So although they have by then had surgery to remove vital parts of their digestive system that make them physically and biologically unable to eat - they are losing weight - the problem of fatness and its solution must be presented as emotionally rooted.

I've been thinking a lot about how this show is structured. Why do they even use the idea of emotionally driven overeating linked to childhood trauma when they're not really solving the problem that way but rather through a brutal physical intervention? I've come to the conclusion that it's again about moralizing about fat people's behaviors. The solution to the problem of weight to be presented to the viewer is that the individual must learn to discipline his emotions, to control his impulses in order to become a responsible adult citizen. Although the operations themselves are a biologically and physically brutal procedure, the emotional problems of the fat people are nevertheless highlighted. This is done through the creation of trauma narratives to show the characters of the fat individuals - that they have been too emotionally uncontrolled in their behavior. Thus, although their weight plummets as a result of the forceful interventions, they are not allowed to be cleared until they have processed their emotions - i.e., admitted their sins. With these stories, even the surgery itself will not be blamed if it fails. After all, it was always an emotionally driven problem, which distinguishes them from thin, rational people.

An important detail in this context is that the photos the viewer sees from the childhood of the ones who had undergone surgery show that the majority of them were fat long before the trauma occurred. This contradicts the whole story that they started eating themselves fat because of the trauma. But with blurry childhood films, the producers are probably counting on viewers to miss that important detail. Most viewers are not critical scientists. Most just want entertainment and a good story.

What I am arguing is not whether overeating is the result of emotional harm or not. There are a number of explanatory models for understanding ourselves, and they are all unique - biologically, psychologically, socially, culturally, emotionally, genetically, and materially. What I criticize is the way such narratives are constructed in reality TV to morally pedagogically arouse the viewer's beliefs about what a good and a bad citizen is. Although fatness is solved by mutilating the biological functions of the body, it is never explained as biological. Probably because that would make fat people innocent and morally unproblematic. Nick Couldry, a professor of media communication, calls these reality shows secret neoliberal theatres, where immoral citizens are portrayed behind various dramaturgical devices.[196] If you are fat, unlike those who are not fat, you are more emotionally driven, a trait that has always been attributed to difficult groups in society.

The search for emotional explanations for fatness is a deep trap. We need to remind ourselves that the fat individual in documentaries is just one ingredient in the producers' moral narrative of right and wrong. It is the producers who build the story, and they do not do it because they want to offer therapy to the fat main characters. Rather, an emotionally driven glutton becomes the excellent "pre-figure" in the story of how failed fat people can become successful thin people. An emotionally driven person can be taught reason and rationality. In this way, viewers really get to understand who is rational and who is unreasonable in the story. It is the difference between fat and thin people that is dramatized when fat people get to play the one to be fixed. It's the difference between thinking and non-thinking people that is portrayed.

The threatening image painted on television will go down in history as one of the most pervasive, fully legal

---
[196] Couldry 2008

violations of a human bodily variation that has ever taken place. In You Are What You Eat, The Biggest Loser, Big Medicine, Fat Kids, Fat Chance, Generation O, Flab to Fab, We Are Eating Ourselves to Death, Inside Brookhaven Obesity Clinic, Obesity Killed Her, Fat Actress, Extreme Makeover Weight loss, The National Body Challenge, My Diet is Better than Yours, Fit to Fat to Fit, Dance your Ass Off, Heavy, Huge, Freaky Eaters, My 600 lb. Life, I Used to Be Fat, Half-Ton Mom, Darling, You've Become a Fatty, Oliver's Ministry of Food, Honey, We're Killing the Kids, Family by the Ton, and Doctor Fat, to name but a few, "ignorant" and emotional fat people are lectured by "knowledgeable" and thin experts. Their fridges, their thoughts, and even their poo are displayed on the screen as horror stories to expose the guilt, stupidity, and disgustingness of the fat. They must, in every show, acknowledge the problem. They must confess that they have turned themselves into something horrible, which can be remedied by disciplining their whole person by more knowledgeable people. We are all witnessing this, but we have not yet realized the extent of what this barbarism can make us do to, say to, and think about fat people.

Mind you, just because I call it barbarism doesn't mean it's not entertaining. It just means it's barbaric - that is, crude and emotionally driven. Humans have always had barbaric rituals where certain types of people are humiliated while the masses watch. The main thing is that we see that it is barbarism, so we don't think that what we are witnessing has to do with science and knowledge. Reality TV does nothing to improve attitudes toward fat people. On the contrary, they are the most barbaric part of the systemic stigmatization of fat people that is played out before our eyes and the eyes of our children. The entertainment value of all the fatness discipline of individuals became enormous. But while the marketers together created fairy tales about how to defeat the fat enemy, the failure to combat the obesity epidemic, in reality, was abysmal.

The Failed Actions

In 2017, the world's largest annual obesity conference, Obesity Week, was attended by over three thousand obesity researchers. The conclusion of the conference was that the results of decades of action against the so-called obesity epidemic were disastrous. No intervention had succeeded. On the contrary, the fat children who had received specific interventions had become fatter than those who had received no interventions at all. On the contrary, no information and no campaigns had made fat adults thin. All that remained, the conference concluded, was even more bariatric surgery. No media reported on that meeting. Shouldn't it have been big news?

The measures and campaigns have not only failed. They have failed miserably. Only one in twenty people who try to lose weight succeed to any degree. Many get fatter. Moreover, dieting has been proven to have devastating effects on the human body.[197] Neither medical science and practice nor public health ideologists have any knowledge of how to effectively, safely, and permanently transform fat people into thin people.[198] Instead, they are cutting out parts of their digestive systems. Or they now try to manipulate peoples' appetite via hormonal injections.

---
[197] McHugh & Kasardo 2012
[198] Greenhalgh 2015

As a professor of communication, Helene Shugart is clear. No campaigns have spent as many resources as those that staged the war on fatness. At the same time, no other campaign has achieved the same total failure. Shugart asks how this is even possible. She gives the obvious answer: "Because the theory on which the campaigns are based is wrong.[199] The medical profession has been tasked with trying to change the behavior of fat people to achieve thinness without that idea being grounded in scientific research.

In the midst of an unprecedented amount of scientific research and an unprecedented information boom, it is easy to be fooled into thinking that anti-obesity measures are evidence-based. After all, they are presented as being based on evidence from a consensus of medical science. This is often referred to as evidence-based knowledge or best available knowledge. This science is supposed to have concluded that the cure for fat people is to, as the then Prime Minister of England, Tony Blair, put it, "close the fridge, get out on the street, and start walking, running and exercising".[200]

In England, a 12-year experiment took place in which ninety-five percent of children in the first and last year of primary school were weighed and measured. Letters were

---

[199] Shugart 2016, p. 19
[200] In Townend 2009

then sent home to parents whose children were measured as overweight according to the Body Mass Index. The purpose of the letters was to make parents aware of the problem and to offer them help in solving it. Few parents took up the offer, and most became very stressed by the letters. After twelve years, it became clear that the experiment had succeeded in alienating the families they had most wanted to engage.[201] At the same time, several studies have shown that children who are slimmed down by their parents are significantly more likely to become obese adults.[202] There are many such failed experiments.

The Starvation Surgeries Should Be Mentioned

Before I go on to discuss the massive failure, I should say something about starvation surgery. They go by many names, but what they have in common is that they involve cutting, bypassing, and sewing up digestive organs so that you can't eat more than the minimum. It is, therefore, an invasive method of starvation. Those who undergo surgery usually lose a lot of weight and do so quickly. I have followed the research results, and I have talked to many people who have had surgery, who want to have surgery, and who are relatives of those who have had surgery. My view is that the results and causes of surgery are so

---

[201] Gillison 2018
[202] Carper et al. 2000

complex that it is not possible to talk about success in general terms.

However, many pounds have been lost. So yes, starvation does work as a weight loss method. If you cannot eat more than a minimum of food a few times a day, you will lose weight. But the complications along the way are so numerous that an entire book is needed just to evaluate the quality of life, self-image, nutritional problems, weight gain problems, and the need for multiple surgeries that follow these operations. The double shame that fat people face when they are finally, mercifully given this help also prevents them from talking openly about the severe side effects, which are psychological, social, and physical. When American sociologist Natalie Boero interviewed women who had undergone various forms of gastric surgery, she interpreted their stories as meaning that they were now living their lives with severe eating disorders. So, even if the public discussion is that the treatments are successful, I remain critical of what we mean by successful.

Psychologist Louise Adams has studied the impact of starvation surgery on the mental health of those operated on. She reports that the number of operations in Australia increased from 9,300 to 22,700 per year between 2005 and 2015. Four-fifths of the surgical patients were women. Adams says that a study that followed 25,000 surgical patients over 15 years shows that two to three times more people than non-surgical patients visited hospitals for mental illness. These included substance abuse, personality and behavioral changes, neurotic and emotional moods, and schizophrenia-like symptoms. In addition, self-harm behaviors increased fivefold, while 10% of all deaths among those who underwent surgery were suicides.[203]

Despite the alarming results of the study, there was no discussion about stopping the operations. Instead, the idea was raised that starvation victims should be offered adequate access to psychiatric care after the operations. In addition, surgeons were accused of not selecting appropriate patients when they apparently failed to turn away people with possible mental illnesses. But at the same time, their own data showed that a full forty percent of mental health problems occurred after surgery, not before. Another meta-analysis of 28 studies found a four-fold increase in suicide among those who had undergone surgery.[204] Again, this study did not lead to a discussion about banning surgery but instead found that the most important thing was to get better at identifying people at high risk of suicide before surgery.[205]

It will be some time before we can or have the political will to, interpret the overall outcome of these procedures. The reason I wanted to mention the procedures here is to

---

[203] Morgan et al. 2019
[204] Peterhänsel et al. 2013
[205] See psychologist Louise Adam's program Untrapped (blogs, x, Insta)

show that I am fully aware that these operations are considered to be a method that works. The vast majority of patients lose weight, and that was exactly what they were promised.

Not until 2022 did the National Board of Health and Welfare Sweden come up with the first preliminary national guidelines for obesity treatment.[206] They will use the term chronic obesity now as the word fatness is considered stigmatizing. In these guidelines, the National Board of Health and Welfare recommends that 220,000 Swedes should now be offered starvation surgery. They justify this by stating that 1.3 million Swedes now suffer from the severe chronic disease obesity and that they have no effective medication. Because of stigmatization, they write, everyone who is weighed and measured and then offered starvation surgery should be treated with respect. Let's hope that by respect, they mean that they will first have extensive discussions about ethics, human rights, and human biopsychosocial vulnerability before this scenario becomes reality. Personally, I cannot escape the thought that deep down, they hope that most people will decline the offer of surgery. After all, they have done their professional duty. They have taken the obesity problem seriously and

---

[206] https://www.socialstyrelsen.se/kunskapsstod-och-regler/regler-och-riktlinjer/nationella- riktlinjer/riktlinjer-och-utvarderingar/obesitas/

offered a kind of medicine. The future will show where all this finally goes.

More Failed Experiments

In the US, the Healthy People 2010 campaign was launched. The goal was to reduce the number of fat Americans from twenty to fifteen percent by 2010. No state achieved this goal. Instead, the percentage of fat Americans increased to twenty-five percent in thirty states. Another example of a failed campaign was calorie labeling on restaurant menus. The campaign was launched in the US over a decade ago. The idea was that restaurant patrons could see on the menu how many calories each meal contained. This allowed them to choose the smarter, expertly informed, skinny option.[207] However, the campaign had no influence whatsoever on what food either fat or skinny people ultimately ordered.[208]

The failure was attributed not to the concept but to the problematic behavior of customers. Experiments such as these demonstrate both a profound ignorance of the social human being and a lack of self-criticism on the part of the creators of the ideas. Statistician Scott Keith and colleagues also explain that a fat person eating large portions of food does not prove that portion size has anything to do with

---

[207] Herman & Polivy 2011
[208] Elbel et al. 2009

fatness. There are no studies showing such a causal relationship.[209]

By studying the long-term consequences of low-calorie diets, Traci Mann and colleagues found that one to two-thirds of dieters gained more pounds than they lost from the diet itself.[210] Another study found that many patients became so sad and anxious when their doctor told them they needed to lose weight that they started eating more than they had before.[211]

Several critical researchers have shown how billions of dollars have been spent on obesity prevention measures without success.[212] One example was the 4.5-billion-dollar fund set up to reduce childhood obesity in the US before 2015, which failed completely.[213] Critical researchers, including myself, now know that many people have become fatter because of the campaigns.[214] In a study of two medical centers in Sweden, ninety percent of the nurses reported that, despite support and advice, their overweight patients never lost weight and that many of them tended to weigh more and more as time went on.[215] That study was done over twenty years ago. All the failures are frustrating,

---

[209] Keith et al. 2006
[210] Mann et al. 2007
[211] Allison 2011
[212] Merry & Voigt 2014
[213] Roberto & Brownell 2011
[214] Meleo-Erwin 2012
[215] Arborelius 2001

but the statistics are probably even worse than that. Remember that the statistics are taken from published studies. The medically funded dieting experiments that have failed never make it into the public domain.[216]

At the obesity unit in Örebro, Sweden, another experiment was recently started whereby weight loss would be achieved by drinking low-calorie powder. I couldn't believe that this could happen again. After all, decades of such experiments have shown that it doesn't work. I decided to follow the process, which was doomed to fail. Every year, I was told that the results would soon be ready. Every new year, I called again to find out how things were going. However, no results were presented. Several years after the study was supposed to be published, I searched intensively for what had happened and found the following note: "The study was unable to analyze the results because too many people dropped out." To me, this is a result that should have been reported and problematized. After all, we can only guess how many such dieting attempts have failed when they are never reported. In another experiment in Örebro, a balloon was inserted into the stomach to make fat people eat less. The first trials showed that the participants lost about 18% of their body weight after 6 months. What the results didn't tell us was that when the balloon was removed, all the weight came back.

---

[216] Tylka et al. 2014

They Made People Sick

Despite extensive research findings that have shown for over sixty years that the simple idea of calories in/calories out is ineffective for fat people, health authorities continue to promote it. They do so year after year, month after month, day after day. At the same time, they have persistently claimed that the reason it has not yet worked is that

- it has not been sufficiently explained to fat people.
- fat people do not understand how to follow this simple information.
- fat people are less motivated than thin people, the proof of which is that they are fat.

Certainly, one explanation for the failure of the campaigns could be that fat people simply do not have the brain power to follow the advice given. Certainly, we could conclude that a billion people are not intelligent enough to control their calorie intake and ensure their calorie expenditure. But why on earth would our explanations go that way? Such a view of human nature must be abandoned. After all, we have spent hundreds of years abandoning exactly such divisions of people. We cannot regard large parts of the world population as idiots for not slavishly following a health ideology imposed by a privileged middle and upper class. The only convincing, humane explanation for the failure is that the theory on which the advice given has been wrong. Not only has there been a lack of scientific evidence to carry out these campaigns. They have been morally panicky, judgmental, and borderline oppressive.

Research shows unequivocally that the majority of fat people feel very bad about seeing doctors and other health professionals - regardless of the condition they are seeking treatment for. The news never presents this kind of research.

Both fat men and fat women are affected by the way they are treated by healthcare professionals and risk losing self-esteem and becoming depressed.[217] The fatter you are, the worse you are likely to be treated.

Governmental health campaigns have played a major role in the promotion of the thin ideal.[218] In fact, effective shaming by the authorities ("the governmental efficiency of shame") ensures that we are kept in a state of anxiety about the risk of our bodies being considered abnormal.[219] This counterproductivity, this thwarting of the very purpose of these campaigns, is ironically the only scientifically established link between health policies and fatness.[220]

---

[217] Puhl & Brownell 2006
[218] Halse 2009
[219] Cobb 2007, p. 360
[220] Campos 2004

When Australian sociologist Sophie Lewis and colleagues interviewed 141 adults diagnosed with obesity, they told us they felt the worst about the kind of contempt that was more subtle and indirect. They found it difficult to challenge it, and so it was precisely such subtle put-downs that made them silently blame themselves. In addition, they avoided more and more situations where such denigration could occur, and they constantly thought of their body in negative terms.[221] In my experience, fat people have exclusively told me about this subtle denigration. In fact, not a single one of them has mentioned overt bullying over the years. However, when I have asked those who want to make fat people thin, they seem completely blind to these more subtle forms of condescension. They truly believe that what fat people are subjected to is overt bullying. Therefore, they completely miss the enormous, and indeed crucial, role they themselves have played in the negative self-image many fat people carry.

The American plastic surgeon Maxwell Maltz, whom I mentioned in the introduction, marveled at how different his patients felt psychologically after their operations. Maltz operated on people who had been severely injured in one way or another and who needed extensive facial or body reconstruction. Some patients experienced an immediate improvement in their quality of life after the

---

[221] Lewis et al. 2011

operations, while others did not seem positive at all. After witnessing for some time, the varying reactions of patients to cosmetic surgery, Maltz left his work as a surgeon to try to understand the human psyche. In so-called experimental psychology, Maltz found that the human nervous system cannot distinguish between an actual experience and an imagined one. This seemed to explain why his surgery did not seem to help some patients. These people, according to Maltz, had a poor self-image even before the injuries occurred. And it seemed very difficult to remedy such already-established self-images.

And how does a poor self-image develop in a person? Well, Maltz said, from all our experiences, successes, setbacks, humiliations, triumphs and how other people have reacted to us, we have mentally constructed an image of ourselves. If that image is negative, it is virtually impossible to change that image in any situation. Maltz went so far as to liken feelings of inferiority to being hypnotized into having false images of ourselves. As soon as we accept an image that others have of us and become convinced that this image is true, it has the same power over us as a hypnotist has over his subject. Instead of hypnosis I turn to human biopsychosocial vulnerability to explain the strong forces we are exposed to in our lives.

The visibility of fatness in contrast to the norm of thinness, together with constant comments, discussions, pressures, news reports, and media debates, have contributed to the creation of a very negative self-image for many fat people. So, how does this negative self-image affect our ability to feel at home and welcome in the world? Maltz answers:

> *"To find life reasonably satisfying, you must have an adequate and realistic self-image and a wholesome self-esteem. You must have a self that you trust and believe in. You must have a self that you are not ashamed to "be", and one that you can feel free to express creatively rather than to hide or cover-up. When your self-image is subject to shame, your creative expression is blocked."*[222]

The Fat Body Were Blind-Folding

So why do they continue to tell fat people that they are no good? That they are ugly, stupid, and imperfect? Why do they continue to portray fat people as sick? I believe that the repeated threat of fatness has blinded their minds. In the book Toscanini's Fumble, Professor Harold Klawans presents various medical cases where medical science got it wrong. One case describes a woman who underwent one of the world's first abdominal surgeries (1960s). Shortly after the surgery, she began to experience a weakening of her legs that made it difficult for her to walk. She was also vomiting. A quick examination revealed that she was

---

[222] Maltz 1960, p. 10

suffering from subacute spinal degeneration - a condition usually associated with severe vitamin deficiency and malnutrition. But here was a woman who was 'obviously' not malnourished - rather well-fed. This puzzled the doctors. She was getting weaker and weaker, and the weakness was even in her arms.

One year after the operation, the woman was dead. The autopsy showed that the abdominal surgery had been too brutal. The woman had not been able to retain food and had vomited up most of it. Fluid had managed to seep through, but the effect was that she had been slowly starving to death ever since the procedure. Although much of the fat had been broken down, adipose tissue does not contain proteins or vitamins that can help a body survive. For example, the absence of a mineral like potassium weakened the heart, and the organs failed one by one due to malnutrition.[223]

So, medical science did not understand that the woman was dying of starvation. They didn't understand it because the woman was fat. This was not the Middle Ages but the latter half of the 20th century. Today, the operations are more sophisticated and are accompanied by lifelong intake of essential vitamins to keep the bodies of fat people from starving to death. The fact that this is the only treatment that has been shown to work (fat people losing weight) and

---

[223] Klawans 1989

that fat people have been queuing up for it shows how difficult it is for fat people to lose weight and how motivated they are to do so. The example of Klawans shows how blinded medical science has been by the fat body. It has actually prevented them from thinking straight.

Instead of healing and uplifting people, the whole approach has pigeonholed fat people as failed and incompetent citizens.[224] Systems researcher Stafford Beer explained that the purpose of a system is what it does, not what it says it does.[225] A system that undertakes to help fat people but instead enacts a pervasive contempt for them is, by definition, not a helping system. It is a discriminatory, degrading, deeply damaging primitive system built on a "ritual exclusion of danger from the pure order."[226] And this "danger" is so visible that it cannot be missed. We already detect it when we measure our babies and start comparing each child with a normal curve. In fact, we get assessments of our children's possible deviations from the desired weight when they are in the womb.

They Ignored Our Biopsychosocial Vulnerability

Already in the introduction, I made clear that the management of the so-called obesity epidemic is based on

---

[224] Ulrich 2000
[225] Beer 2004
[226] Douglas 1992

and maintains a dehumanization of fat people. Dehumanization has four technical components: differentiation, symbolization, organization, and polarization. All aim to distinguish the fat person as something other than an ordinary human being. As something undesirable. Dehumanization could be seen as a method whereby those in power consciously or unconsciously set aside knowledge of human vulnerability to achieve specific conscious goals. The worst examples of dehumanization can be seen in mass murder, war, torture, and extermination of populations. In classical warfare, the method of ignoring the biopsychosocial vulnerability of the enemy is crucial for soldiers to be able to hurt their opponents.

But such dehumanization is also embedded in various forms of oppression, stigmatization, and discrimination against people who are not considered to be quite as worthy as those who identify them.

Dehumanization is also inherent in targeting groups of people. For example, moralizing about the unwanted behavior of fat people is dehumanizing in several ways. On the one hand, it gives those who identify fat people a kind of superior position that gives the impression that they themselves would engage in "good" behavior, and on the other hand, the concept of behavior, when directed at undesirable people, tells us that these people's vulnerabilities should be ignored. They are not relevant. They are just "excuses" to avoid addressing the behavioral problem already identified. The focus on human behavior simply shuts down, on a morally dehumanizing level, any understanding of human vulnerability of a biological, psychological, and social nature.

Human Vulnerability Is Partly Biological in Nature

What distinguishes fat cells from other cells is that they can continue to grow even after reaching full maturity. They can store more and more fat and thus continue to swell. From thinking that fat cells are passive storage depots, researchers now know that they are active, playing a major role in their own defense. This makes it very difficult to influence them through behavioral changes. Biological life has no moral guidelines. If nutrition is lacking or too much energy is expended, the organism shuts down peripheral processes and devotes all its energy to survival. No hocus-pocus, just pure survival. Nature saves energy. It does not waste it. The more numerous and larger the fat cells, the better they are at saving.

If the biological body lacked energy-conserving survival instincts, we would live dangerously. We would die quickly if the body continued to use as much energy as usual during long periods of starvation. Researchers have shown how the heightened ability to store fat in those who become fat again after weight loss sets a new, higher starvation threshold, with any effort to go below that threshold being fought by the metabolic system.[227] Few systems in the world are as adept at survival, says Rudolph Leibel, Ph.D., at Columbia University, as the energy-preserving body system. This includes not only adipose tissue but also the brain, digestive system, liver, pancreas, and thyroid.

> *"People can exert a level of control over their weight within a 10-, perhaps a 15-pound range. But expecting an obese person to decide to simply eat less and exercise more to get below the obesity range, below the overweight range? It virtually never happens. Any weight that is lost almost invariably comes right back. The control mechanisms for body weight operate over months, even years, not day-to-day or meal-to-meal. People live in the moment. They lose weight over the short term and say they have exercised willpower, but over the long term, the body's intrinsic controls win out. And just as willpower cannot make fat people thin, a lack of it does not make thin people fat."*[228]

Biological vulnerability is vital knowledge for fat people who have been trying to lose weight for decades.

---

[227] Sumithran et al. 2011
[228] Friedman, In Kolata 2004

Knowledge of the biological body's own resistance mechanisms to starvation has not only been omitted in research and the media. This knowledge is also openly mocked by the most vocal fat-haters in social debate forums. Those obsessed with the behavioral perspective call it simple excuses. Nor have public health authorities been particularly interested in the biological body. That knowledge would prevent them from flexing their political muscles. In its current neoliberal form, public health science relies on the free will of people to make the nation healthy through behavioral change. But if we had really understood or even discussed how biology fights against being drained of energy, we would also understand that fat people have to go far beyond normal will and motivation to manage weight loss and make it permanent. I remind you that many people, after years of unsuccessful dieting, eventually choose to have large parts of their digestive system cut out in order to have a chance of becoming thin.

Human Vulnerability Is Partly Psychological in Nature

Earlier, I described how Maxwell Maltz left his job as a surgeon to devote himself to understanding the human psyche. He presents how sensitive the human psyche is in the construction of the self-image that is slowly established in each person's life. It has long been known that chronic diseases increase the risk of anxiety, social phobia, depression, and suicide.[229] The fact that an entire surrounding society suddenly decides that fat people suffer from a severe chronic disease is naturally absorbed into the psyche of these people. When this idea of illness also moralizes fat people's behavior, abilities, and choices as causes of this illness, it naturally builds up an increasingly damaged self-image among fat people.

Here, I would like to return to the fact that starvation surgery is claimed to be a medical cure for obesity. But what the surgeries actually reinforce is the widespread belief that obesity is about unconscious behavior. The operations are primarily designed to force starvation behavior, not to repair a disease. The fat people queue up for surgery mainly for the chance to feel like normal people - not because they want to be medically healthy.[230] Here, they do everything they can to try to repair the damaged self-image built up by the singling out of their bad behavior.

Unfortunately, starvation surgery does not eliminate an already established negative self-image. Many people who have undergone surgery have told me how the expectation of a new view of themselves did not materialize and that this was extremely painful to realize. Plastic surgeon Maltz operated on people severely injured in accidents. These

---

[229] https://www.dagensmedicin.se/opinion/debatt/vart-psyke-paverkar-var-kroppsliga-halsa/
[230] Boero 2012

patients had very different self-images before the accident. Fat people undergoing starvation surgery to improve their lives is a completely different story. The fat people who finally end up deciding to have surgery are almost exclusively carrying a negative self-image. In fact, it is often this negative self-image that forces them to have the operation in the first place. This explains, I think, why so many people who have had surgery never experience any increased zest for life when the weight is reduced. The health service has, of course, seen this. They have, therefore, tried to screen out people who do not appear to be mentally strong enough to be satisfied with the operation. At the same time, the National Board of Health and Welfare now wants 220,000 Swedes to be offered a starvation operation. This shows that they are ready to put people's vulnerability aside to achieve a so-called public health goal.

Our psychological vulnerability is also evident in the phenomenon known as eating disorders. In a study, researchers Eric Stice and Mark Van Ryzin identify the risk factors that shape the development of eating disorders in adolescents. It is, they show, a one-way street in five stages:

- the pressure to be thin
- the incorporation of the pressure to be thin

- contempt for your own body, which can always get even thinner
- dieting
- eating disorder, when the body no longer wants to accept food.

Once the contempt for one's own body has turned into active dieting, it usually takes more than two years until the eating disorder is a fact. The process is, therefore, difficult for healthcare professionals to understand and link together. Dieting does not in itself mean an eating disorder. Rather, the young people's dieting, with increasingly poor self-esteem and attempts to take control, escalates into something that only after more than two years is established as a deeper psychological and physical disorder.[231] The five steps to an eating disorder show how biology and psychology are in direct communication with human social vulnerability.

Human Vulnerability Is Partly Social in Nature

Socialization is the very process that affects our psyche's ability to build a good or bad self-image. In the social world, we are exposed to relationships from the very beginning of life. They may involve attraction or repulsion, understanding or incomprehension, adaptation or deviation, and success or failure. When we perceive these differences,

---

[231] Stice & Van Ryzin 2019

we also perceive who we are. Here, we adopt the world's summarized view of ourselves so that it becomes our own view. When people who are already undesirable face even more contempt, the stress develops into something much more serious than for others.[232] Researchers have shown that the high level of psychosocial stress that many fat people report, as a result of their deep contempt for fatness, contributes to negative changes in the body's metabolism.

The words, attitudes, and actions of your social environment have an indirect impact on your mind and body. The same is true from the other direction. Our bodies affect both our psyche and our place in society. We could talk about three anxiety-driven interacting feedback systems. By anxiety driven, I mean that the different parts of the vulnerable person are constantly trying to reduce anxiety. Socially, we don't want to end up on the negative side of a society's values. Psychologically, we struggle to maintain as secure a self-image as we can. Biologically, the body fights for pure survival. These anti-anxiety mechanisms kick in automatically when a problem arises. These are problems such as social exclusion, psychological degradation, or biological starvation. A person who does not succeed in reducing any of these anxiety-producing states is placed in an existential, chronic anxiety that

---

[232] Kira et al. 2014

becomes increasingly difficult to escape. A person who has the resources to keep the anxiety away can experience flow.

Today, fatness is claimed to be a medical problem, while its solutions are behavioral.[233] Those who want to fix fat people have thus been given a large moralizing space to influence their (fat people's) self-images. Moreover, a whole market has been opened up to exploit the full extent of this human vulnerability. As a result, fat people have an increasingly anxious relationship with themselves and their own bodies. Ethics researchers describe that in order to get any kind of relief, people, patients, and clients must experience being treated as autonomous, competent, and belonging human beings.[234] Today, fat people experience the exact opposite. In a pervasive way - biologically, psychologically, and socially – they are treated as non-independent, less knowledgeable, chronically ill deviants.

---

[233] Herman & Polivy 2011
[234] Lewis et al. 2011

Stigmatization

Being fat has acquired a kind of status that has overshadowed the more positively charged characteristics of individuals. They have become carriers of a stigma. A stigma is a marking of an unwelcome identity. It is about making it clear that something about a person or a group is unacceptable. Many such labels have been documented in human history. For example, a mark could be burned or carved into the forehead of individuals who were considered a danger to others.

Stigmatization also worked by frustrating the public's beliefs about what is right and what is wrong. Public hangings, whippings, stonings and being shackled and shamed. These are all examples of how the unacceptable could be made visible to everyone. Today, in modern society, people are not marked in the same concrete way. For ethical reasons, the stigmatization of unacceptable people is less tangible. Instead, the stigmatization of people is shaped by the popular court that has emerged in the mass communication society.

Along with an increasingly harsh court of public opinion, where more and more people are taking up space to judge people who they feel do not belong in society, there is an additional dimension to today's stigmatization. Unwanted variations such as fatness are now claimed to be managed from a care perspective. This has allowed the loud-mouthed court of public opinion to invoke care when they openly despise fat people. They can imagine that they are thinking about the health of fat people. When, in fact, they are thinking that they need to get thin.

Moreover, once established, stigmas are self-reinforcing. One experiment showed that individuals who were shown negative images of fat people afterward expressed themselves more negatively about fat people than those who were shown positive images.[235] In reality, the same experiment creates incalculable avalanche effects. The more people present their negative evaluations of fat people, the more negative images are circulated.

Some stigmas are considered more serious than others. In the legal system, for example, there are gradations of the severity of the crime, which in turn determines the length of the sentence. Quite simply, we make different moral demands on our fellow human beings so that we can coexist and make society work. But outside the concrete legal system, it becomes more complicated to evaluate immoral crime in human variations. Here, beliefs are formed by sharing the same images (such as threats), the same political statements, and the same moralizing texts and films. We slowly grow into the opinions that are pushed the hardest by those who have the most room to

---

[235] McClure et al. 2011

speak. Eventually, we may be so convinced of the reprehensibility of a particular deviation that we no longer need to think. The more extensive the system of beliefs, the more it thinks for us but is kept alive by us. In this sense, being fat has become a full-blown stigma.

Ignorance of Stigmatization

The stigmatization that followed the large-scale launch of an obesity epidemic has reached deep into the self-image of our children.

In 2014, a teenage girl with anorexia wrote a short post in the local newspaper. It went something like this:

As children, we went to the school nurse for health checks. Among other things, we were weighed. If it turned out that you had grown too much, they became very afraid of you being overweight. This happened to me when I was nine years old, and the nurse gave me a booklet with different eating advice. There were pictures of different food products and information on how much sugar they contained. Since then, not a day goes by that I don't worry about eating too much or the wrong things. Not a single day has I enjoyed my body, and I struggle every day to prevent these thoughts from taking over my life completely...

The above post made a deep impression on me. And because it was so close to my own research, I wrote a response. In turn, my response led to an invitation to appear on the radio. I told them that we need to stop weighing our children's bodies because we are making them feel that there is something fundamentally wrong with them. One of our most famous obesity doctors was asked to respond to my criticism, and he said: "Brandheim (that's me) is completely out of line. Of course, we should do everything in our power to protect these children from the obesity that causes so much suffering." He argued that any steps taken to prevent obesity are right because the condition of obesity is so terrible to suffer. So here he turned directly to the fifth and final step of the fear hypothesis: "We must do something, and anything we do is better than nothing."[236]

Research on fatness as a stigmatized variation has increased since I started researching. However, far too little attention has been paid to how the measures themselves harm individuals belonging to an already stigmatized group.[237] Yet it is not difficult to understand that the idea of calling people sick carries with it fundamental ethical issues of identity and human rights. Such ideas about determining that a particular human type is sick require careful investigations into the difference between real illness and human abnormalities we find merely disturbing.[238] We simply cannot "do everything" to save

---

[236] Diprose 2008, p. 142
[237] Hatzenbuehler et al. 2013
[238] Leach Scully 2004

ourselves from an obesity epidemic. We must, of course, avoid harming the people we claim to want to help.

Those so-called obesity experts must know what stigmatization is and what it means for fat people today. In fact, doctors themselves tend to emphasize stigma as one of the major problems of being fat in today's society. However, it is as if they do not want to understand where the stigmatization of fat people gets its basic legitimacy from - namely, from the constant launch of an obesity epidemic by healthcare, authorities, and medicine. The control of the body that takes place in our schools does not reduce stigmatization but increases it.

But surely the thin people just want to help the fat people to be healthy? This is by far the most common question I have been asked over the years. In line with the philosopher Georges Canguilhem, I would like to point out that ill health, and especially attributed ill health, is automatically a cultural devaluation. That is to say if a child who feels healthy and strong is taken into a separate room and treated as if it carries a dangerous disease, a new devalued identity is created for that child. That's how sensitive we are socially. Obesity doctors seem to think that control is perceived as care and that this care leads to the child becoming thin. But humans don't work that way. People are born into very different environments where their self-esteem depends on the social, cultural, and economic resources that surround them from birth. Over time, they conquer others' views of them. Children with fewer resources will experience the singling out of their bodies more harshly than children with many protective resources. The irony is that most people who are singled out in their fat bodies are precisely people with far fewer resources than those doing the singling out. Campaigns against fatness should also, according to the public health authority, take place primarily in socio-economically disadvantaged areas.

The teenage girl who wrote the report adapted to the so-called care shown to her by the school nurse. She lost weight and became thin. But the price of adaptation was a body contempt and an eating disorder that she now struggles every day to keep at bay. All the steps taken to counteract fatness are simply not good, and sometimes they are downright disgusting. In a culture that despises fatness, it is not possible to start helping people stop being fat without invitation. In a racist context, you can't gently tell the victims of racism how to repaint their skin to avoid racism. Well, you can, of course, but it reinforces the racism that singled them out in the first place.

I've already told you about the doctor who told me that "we can't have it like in the US, a lot of fat people walking on the sidewalks." In this sense, all problems with the treatment of fat people reach a kind of climax. Thus, despite the fact that contempt for fat people has grown with the measures, despite the fact that the interventions have failed and even been counterproductive, despite the fact that people wage daily wars against their own bodies to try to avoid devaluation, we "can't have it this way" with a bunch of fat people walking around in our midst. And that's why we keep picking up fat kids from the classrooms, weighing them, and giving them advice on how they can be as good as those who remain in their school desks. A little thinner, a little better. All this reflects a huge ignorance of the real social drivers of stigmatization.

Driving Forces Behind Stigmatization

Stigmatization is not about the victims feeling a little offended by the negative attention. Jo Phelan, a researcher in social medicine and stigma, and her colleagues summarize three of the basic drivers of stigmatization:

- exploitation and domination - keeping some people down.
- social reinforcement of norms - keeping some people within certain boundaries
- avoidance of disease - keeping some people out.[239]

Thus, stigmatization does not occur automatically for every new human variation that is suddenly noticed. For stigmatization to occur, an internal image must be created

---

[239] Phelan et al. 2008

of why a specific variation is an unacceptable deviation. The process does not arise because fat people are made visible by themselves. Rather, there is already a layer of images of right and wrong in all of us that is constantly ready to be pulled out. Once the fat person has been identified as bad and wrong, the next step in the process begins, where the image is reinforced by fitting into larger narratives of badness. For example, the fat person may suddenly seem stupid in their fatness. At a time when everyone should strive for thinness, fat people continue to be fat. At the same time, we are told that fatness costs money. Then, those who don't seem to be doing anything about their fatness are portrayed as stupid, inconsiderate, and selfish. And so the negative image of fat people is further reinforced.

Negative attitudes towards fatness are overwhelming in our part of the world. They are pervasive throughout society: in our workplaces, in healthcare, in government, in education, in social media, in traditional media, and in the pub. At the same time, it is in the intimate sphere, among family, friends, and life partners, that the greatest wounds are created. In our closest relationships, the intimidated act as a kind of ground soldier in the ideology of thinness and health.[240] Even those who have a relationship or proximity

---

[240] Carr et al. 2008; Puhl et al. 2008

to someone who is fat risk falling victim to the same stigmatization.[241]

Discrimination against fat people has grown steadily since the launch of an obesity epidemic and is now comparable in scope to racism, Islamophobia, and prejudice against people with mental illness. Furthermore, contempt for and prejudice against fat people has been found to be more prevalent among health professionals than among the general public.[242]

A further dimension of the management of fatness is the collective perception that everyone is at risk of becoming fat today. Everyone is at risk of turning into costly, unhealthy, and unattractive people. The bathroom scales acquired as small confessional booths out of guilt testify to this imminent threat. "How much do I weigh today?", "How close am I to being called fat?" and "Do I look fat?" are questions that preoccupy large parts of the Western world's population. It creates a culture of judgment that is perpetuated every time an extra kilo appears on the scale. These numbers provoke anxiety about the unacceptable person we are becoming. Here, we are all almost unknowingly driving the stigmatizing process.

It is now impossible to take measures against fatness without simultaneously degrading fat people, as they are

---

[241] Hebl & Mannix 2003
[242] Forhan & Ramos 2013

already long-standing cultural undesirables.[243] Some researchers go so far as to speak of a fascist structure. By this, they mean that anti-obesity measures have been shaped by processes of ideology and intolerance of alternative research findings on the fat body.[244] Specific power relations tend to highlight only those scientific results that point in one direction - the dominant idea of the healthy, slim, and self-disciplined citizen.

The public's drive to self-actualize as thin is very strong today. You are rewarded for looking like an active self-producer. But this drive also becomes a driver for stigmatization of those who fail to look self-actualized. Moreover, in contrast to the stigmatization of race or sexuality, for example, the contempt for fatness is reinforced and encouraged by our authorities. The contempt for fat people does not have to be hidden in dark back alleys but has been planted in our democratic institutions under the slogan of health. The health ideology is, therefore, undoubtedly one of the strongest driving forces behind the stigmatization of fat people. Although there is no pure correlation between body weight and health, fat people absorb the shame of being identified as unhealthy in their own self-images. In the wake of this shameful silence

---

[243] Merry & Voigt 2013
[244] Rail et al. 2010

among fat people themselves, the stigmatization often flies under the radar for those who are not fat.

The Extreme, Oppressive Consequences of Stigmatization

> *"Stigma leads to suffering only when the person takes up a subject position where the messages about ugliness, failure, irresponsibility, and blame become incorporated in self.[245]"*

Stigmatization always strikes downward. It even has a direct impact on the purely physical fat body. I am thinking of the surgical procedures that are done to cure fatness at the individual level. Surgeons who operate on parts of fat people's digestive systems are clear - they want to perform the operations on people who are healthy, people who can tolerate invasive surgery, people who can be expected to survive. Sociologist Natalie Boero has shown how surgeons, therefore, cite not only possible future illnesses but, above all, stigmatization as the most compelling reason for surgery.[246] And because the shame of being unwelcome in the world is unbearable, fat people themselves queue up for these operations.

As I mentioned earlier, societies work by wanting to control, organize, and help people - either for the sake of those people or for society. In some cases, says Ian

---

[245] Malterud & Ulriksen 2010, p. 51
[246] Boero 2012

Hacking, like with obesity, we also want to change people. In order to change, we use science to create new human types that, in some sense, did not exist before.[247] We begin to medicalize human differences. In a five-step process, being fat is slowly being equated with being a human being who must change to be good enough. The first step is to label human variation as sick or abnormal. The second step is to identify the suffering people as incapable of managing their lives in the best possible way. In a third step, the idea is embedded in the existing institutions of society. The fourth step is to focus and reinforce knowledge about the identified people within the framework of institutions - such as health care and universities. Finally, in the fifth and final step, experts on this specific category of people emerge. The experts can then validate both the knowledge and the practice that is then in full swing.[248]

When the public sees the entire war machine orchestrated against a looming obesity epidemic, it is hard for them to think that it could have been a mistake from the start. There is too much invested to be a mistake. But what they never learn is that people who suffer weight discrimination are sixty percent more likely to die, regardless of BMI.[249] Although such research should be of great interest to public health, it never appears in the news.

---

[247] Hacking 2006
[248] Ibid.
[249] Sutin et al. 2015

Part of the explanation for the higher risk of death is that the dehumanization associated with stigmatization undermines one's entire self-image as a fully functioning human being.[250] The stigmatized lives of fat people have been linked to devastating psychosocial stress with health problems such as depression, severe eating disorders, poor self-image, and purely physical stress symptoms.[251]

Stigmatization is different from other types of psychosocial harm. The person who is stigmatized is harmed publicly, privately, internally, in relation to others, economically and socially.[252] To feel mistreated on one or two occasions or to have many bad days in one's life is not to be oppressed and stigmatized. When a group or a type of people are stigmatized, their actual space for action is closed off. When faced with pressure from so many directions, they are forced to follow certain rules that others don't have to. They are more ashamed to take up space, to eat food, to apply for skilled jobs, to get health care, to dare to have romantic relationships, and even to have children. The core of stigmatizing oppression is, therefore, an existential restriction of freedom.[253] Dealing with one's own fatness today is about coping with the constant denigration of one's character.

---

[250] Shafer & Ferraro 2011
[251] Friedman et al. 2008
[252] Eller 2014
[253] Frye 1983

Two of the most serious consequences of stigmatization are that the health care system, in its emphasis on the smallest fat deposits, fails to provide care for severe obesity that is truly dangerous and fails to provide care for the severe diseases of the fat body they seem unable to see past. Several studies have also shown how stigmatization itself increases fat people's tendency to avoid all areas where their weight is discussed, such as health care.[254] There is also evidence that fat people who experience discrimination lose the motivation to eat healthy and strive for better health.[255]

Stigmatization is a moral communication that directly threatens what is essential for a good life - our social relationships. Social psychologists explain shame and guilt as order-preserving functions that are there to inhibit socially undesirable behaviors.[256] These emotion-inducing functions can be seen as a moral system that is a prerequisite for the functioning of social life. The fundamental reason why guilt can be so quickly established in people is our awareness of ourselves as social members and users of the commons.[257]

---

[254] Walls et al. 2011
[255] Vartanian & Smyth 2013
[256] Tangney 1996
[257] Misheva 2000, p. 89

The Silence of the Stigmatized

The stigma of being confronted with their body on a daily basis and oscillating between starvation and weight gain has had devastating consequences for the psychosocial ability of fat people to create a meaningful life. Most of the fat people I have spoken to chronically struggle, every day, to get to bed every night almost in one piece. Others go to bed broken and get up broken, not because of the fat cells but because of the stigmatization. We are all just trying to feel at home in the world through rationality. We are all just trying to feel at home in the world via rationality, emotions, desires, pleasure, duty, freedom from guilt, shame, and much more.[258]

With the exception of a few countries, fatness is not yet included in anti-discrimination laws. I interpret this to mean that those with the power to legislate do not yet consider fat people as a vulnerable group in need of legal protection. Yet, as several analyses have shown, weight discrimination is as widespread a problem as the prevalence of racism and sexual discrimination - especially for fat women.[259] While the public condemns - and legislates against – racism, sexism, and homophobia, weight-based prejudices are freely circulating, not least in the media.[260]

---

[258] Shugart 2016
[259] Puhl et al. 2008
[260] Ware 2013

This leaves fat people powerless in their stigma. They are deprived of the opportunity and freedom to legally and formally fight for their dignity. They are silenced from all sides.

In the spring of 2012, I went to meet members of the then -Swedish Overweight Association. The purpose was to discuss how we could next organize fat people to heal from their interactions with health care and how they could become more knowledgeable about their own situation. I had expected to meet angry people, people who were tired of being treated badly. But I found that few actually work that way. None of the people I met were angry. Rather, they were sad and wanted nothing more than for doctors to help them in their situation. I was surprised that they were not angry with those who showered them with ignorance. However, after spending a few days together, it became clearer and clearer why they still put their trust in health care.

In order to get any help from the health care system, they felt obliged to admit to some kind of disorder of the mind. They would admit that they were emotional overeaters, that they lacked the ability to discipline themselves in everyday life, or that they lacked knowledge of nutrition. The best thing to do was to admit them all. Because then there was help available. Even though we now know that this help never worked, the fat people still felt welcomed into the healthcare system. While waiting for the cure, they went to a dietician and were given schedules, diaries, and nutritional powders to control their supposed wild eating habits. Eventually, they were offered surgery. Although most of the people who needed help and support from the Swedish Obesity Association were people who had just undergone surgery and still had a damaged self-image, most of them still seemed to want more of it.

Listening to their reasoning, I could hear the trap they had fallen into. As soon as they had admitted their illness to their doctor or lifestyle nurse, that admission became an obstacle to their ability to feel dignity despite their weight. They had sought out health care to get some kind of relief from their stigmatized bodies. But the price they had to pay was to be constantly informed that they themselves had to get rid of the exact problem they had sought help for. Trapped in that double bind, they could not feel anger. It was not on the agenda. Rather, they struggled to avoid even more pain by desperately clinging to what little relief they got from being listened to at all. They felt that the doctors who felt sorry for them were at least giving them some kind of attention that wasn't contempt.

Now, I saw the fat people from yet another new perspective. Before the meeting, I had already devoted several years to my dissertation project. In all the intellectual and theoretical discussions about fatness with colleagues in academia, I had been able to distance myself from the severe personal consequences of fatness stigmatization. The environment at university was so open and so reasoning, and it allowed me to look at the management of fatness from the outside as a phenomenon rather than as a feeling inside myself. In that realization, I thought that what fat people would need – to be liberated - would be to see their whole situation from the outside. To see their position in an oppressive system.

The Stigmatization of Fat People Is Systemic

Every society has unwanted deviations. These may be diseases, criminality, perversions, or other forms of "filth" that need to be cleaned, corrected, cured or kept out of the social order. With the designation also comes a picture of the deviant's responsibility and intentions. Is he or she an innocent victim of the deviation? Has he or she gone wrong? Is he or she even malicious? Together, these images form ideas about what should be done about the deviance.[261] Once a society starts to develop concrete policies against deviance, the problem seems to emerge by itself. The chain of steps erases the fact that the problem was created.

The American sociologist Howard Becker has described how deviance is not something that suddenly

---
[261] Cohen 2002

appears but is created by society. Not in the sense that society pushes deviant behavior but rather by creating rules where the breaking of the rule becomes the deviation itself. If your life is considered deviant, it is because your life breaks norms and rules that others have previously set. When you break these rules, those who set the rules and those who blindly follow them call you a deviant.[262]

Social worker Stanley Cohen was born in South Africa. He witnessed firsthand how a corrupt legal system, together with the media, had the power to create criminals in the disordered part of the population.[263] While older sociology seemed to rest on the idea that it is deviance that leads to demands for increased social control, Cohen, like Becker, argued that it is social control that automatically leads to deviance. When social control identifies the thin body as a good, healthy body, fatness becomes a deviation.

A stigmatization that is not carried out by criminals but through the democratic institutions of a society's core activities takes on even more serious overtones. In order to exercise social control, welfare measures legitimately sort people into different identity categories. Categories have concrete effects when they actually shape the life chances of those targeted by interventions. Identities in need of care, purification, hygiene, and medicine are created, and

---

[262] Becker 1963
[263] Cohen 2002

with it, social boundaries and unequal access to freedom, resources, and opportunities.[264] Some of those categorized as in need of help are considered morally deserving of sympathy and assistance. Others are considered immoral and in need of condemnation and punishment. Some consider fatness to be in a gray area between these. I argue that it leans steeply towards the latter.

In the media, fat people are constantly portrayed as unattractive people with a lack of self-control.[265] The mass media's way of reframing reality has a direct effect on our view of the world and ourselves. In her study of how fatness is represented in the Swedish media, Helena Sandberg discovered how even those fat individuals who managed to become thin continued to despise and loathe the fat body they once had. As a result, they themselves added to the stigmatizing attitude that the media displayed towards fat people.[266]

Despite legislation, ethical guidelines, a belief in human rights, the condemnation of hate and intimidation crimes, democracy, and a constant focus on equality, the stigmatization of fat people persists. It is, therefore, about deep-seated systemic and primitive forces. While other deviants do not have total institutions dedicated to curing them, the war on fatness is waged openly and powerfully. It

---

[264] Loseke 2007
[265] Merry & Voigt 2013
[266] Sandberg 2004

can continue because the pervasive prejudice about fat people is that they can choose whether or not to be stigmatized. They can choose to be fat or thin. The prejudice is so strong that some psychologists believe that fat people have some disorder in their cognitive functions. Therefore, they are attributed more pathology, more severe symptoms, and worse prognosis than thin people with exactly the same psychological profile.[267] The prejudice is so strong that doctors moralize instead of relieving pain. Moralizing opened the door to a weight loss market that could freely exploit an already built-up contempt for fat people. And the stigmatization was complete.

---

[267] Davis-Coelho et al. 2000

A Distinguishing System

"Interventions will never work as long as they follow the same parting pattern that once caused the 'epidemic', namely the distinction between people and people."[268]

As I write in the chapter on the health ideology, the appearance fixation of the obesity epidemic is crucial to its impact. The visibility of the fat body has caused enormous problems for fat people. In a 1950s study, 10- and 11-year-olds were shown pictures of other children and asked to rank them according to which child they liked best. The pictures were of a 'normal' child, a fat child, a child in a wheelchair, a child with crutches and broken bones, a child missing a hand, and a child with severe facial injuries. The fat child was ranked last.[269] We have to speculate whether the type of visibility played a role here. After all, fatness is not an injury to a normal body. It fills up the whole body and thus merges with the person. Fatness becomes a character in a completely different way than a person walking with crutches. Anyone who is considered to have been injured has suffered something. The fat person is someone with a particularly immoral character.

At the same time as the study of the children was published, the study by Albert Stunkard was also published.

---

[268] Wallace & Wallace 2003
[269] Richardson et al. 1961

The study showed that the advice on diet does not work on fat people because the ability to store fat is genetically and metabolically predetermined.[270] There is no doubt that those in power since then have completely ignored Stunkard's discovery. Although studies have continued to show that dieting does not work for fat people, it is dieting that is prescribed. To understand something that seems so illogical, one must understand the composition of the larger system.

Primitive systems are not held together by knowledge. Rather, it is myths and moralism that order society by punishing the undesirable and rewarding the desirable. To achieve this, certain beliefs, convictions, values, and behaviors are dramatized and intensified to make them more palpable in normal life. The mindless focus of doctors and nurses on the visible fat body has led them to prescribe dieting no matter what condition the fat person is seeking treatment for. Parents, school, friends, media, work lunches, gym commercials, lifestyle appeals, and during weekend nightlife. Everywhere, the judgmental gaze has been attached to the fat body.

The philosopher Thomas Kuhn defined a scientific paradigm as the set of ideas, concepts, values, and beliefs that form the basis of the questions, curiosity, and methods

---

[270] Stunkard 1958

that are put forward about a specific phenomenon.[271] If all goes well, if problems are solved, and if knowledge is developed and used for the benefit of mankind, the persistence of a paradigm can be a tremendous asset. But when a paradigm instead stagnates and becomes a ritual repetition without solutions, the logical thing to do is for paradigms to die out and be replaced by new ones. It is then slowly discovered that the old research questions are not fruitful but only hold together an already broken paradigm. However, history has shown that such death processes often take time. There is so much invested in the old questions. Especially those that have been distinguishing. It is extremely difficult to change a culturally established distinction between folks and folks. It requires efforts and innovative solutions designed to assess what and how people think.

Those who have tried to cure fat people by telling them to stop being fat have long been engaged in doomed rituals within a fruitless paradigm. This applies not only to the targeted health advice of authorities and the motivational talks of healthcare professionals with their fat patients. The rituals extend into all relationships. Every individual who enters a social relationship is automatically drawn into a negotiation about what the relationship looks like and how it is expected to continue. In this negotiation, we form

---

[271] Kuhn 1970

categories of each other that fit the expectations. The function of social relations is to maintain the form of a shared society.[272] By form, I mean that we strive together to carry on the prevailing values of society. When it comes to human fatness, the categories are extremely polarized. In health ideology, the thin counselors, in contrast to the fat people they address, have been transformed into what I would call superhumans. The stubborn perpetuation of a totally failed epidemic paradigm can best be understood by looking at the very superhumans who have invested and profited most from the distinguishing system.

The Self-Proclaimed Superhumans

When I was in my 20s, I went on a cruise with my study group, which consisted mostly of young, fit guys. One of them was called Mats. Mats staggered up to my table during the night and wanted to talk seriously with me about my fatness. He had also been fat, he told me. But he had eaten rice every day until he became thin. Now, as he looked at me, he wanted to help me come to the same realization. He had no problem with fat people. People can be as fat as they want, he said. At the same time, he told me how beautiful I could be, that I was worthy of a life of thinness, and he concluded with the totally surprising notion that if I were to become thin, I could have someone like him!

---

[272] Douglas 1992

It was a shocking experience. Not for one second had I considered him as a potential partner. I was simply unattracted to him, both visually and intellectually. I sipped my drink and listened to him politely. I didn't want to interrupt him and tell him what I thought of him. I was very tolerant. I couldn't think of a single kind word to say to him about his personality, self-image, outlook, or taste. So I was silent. But I looked at him differently after that trip. We sat together in the classroom; we were a small group. I wondered, what did he really mean ... that I could have someone like him?

A friend of mine who is a personal trainer used to ask me why the amazing popular movement of bodybuilding, nutritional science, exercise, and health care was not reaching fat people. Rather, it was the thin and already fit who came to every training session. "We wish you so well, and we have the knowledge," he said. "We can help you live longer for the sake of your children", he once told me. This is another one of those phrases that has stayed with me. So, people wanted to help me live longer for the sake of my children. Almost like a ... gift?

What they do not understand - those who believe they have knowledge - is that they are not asked to be the saviors of fat people. They seem to think that what they offer is a heroic effort that will create basic existential revelations for the fat individual. These revelations could be "having someone like him", "being there for your children," or "being able to walk several kilometers". As if fat people are not busy living their lives, being there for their children, choosing their days, trying to understand the world, trying to feel good, walking, being in love, being sad, being educated, being novel lovers, being dancers, being simply living people in the midst of life. With one foot in the grave like everyone else. Most fat people do not have body production as their main interest. The ones I've talked to usually just want to be thin to feel normal, not to get existential revelations from exercising all their remaining time in the world. Most superhumans claim to be able to help. They are not bullies in the true sense but carry a more subtle fear of fatness.

Another person close to me once told me that he would never allow himself to get fat. It was incomprehensible to him that there were people who didn't care about their bodies. For him, it was simple. One. Don't get fat. Two. If you get fat, lose weight. Three. If you don't get thin, get on an exercise machine 8 hours a day until you do. It was that simple, he thought. He was a so-called fridge eater. Every day, he ate huge amounts of food. In addition to large meals, he ate cold sausages straight from the fridge every day, chocolate in the car to and from work, and coffee with buns and cakes several days a week. He loved beer and mashed potatoes with butter and cream. He died of his advanced angina before he turned 65. But he died thin. And active.

He is not the only one. I have met many people with the same attitude. Those who could never imagine being fat.

Once, I sat down on a park bench. Next to me sat an emaciated, toothless heroin addict with a huge rash on his face. He smelled bad and looked really sick. He told me that he thought I looked too damn fat and that I should lose weight and get pretty instead. I walked away. I could never talk to another person the way he did. At the same time, relatives have said in all seriousness that they would kill themselves if they walked in my shoes. How did they think I would react to that? But above all, what do all their words say about their own self-image?

It is not uncommon for people to condemn what they once were as they move up the hierarchy. In southern African countries, where the apartheid system once emerged, you could see how black, oppressed people were naturally in open opposition to the white people in power. When, after the end of apartheid, some blacks came to power themselves, along with whites, they became part of the system that continued to oppress blacks. They crossed a boundary, became more valued, had more resources, and automatically felt more distance from those with fewer resources.

Let's also return briefly to chef Jamie Oliver. Oliver's experiment to fight the obesity epidemic in the poorest part of England with megalomaniacal cooking classes did not succeed, of course. I could have told Oliver that in advance. But Oliver's reaction to the failure was immediate and clearly reveals the self-image of the superhumans. Oliver took the failure as an affront to his potential to improve the health of the entire nation. Instead of becoming good citizens and following his teachings, the population proved incapable of helping themselves. Not only that, as they continued to eat their own 'junk food', they deprived him of the possibility of hero status.

He, the savior who knew what needed to be done, had expected some kind of respect.[273]

Superhuman Fantasies about 'Those Others'

The feminist professor and researcher in disability Rosemarie Garland Thomson would probably call these superhumans, the saviors, "normates". She describes the normate as a citizen ideal whose very identity is dependent on maintaining the boundary between itself and all those who do not live up to the ideal.[274] The deviant is problematized, made into a policy area, and the object of efforts instead of questioning the norms that have created

---

[273] Warin 2011
[274] Garland Thomson 1997

the problem areas.[275] But when the designated group has not really done anything wrong, when the group is worse off from the attention, and when the efforts have both failed and been counterproductive, then we must turn our attention to those who have created and maintain the problem area - the self-proclaimed superhumans.

Numerous studies show that health professionals who are supposed to know things about illness carry deep prejudices and deep contempt for fat people. This is true even among those specialists who are appointed to deal exclusively with fatness.[276] Even health professionals are colored by prevailing ideologies and make their own daily efforts to remain thin and dignified. According to Lindsay Wiley, a professor of health law, many thin people feel that their own thinness would indicate that they somehow exercise a very high level of self-restraint in their lives. They like to talk about how they can't just relax and eat as they please because then they would get fat immediately. But, she continues, it is easy for thin people to feel like they are doing something right. Most people think that fat people eat much more and move much less than they actually do. It's a mistake, says Wiley, to think that if only

---

[275] Berg & Grönvik 2007
[276] Lawrence et al. 2012

fat people could exercise the same kind of self-restraint that thin people think they're doing, they'd be thin too.[277]

Wiley calls it a mistake. I would call it delusional. What it means is that people who have never been fat themselves believe they have a capacity to transcend the body's natural tendency to store fat, a capacity they must teach to those who lack it. About their own thinness, they may say: "If only you knew what a huge amount of work it takes to look like this." So what do they really mean, the self-proclaimed superhumans? Is it easy, or is it hard? Does it require a lot or not? Is it hard for thin people to stay thin but easy for fat people to get thin? Wiley argues that the most prevalent notion that fat people can easily control their problem is comforting to the superhumans because it gives them a higher value for themselves.[278]

"Obesity is caused by 50 to 100 decisions you make every day," said an associate professor of behavioral medicine. Since no one would choose to be fat in a world that despises fatness, he must mean that those who do make the decision to eat fat do so without thinking. In such formulations and statements, the degrading image of fat people as human beings lurks. Fat people would thus, without thinking, if we exclude eight hours of sleep, make

---

[277] Wiley 2013
[278] Ibid.

between two and six wrong decisions every hour, every day.

No one has listened to the fat people who say they eat well and feel good. Neither in healthcare, nor in the media, nor among superhumans, fat people have conquered any positive voice regarding their life situation. Instead of asking fat people something and then listening to the answers, healthcare relies on the imaginary fat patient they carry around in their heads. This imaginary stereotype is imbued with the moral and cultural values of the superhuman. In fact, the moralistic approach to care is only possible because of these beliefs. Dehumanization is impossible in equal conversations between real people.

But why do so-called experts imagine that fat people have trouble thinking? Well, because it is impossible to imagine anything else. It's a kind of reverse logic. If they are to continue to give infantile advice on calorie balance and physical activity, then the imagined image of fat people as dummies is the only way to justify this advice. Because the fat people, obviously, do not understand this advice. If they were to start talking to fat people as if they were intelligent, they would not have the nerve to try to tell them that there is a difference between chips and kale.

When a professional without knowledge, driven by fantasies about fat people, tells the fat person to go home and get thin, the power relationship between the professional and layman is maintained. But the relationship is emptied of healing content. The shame, and even the anger, of being advised at the level of a five-year-old means that fat people are just happy to get out of there and try to heal from the experience in private. And to try to never have to return.

Superhumans Are Useful Idiots in Stigmatization

Since it is behavior that is focused on in the image of fat people, fat people have been imagined as immoral deviants. As a result, they have been denied a voice in the dominant health debate.[279] Health authorities increasingly discuss stigma, discrimination, bullying, social marginalization, and negative self-image as consequences of being fat. But they seem blind to the role they themselves have played in this. Many fat people experience social isolation, loss of status, and discrimination at work, at school, in the family, at the doctor's office, in grocery stores, in clothing stores, and in virtually all forms of social encounters with other people, beginning in early childhood.[280] They cannot go unnoticed in their exposed bodies because of the massive negative attention they have received through socialization. The more the public believes that everyone can control their bodies through various eating and movement techniques, the more anxiety

---

[279] Brandheim 2012b; Rail & Beausoleil 2003
[280] Wiley 2013

is created by the sight of those bodies that display human vulnerability.[281]

The medicalization of unwanted vulnerable bodies provides a secure base for superhumans. Not only does medicalization allow them to continue to comment on the behavior of fat people, but it also gives them the right to try to keep fat people in check. Through tips and advice, for example. Since health is equated with thinness in health ideology, the contempt for fat people can hide behind well-intentioned, caring, and scientifically subsidized interventions.[282] But the devaluation seeps through. It permeates everywhere, in small, every day, repetitive rituals that form larger processes that eventually coalesce into a chronic sense of being unwelcome in society.[283] The more devalued fat people feel, the quieter they become. Therefore, the superhumans can happily continue to give advice unchallenged.

The stigma scholar Erving Goffman described how a negative human identity is formed in relation to the dominant norms and values of society. Superhumans are, by definition, always careful guardians of such norms and values. That is exactly where they are, like soldiers at the abstract and invisible border where the normal is threatened by less normal intruders. At that border, groups of people

---

[281] Shildrick 2002
[282] Rice 2009
[283] Brandheim 2012d

are excluded by soldiers constantly treating them as slightly less human.[284]

In their struggle to defend certain norms and values, superhumans cause deep damage to the self-image of fat people. Every person forms a "biographical competence" from all life experiences.[285] We eventually become experts on who we are in different power systems. When useful idiots constantly show and point out to fat people that they are "wrong", the singled outs eventually begin to accept, and even cooperate with, the oppressive aspects of the system.[286] This is because, as I said earlier, our social desire to be welcomed is so strong that we would rather admit our guilt than be excluded altogether.

The ever-present trauma of being culturally devalued can be likened to being under chronic stress.[287] Being able to put up concrete resistance in that situation is rare.[288] Most people do not start arguing against people who do not welcome them. Rather, a piece of the self-image that gives us value comes loose, and life becomes a struggle to hold together the pieces that are still there and to avoid the people who hurt you. Fat people may also try to obey those

---

[284] Goffman 1963
[285] Jansen et al. 2006
[286] Cannella & Lincoln 2009, p. 55
[287] Kira et al. 2014
[288] Shugart 2016

who stigmatize them through constant attempts to starve their own unwanted bodies.

It becomes like a stigmatizing pecking order, with the bottom ending up attacking the body itself. If fat people weren't so vulnerable to superhuman devaluations, they would question those devaluations instead of sacrificing parts of themselves. It's a pretty old story about how abusive relationships affect the abused. Why don't we leave? Why don't we fight back? Why don't we resist? In simple terms, it is about the normalization of devaluation. We allow it to pass. And then it is also normalized in the person being devalued. This is not hocus-pocus. In long-standing processes, fat people have been identified as being in need of simple information. Thus, they have been made deviants,[289] abnormal[290], or bearers of a devalued identity by superhumans.[291] This happens gradually. The self-image takes a beating over time, not by individual actions. Eventually, we learn not to question. Ultimately, fat people flee the degrading relationship and try to build their self-image elsewhere. Or maybe they can't do that either. The superhumans walk free. No one asks them why they act the way they do, why they hurt fat people.

Attitudes towards fat people have been exclusively negative among health professionals. At the same time,

---

[289] Scambler 2006
[290] Goffman 1963
[291] Rice 2007

fatness has become the task of the same professions to cure. This creates a toxic relationship that makes it difficult to establish trust and confidence. One study found that most general practitioners do not even consider that fatness is something the medical domain should be responsible for.[292] This is likely to cause major problems in the relationship between health professionals and fat patients. If healthcare staff despise fat people for their lack of willpower, for their inability to take responsibility for the obesity epidemic, and if they themselves do not believe that they, as a profession, can do anything about it, this naturally has consequences for communication. Contempt and incompetence, in combination with authoritarian communication with an individual, cannot be masked for the socially and psychologically vulnerable person.

Science is also the useful idiot that has participated in the devaluation. The questions asked by science have been based on the premise that fatness is a human variation that must be combated. They have consistently proven the futility of looking like fat people do. They have claimed that fat people do not really live fully until they become thin. This is no small abuse. An entire culture today encourages fat people to feel bad about their bodies.

---

[292] Ogden & Flanagan 2008

Caring For the Fat Is Really Caring for The Thin

Some of our most famous obesity doctors try to side with fat people by saying that fat people are to be pitied. You never say that about people you equate with yourself. Anyone who stands on the side of a designated group, who respects their vulnerability and wants them to feel good, is also taking a stand against everything that hurts them.

Imaginations that fat people need help in the form of advice on calorie balance are practiced in order to get the problematic fat person to adapt to an unchanged and unchallenged structure.[293] It is a matter of reversing the logic that professions are supposed to follow. They are supposed to have more knowledge than the client and also the power and resources to apply that knowledge to solve the client's problem. When the entire problem is instead placed in the character of fat people, they are portrayed as having a problem because they are immoral rather than because they are fat.[294] Studies have shown that children as young as three years old already carry negative images of fat people, seeing them as stupid, ugly, sad, and lazy.[295]

The active pressure on fat people by self-proclaimed superhumans, supported by authorities and social institutions, naturally makes fat people feel unwelcome in

---

[293] Maranta et al. 2003
[294] Townend 2009
[295] Wiley 2013

the world. Screening fat children's BMI, constantly launching new deceptive medicines, and constantly raising the tone of fatness as a socially threatening disease are obviously dehumanizing to those who are fat. The only people who get a positive charge out of the treatment are the thin people themselves. In the chronic pressure against fatness, it makes no difference whatsoever that they claim to 'fight obesity, not fat people'. All the public negativity and moralism, and all the threats and stereotypes about the inability of fat people, have made it impossible to separate obesity management from the stigmatization of fat people. Thus, it has also become impossible to separate the management of obesity from the celebration of thin people. Fat people find it difficult to feel at home, both in society and in their own bodies.

Moral guilt is not only something we feel ourselves but also something we place on those we feel are abusing the common good in one way or another. Some researchers have shown that contempt for fat people is justified by an underlying ideological belief that in a just world, people get what they deserve.[296] The underlying ideology is particularly evident among those who are most vocal, in various social forums, in demanding that 'something be done about fatness because we can't have it this way'. These attitudes reflect a kind of Protestant ethic where those who

---

[296] Ebneter et al. 2011

believe they are doing the right thing in some way also have the right to judge others who they believe are not doing the same.

Within this perspective, contempt and degradation are twisted into a perceived response to what some believe fat individuals have implicitly 'asked for'. My whole point, however, is that these attitudes really stem from within those who see themselves as 'superior' and nourish a strong ideological disdain for weakness. There is a huge ethical difference between a *negative response* to a threat, and an *active pointing out* of a threat stemming from some's deeply seated judging view of other humans.

In the reality show The Secret Lives of Thin People, the imagined abilities of thin people are clearly portrayed in high esteem. The producer of the show goes to great lengths to portray the so-called truth about how thin people actually behave around food. By pretending to surreptitiously film thin people, saying they eat all the time, and then showing them not eating all the time, the producer wants to dispel the myth that there are biological and genetic explanations for thinness and fatness. Directed film clips show thin people taking only one bite of the chocolate bar when they say they "eat a whole chocolate bar" and taking one chip when they say they "eat chips every day". The portrayal is that thin people are constantly exercising self-restraint and that it is this characteristic that keeps them thin. It is not a biological body constitution but an inherent sense of reason in relation to eating. A sense that fat people are said to lack.

In Greek mythology, hubris was an attempt to emulate and surpass the gods. In the real world, hubris can be described as having an overly positive view of one's own abilities. Many of the patronizing superhumans undoubtedly have hubris about their own character and abilities. They may eat an apple and imagine that their thinness is the result of a characterful choice of fruit. At the same time, they can see fat people eating a chocolate bar and imagine that fatness is the result of a character-weak choice to eat sweets when it is actually about fundamental differences in biopsychosocial conditions. With the exception of fat people who have voluntarily starved themselves thin, neither fat nor thin people have chosen their bodies.

The Medicalization of Fatness Is Similar to Eugenic Values

An ideological system has unrestrainedly painted a distinction based on people's appearance - a 'pure' appearance and a 'dangerous' one. The creation of the fat person as a suitable enemy for medicalization has certainly had results. In Sweden, more than one in two fat women feel deeply offended after meeting with a doctor.[297] In Australia, one in three women are on a constant diet[298], and throughout the Western world, more and more girls are starting to diet hard before the age of 14.[299] Fat people have been shown in several studies to have a hugely negative view of themselves, and they blame and shame themselves completely for every pound above normal that the scale shows.[300] This is because the way in which fat translates into unhealthy is unabashedly ideological.[301] Ideology makes us want to be thin.

An accelerated field of research has created interventions that, instead of addressing real diseases, seek to influence social norms. They want to change the attributed behaviors of fat people within a medical framework. The consequence is that dominant ideas about the ideal body are maintained, and the disdain and fear of fatness are cemented. The medical science surrounding fatness has become so entangled with moral ideas (of beauty, dignity, and citizenship) that it can no longer speak for itself.[302]

Much research has been done on the negative side effects of medicalization. Medicalization can not only

---

[297] DN 2013
[298] O'Dea & Abraham 2001
[299] Ikeda et al. 2004
[300] Lewis et al. 2011
[301] Campos et al. 2006
[302] Guthman 2007

exacerbate a stigma but also create barriers to the healing process itself when medicalization takes the form of exclusion.[303]

Critical scholars argue that the epidemic is a cultural phenomenon rather than a public health crisis. In The Obesity Myth, lawyer Paul Campos describes the obesity epidemic as a moral panic. In Fat Politics, Eric Oliver, a professor of political science, argues that fatness is not an epidemic disease at all but rather a product of prejudice, politics, and profit motives. He shows how the combined forces of public health authorities, the pharmaceutical industry, and the dieting industry came together to turn obesity into a disease. Medicalization can be described here as a means to secure certain interests. I urge everyone to try to see where these interests lie. Who has benefited from this hysteria? Who has lost out?

Researcher Roel Pieterman is highly critical of the management of the so-called obesity epidemic. He asks whether the medicalization of fatness is really about turning those considered different into patients. At the individual level, he argues, medicalization opens up a stigmatization far beyond the already established ones based on beauty and fitness.[304] Public health experts often repeat that they are waging a war against fatness - not against fat people.

---

[303] Kvaale et al. 2013
[304] Pieterman 2015

But, as Pieterman points out, the very fact that they have to constantly remind themselves of this shows the risks of a health-driven de-normalization of fat people.

Not all medicalization is automatically bad, which is important to remember. Few people nowadays want to give birth at home, preferring to do so within the medicalized framework of the healthcare system. For many, this has become an extra security without shame. Paradoxically, the medicalization of concentration difficulties has led to children, via diagnoses such as ADHD and ADD, being entitled to the individual support that schools were already obliged to offer all children. But when it comes to the medicalization of the fat body, it is very difficult to see any benefits. Especially if we consider the total absence of useful medical knowledge, together with the loud presence of a profit-driven slimming market. What the medicalization of fat people has achieved instead is a bodily hygiene distinction between the thin and the fat person. How could we let that happen?

To Be Able To See How We Have Participated In Our Own Oppression

"Oppression occurs when individuals are systematically subjected to political, economic, cultural, or social degradation because they belong to a social group. Oppression of people results from structures of domination and subordination and, correspondingly, ideologies of superiority and inferiority."[305]

The quote by James Charlton above is taken from his groundbreaking book *Nothing About Us Without Us: Disability Oppression and Empowerment*. It was the first book to address the oppression of disabled people. Charlton's conclusion was that oppression can only be resolved by the group itself clarifying its own history and asserting its fundamental rights to self-determination.

Fat people are undoubtedly a degraded and singled out group, with thin people considered superior to fat people. When fatness is constantly portrayed as the opposite of willpower and self-control, fatness is linked to existing cultural and political power relations that reward visible self-production. As explained so far, fat people are denigrated for their alleged apparent inability to make

---

[305] Charlton 1998, p. 8

morally correct decisions. Fat people, therefore, meet the criteria to be considered an oppressed group.[306]

In the quote, Charlton describes an oppression that is systematic. In contrast, I argue that the oppression and stigmatization of fat people is *systemic*. There is a difference. Systematic oppression means that there are clear oppressors. That there are plans, methods, and structures to dominate a particular group. Slavery is perhaps the most obvious example. Systemic oppression is more subtle. It is the result of a variety of discriminatory processes that interlock with each other so that, in the end, there is no direct starting point. Therefore, there is no clear oppressor to resist. To find American slavery, you just had to go to the homes of the slave owners and witness who dominated whom. In the case of fatness, everyone denies participating in the stigmatization of fat people. They are doing science, they say. And social care. And care. And health.

There is not only a difference between systematic and systemic oppression. Unjust oppression is also different from moral oppression. The difference has to do with whether the deviation is considered to be due to the natural lottery or not.[307] Being unfairly oppressed provides a position in which injustice can be invoked. Since fatness is considered to reflect an immoral individual who has made

---
[306] Lawrence et al. 2012
[307] Eller 2014

immoral choices that burden others, the stigmatization of fat people is a matter of moral oppression. It is difficult to resist a widespread moral devaluation of one's person. Because where to start?

Critical researchers list several key areas where public health measures against fatness border on oppression:

- The measures emphasize a prevention model of fatness that does not make social and cultural distinctions about fatness.[308]
- The measures' focus on personal responsibility creates a stigmatizing "blame the victim" mentality.[309]
- Instead of creating solutions in the environment and society in which people live, the initiatives focus on the ill health that is allegedly the result of this environment.[310]

Despite the fact that these measures border on oppression, few nations in the world allow anti-discrimination laws to involve contempt for fat people.[311] Thus, fatness is still contemptuous in a political and government-controlled way. It is, as it were, legal to stigmatize and discriminate against fat people in both the medical and moral systems of society. At the same time, the oppression is not an unfortunate coincidence. Many

---

[308] Greener et al. 2010
[309] Townend 2009
[310] Smith 2009
[311] O'Hara & Gregg 2012

people genuinely believe that fat people are unintelligent and that they lack willpower and self-control.[312] In fact, many fat people deep down think so, too. Many fat people are ruthless towards other fat people and inherently judge them very negatively.[313] The fact that fat people actively contribute to their own oppression in this way makes this oppression different from other types of injustice. For example, while structural racism was highlighted to show that it was not race but racism that was the problem, fatness is still openly and legitimately described and talked about as the problem itself.

In the case of fat people, we haven't got there yet because a) no real power has taken away the formal rights of fat people, and b) the power of medicine to pronounce the danger of fatness has not yet been seriously challenged. I am not saying that racism and homophobia have disappeared. What has happened is that the victims of these aberrations have been built into and are supposed to be protected by a legal system. Everyone is still trying to cure fatness with the law on their side. This makes moral oppression, the guilt system that takes place in interpersonal relationships and not in political decisions, extremely difficult to challenge.

---

[312] Puhl & Brownell 2006
[313] Hebl et al. 2008

The Weight of Not Being Welcomed As A Moral Person In Your Own Society

The philosopher Samuel Todes was convinced that man's basic need is not to be self-actualized but to feel at home in his environment. Therefore, he said, in every situation we face, we try to relate and orient ourselves to it. We strive to achieve balance and become physically ready to respond to the "calls" of the situation.[314] In every situation, we search for who we are and who the others are. Subconsciously, we ask ourselves whether we are in a safe place or not. Through encounters with social institutions, we learn whether we are welcome or not. In the family, in the classroom, in images, at work, in texts, speeches, petitions, official statements, money, and political statements, we will know. How we respond depends on our life experiences, our self-esteem, and the biographical skills we have already built up. Above all, we orient ourselves according to our society's order of purity and danger.

What does it mean then to live in a body that is not welcomed in its own society? According to the Swedish etymological dictionary, the word welcomed means "to come according to someone's desire or will."[315] Not being subject to someone's desire or will is a deeply painful experience. The feeling is so strong that after touching it,

---

[314] Todes 2001
[315] Hellquist 1922, p. 1163

we do anything: hide, change, adapt, or sell our soul to never have to experience it again. It is so strong that we do not resist.

To be welcomed in healthcare would be to be taken seriously and respected and to know that you are part of a profession whose purpose is to help you feel better. Fat people give a clear picture of how unwelcome they have been in healthcare. They describe how doctors ignore pain and how they aggressively and condescendingly confront their bodies. They tell how the healthcare system has missed a number of diagnoses and how trust in the healthcare system has been broken when the treatment has made them sicker than they were before the doctor's visit. One doctor, who is himself critical of the healthcare system's fat phobia, told us how a patient arrived at the emergency room because she had difficulty breathing. They ignored the condition and said it was because she had too much fat on her chest. Later, a life-threatening blood clot was discovered in her lung, requiring emergency treatment. "It was just lucky that the woman survived," says the doctor.

I have heard many similar stories. A social work student told me how she was persuaded to have bariatric surgery because of her severe hip pain. "The pain is because you are fat," the doctor said. The young woman protested, telling the doctor that the same hip pain ran in her family and that not one of them was overweight. But he was sure. There was bariatric surgery. The student became thin, but the hip pain got worse and worse. Being thin, she finally got the pain treatment she had asked for before.

In a survey of fat women, more than eighty percent said that their weight prevented them from seeking the care they needed. At the same time, seventy percent said that they hesitated to seek care because of the disrespectful treatment by health care professionals, the shame of having to be weighed, and the risk of having to receive tips on weight loss that they never asked for.[316] As I said earlier, health care professionals have, in several studies, been shown to carry remarkably high levels of prejudice and contempt for fat people. Among other things, they think fat people are lazy, irresponsible, lacking in self-discipline, dishonest, unintelligent, difficult, and hostile to treatment. I am convinced that the failure of health care to cure fat people has spilled over into contempt for those they have not helped.

Healthcare professionals do not engage in open contempt. They do not tell fat people that they are not welcome in healthcare. Rather, the treatment is characterized by a profound moralizing omission and neglect. Health professionals simply fail to show respect when they do not feel respect. They cannot give what they

---

[316] Wiley 2013

do not have. Large parts of healthcare are simply intellectually blocked from treating fat people with dignity. They are, as I have already described, so blinded by the fat body that they do not think rationally and clearly. Therefore, they do not examine fat people as thoroughly as they examine thin people. That's why they don't listen as carefully to fat patients as they do to thin patients. That's why they dismiss more symptoms of serious diseases in fat people. All this makes fat people feel and know that they are unwelcome. But because this neglect or omission is not expressed openly and verbally, it cannot be answered openly and verbally either. Instead, fat people leave these encounters with an increasing sense of existential impotence.

My Own Journey in Brief

I hesitated for a long time whether to include a personal section at all. Personal suffering is certainly important to portray, but other authors have already done this very well. Fat people need self-healing, recovery, and shared experiences to have a chance to regain the dignity that has been taken from them. But I wanted so much to contribute with a different, not personal, picture. Not a picture of the victim but a picture of the perpetrator. Because if people who have not harmed anyone have to fight to regain their dignity, then something has actively taken their dignity away. It is this "something" that I have chosen to try to understand, criticize, and explain. After much reflection, I have finally decided to briefly share my personal journey. It still provides a unique perspective to my critical questions. This personal journey has already been published.[317]

When I was in middle school (in the 70s), there was one fat girl in the whole school. Let's call her Siv. There was really nothing extraordinary about Siv. Some kids had red hair, some had big front teeth, some were tall, had short legs or protruding ears, and Siv was simply fat. I never saw her being teased. I hope she got away with it. Teasing was completely unthinkable to me. Then you hurt people, people who haven't done anything wrong at all. Siv was just like the rest of us, doing the same things, laughing just as loudly, reading aloud just as nervously as others. She was bad at bandy, just like many others. I myself was good at bandy. Siv couldn't get up on the platform in the gymnasium, so she had to bounce once on the dumb trampoline and then walk around the platform. That made me a bit jealous.

There were some girls with nice ponytails and expensive gymnastics costumes who sailed high, high above that platform with the nasty, rough padding. They landed as if they were competing in the Olympics, perfectly level with their arms up as a sign of victory. The rest of us hated the plinth. It was like a punishment. Even today, I

---

[317] Brandheim S (2012c)

feel sick when I see and smell a plinth. But Siv was allowed to walk alongside. What luck she had there, Siv. With her freckles and her bear-brown velvet pants.

When I was fourteen, at my own request, I was prescribed birth control pills. They were strong hormone pills in those days, and I gained about ten kilos in one year. The midwife said "oops" when she saw what the scale showed. She added that gaining weight on the pill is not good at all, so I should really lose the ten kilos I had gained. That was enough for me to immediately stop eating and lose ten kilos in three weeks. I didn't want to hear an "oops" in dismay at my body. I, who had always liked myself and enjoyed life, immediately became negative about my body. It only took two seconds. Since that day, my relationship with my body changed. Suddenly, the eyes of others said something more about me. You had to be careful not to get fat. I lost the pounds by stopping eating. Over the next few years, the pounds crept back on, and a few more were added.

Sudden, Severe Illness

When I was nineteen years old, I had been suffering from cold asthma for a year (I have had asthma since childhood). One hot day, I collapsed while chopping wood in the scorching sun. Thinking I had sunstroke, I found it very difficult to breathe and tried to calm down. During the night, the panic increased, and the asthma medication didn't help anymore. I woke up my then-boyfriend, and we rushed to the emergency room. No asthma medication helped, and no injections. Everything just got worse. My relatives were called in. I stopped breathing, and they ran with me to a machine that they plugged into my mouth and told me to breathe out. I couldn't. There was no air to breathe out. Suddenly, I knew I was going to die. I stared at the terrified nurses, unable to speak, unable to breathe, feeling myself slowly suffocating to death. Then they pressed a button, and air pressure was injected into my lungs with full force. I felt like a balloon; it spread like sugar water throughout my chest, and I fainted. There was no light in any tunnel. Just a single thought. It's just animal primitive terror. Now I am dying. I still wake up today, almost forty years later, in the middle of the night with the same terror.

But I came to life. I was lying in a bed in the intensive care unit. The alveoli that suck oxygen from the air into the bloodstream had burst, and all the air was in big bags just under the skin over my neck and breasts. For days, I was the most exciting case in the hospital. Everyone was there and got to squeeze the air sacs. No one had ever seen anything like it before. Everyone was amazed. Some nights, nurses cried openly as they washed me of sweat and watched me struggle to breathe. They pumped me full of cortisone shots, but I kept getting worse. Finally, a specialist in internal medicine was called in, and she wanted to try one last thing. She added pituitary hormone to my IV. All the cortisone they had injected into me had knocked out the body's own cortisone production, so she wanted to try to trigger it with the hormone-stimulating substance Synachten.

The healing process was, in short, absolutely amazing. The very next day, I felt my life coming back. The treatment saved my life. When I was eventually discharged, I had to take cortisone for a long time to heal my lungs. After a year, I had gained 30 kilograms. Those around me thought I had become a food addict. It didn't matter how much I explained that something had happened to my body, something that made it store fat. But no one, absolutely no one, believed me. Not doctors, not friends, and not family members. They just told me that I had to stop eating.

Eventually, once again, they won me over. I would win over my body by sheer force of will. I dieted, lost 20 kilos, gained 30, dieted even harder, and gained even more.

Every time I got up, everyone told me I had to eat even less. The doctors treated me like I was insane when I insisted there was something wrong. They said things like, "You can eat everything, but not always," "Yes, we'd all like to eat all day, but you can't. You have to move too," and "All you need is motivation." I had spent so many days in pure starvation over many years that I knew what motivation was. I moved a lot. I liked to work my body. I knew that I didn't eat more after the diet than before. With every conversation, pieces of me were torn apart. It was like a nightmare. I became rock-hard. But only to myself. Never to the people who hurt me. I starved, started eating, and starved even more, and in the end, I gained 80 kilos of weight. Then, I couldn't stand having conversations about my weight anymore and committed what I call social suicide.

I Committed Social Suicide

For years, I avoided people, mirrors, shops, and phone calls. They hurt me. Instead, I read. I read books on endocrinology, psychology, nutrition, and physiology. I borrowed them from the library. Eventually, I learned that fat storage is a biological phenomenon that can be further stimulated by dieting or other forms of trauma. It was not the result of unmotivation, unintelligence, or ignorance but was a biological, bodily phenomenon where the body stores different amounts of fat in different people for different reasons. The starvation I had undergone with each diet had left me shivering and cold all day long, and I had to take five to six walks a day to get my breathing and warmth going. I had four blankets in bed to stop the shaking before I could fall asleep.

My poor body. When I told them about my coldness, the doctors said, "No, being fat doesn't make you cold. It makes you hot." I stared in horror at all these people who didn't hear what I was saying, and I realized that no one really knew anything about this. Then, I stopped listening to them.

In the late 90s, the internet came to me. My search for knowledge changed overnight. With the computer, I went out into cyberspace and read all the new knowledge I came across. I read about the new obesity epidemic that had hit the world, and it was a terrible experience to watch from a distance how this new danger was portrayed and over-dramatized. I read about how people were losing weight, getting fatter, losing weight, getting even fatter. I read about how the so-called obesity epidemic had exploded in the Western world and that it was due to things like McDonald's popping up in every city or people living too far from the tracks. Information on nutrition began to flood in. People bought billions of dollars' worth of slimming products. Both thin and fat people lost weight. The thin people got thinner, and the fat people got fatter. So-called experts said that fat people got fatter from dieting because they ate even more after dieting than they did before. I knew they were wrong. My biological body was altered by the starvation experiments. But not a single expert said anything like that. They just said it was a lack of motivation, self-control, and knowledge - all things that thin people apparently had.

I left biology and endocrinology and started reading up on sociology, psychology, and social psychology on the internet. I found trauma research showing that people exposed to severe trauma gain weight because the biological body does not distinguish trauma from starvation. In fact, starvation is, by definition, trauma to a living organism. In starvation, the life of the organism is threatened. Therefore, it becomes more adept at extracting nutrition from the next meal to survive. It was easy to understand, I thought; rather, I started reading up on how knowledge is created, how knowledge can be resisted, and who gets the right to call themselves knowledgeable. I read about science and power. One day, I no longer had a choice. I would become a scientist. I would go into the nest of knowledge and see how it was done and, above all, find out why nobody seemed to know anything about thickness. Why had scientists only made things worse?

I Started Pointing at Those Who Hurt Me

I decided to break my social suicide, move to a university town, and start studying. But there were two problems. I had been treated so badly in terms of my self-reliance that I didn't know if I dared. I had been treated so badly about the appearance of my body that I couldn't go out. But I had to take a college test. I did it and got high scores. I then decided to do something I had promised myself I would never do again. I had to lose weight. Again.

I was too afraid to apply to university as a fat person. I knew that my body would not agree to another diet, but temporarily, I could dare to go to university as a thin person. When I would then gain all the pounds again, I would already be in the system and thus cope better with the pressure. That was my reasoning.

Before this final diet, I had read both endocrinology and physiology. I had come to the conclusion that it was the processed food that had to go. What was left was rice, potatoes, vegetables, fruit, and water. An occasional piece of meat or tuna. But I ate no fat, which I later realized was devastating. I was sick 24/7 for a year while I was losing weight. I was sleeping, freezing, walking, freezing, and fainting all the time. My goal was to have the courage to go to a university town. But I was so sick. Finally, I couldn't eat at all. I couldn't drink water. My body didn't want to take anything. My blood pressure dropped, my blood sugar dropped, my liver showed high levels, and I was rushed to the intensive care unit, where I spent an entire summer in and out with severe heart palpitations and adrenaline rushes.

I had lost 55 kilos but was dying again. This time, the doctors thought I was anorexic, that I didn't want to eat, and that I wanted to get even thinner. Again, they didn't listen. I wanted to eat, but my body refused. It had shut down, and I felt constantly stuffed. Still, I pleaded with the doctors that something was wrong. I told them that I had felt physically sick every second of the diet, but they said that, no, you don't feel sick from eating rice and vegetables. You feel fine. And the fact that I had managed to lose 55 kilograms had only been good. So, if I just pulled myself together and started eating, everything would be fine.

I was ready for university and had no time to be sick or to continue dieting. But I couldn't eat. Water and a piece of apple gave me breathing problems. But the values were critically low, so they had to make me eat. They forced me to take a nutritional drink. I was so exhausted that my intestines were aching and shaking. But eventually, I did it. Slowly but surely, I started eating again, and at the same time, I started university. I went for about 7 walks a day to keep warm. And I could slowly start eating real food again.

A year later, I had gained 55 kilos. After another year, even more. The endocrinologist was shocked. He had never seen such rapid weight gain ... he muttered something about something being wrong with the liver ... but referred me to psychiatry instead. I don't know why. My only educated guess is that he thought I didn't realize I was eating too much food - that I was going into some kind of psychotic coma. The psychiatrist talked to me for an hour, telling me that there was nothing wrong with me but that I was probably biologically, hormonally, and psychologically traumatized, not only by the treatment but also by all the dieting I had done over the years. He also talked about research on war veterans and road accident victims whose metabolism was switched to more fat storage later in life. There was nothing strange, he said. It's just pure survival biology. "I've read about it, too," I replied. "But nobody listens." "Doctors," he said, "don't know as much as people think. They mostly read about which medicine to use for which condition. In order to understand the biological life of the bodily system itself, they need to have a special interest."

Encountering the Concept of Stigmatization

Once I ventured into a university, I dared to stay there despite the weight gain. I gained even more weight while studying for a bachelor's degree in psychology, a master's degree in sociology, and a doctorate in social work. All the while, I linked everything I learned to society's relationship with human fatness. Over the years, I circled narrower and narrower toward what would eventually result in my dissertation: *A Systemic Stigmatization of Fat People.*[318]

In the dissertation, I was not allowed to criticize medical science's ignorance of starvation or fat storage mechanisms. Because, as the supervisors said, I was not a doctor. The respect for medical science was incomprehensible to me. It is there for all of us, and in my opinion, it must develop in reflection with the surrounding

---

[318] Brandheim 2017

society. It must be criticized, especially by the groups that are exposed to it. In my thesis, I was at least able to show how pervasive societal ignorance was intertwined with ideology, moralism, market forces, and medical power in a way that not only failed all interventions against obesity but also made fat people sick in the wake of these failures.

During the years I worked on the thesis, I also taught social work students about stigmatization. There, I often used my own fatness as an illustrative example. Not only is knowledge about stigmatization an important part of their professional life with vulnerable people. The students were also always very interested in discussing the role of body weight in their lives. The issue of the body and the ever-looming risk of being unattractive is an existential part of young people's social lives. There was never enough time for these discussions. After the lectures and seminars, many came forward to continue the discussion. Others, who had been sitting quietly for hours, wanted to talk without so many people listening. Many wanted to talk about their own experiences. Others wanted to talk about people close to them. The experiences they shared were all unique, but the message was identical. They testified to the profound pain inflicted on them by other people from the perspective of knowing about their fatness. Among the many students who had lost weight through gastric surgery, many still carried painful memories and a damaged self-image from their years as fat. They now carried a double shame because they still felt bad despite the surgery they had received. Sixty years ago, plastic surgeon Maxwell Maltz described how a damaged self-image persists even though the stigma itself has been partially corrected.

The students told me about the ignorance of those around them, the unawareness of those who hurt them, the prejudices, and, not least, all the condescending comments from the health center staff. They all expressed a deep lack of trust in the medical profession, which, instead of comforting and healing them, filled them with shame about their body and person. Sometimes, they had been subjected to overt contempt, but most often, they described a more subtle, moralizing paternalism, such as when doctors could give diet and exercise advice at a level that five-year-olds could understand. They talked about the things that cut the deepest wounds: the loved ones who said things in good faith while their eyes signaled everything from shock to outright contempt. And how loved ones had derived their right to discriminate from a medical profession that had claims that the dangers of obesity were scientifically proven.

One student told me how her fat father, who had been a happy and safe embrace for her since she was a child, was forced into a powder diet by his medical center. They believed that his fatness endangered his future. Over the course of a few years, the daughter saw her father's whole person disappear as he sucked on his powdered soups. His zest for life faded, and he had no power to protest. He became deeply depressed and lost interest in everything. He died of a stroke when he became thin, and to this day, the student is convinced that what caused his death was the loss of his zest for life through starvation. He suffered in silence at home and never showed the health services how badly he was suffering from chronic hunger. They told him that they made him feel good. And he obeyed.

I carry that story with me as a constant reminder of why we must engage in a battle for the very knowledge of fatness. Because fat people are not legally protected from the discrimination and stigmatization of forced starvation, the dietician could easily injure the man so badly that he actually died from the injuries because starvation for fat people was considered a treatment based on knowledge. It is, of course, completely unacceptable to call it knowledge.

So why did the man obey? Why did he suffer in silence in the face of an eager dietician's recommendation that he drink powder and broth? Because they are stigmatized and, therefore, subordinate, people let institutions that claim to have knowledge choose their lives for them. Stigmatized people conform to the social order. Through their silence, they admit guilt for crimes they did not commit. They believe that the punishment is justified. "If I've eaten this much, it's probably only right that I should starve and feel like shit," they tell themselves. And precisely because of this enormous human vulnerability of those who are singled out, our demands on the knowledge that is directly applied in people's lives must be rock solid. A battle for knowledge itself is now required because the knowledge that has been given free rein so far has been completely misguided.

A Struggle for Knowledge

I have argued that knowledge of the vulnerability of the biopsychosocial human being has been rejected in the management of fat people. In a broader perspective, I believe that we as a society have rejected this knowledge in most treatments of ourselves. But here I want to show the consequences of this for fat people in particular.

Most anti-obesity campaigns and interventions could not have been implemented if the creators, in their impact assessments, took into account the complexity of the biopsychosocial human being. Therefore, the words behind the measures are about the behaviors and choices of the fat individual. The individual could have chosen health. She could have chosen not to get sick and be a burden to society. At the same time, the same people who created the measures have themselves decided what concepts such as health and illness should mean. A struggle for knowledge must, therefore, not only criticize the ignorance that those in power have relied on but also highlight the knowledge that has been excluded. The ideology and market thinking behind these choices of knowledge must be exposed.

Unfortunately, knowledge is rarely formed in some kind of natural process where only the most valuable knowledge is crystallized. Knowledge is so deeply associated with power that they are essentially merged. Those who have power decide which knowledge should count. As mentioned, Michel Foucault defined the relationship between knowledge and power as an integrated one where power is based on knowledge and knowledge is based on power.[319]

What Foucault later called governmentality indicated even more clearly how knowledge and power are linked. People are to be steered to become the desired citizens, and this is done by extracting certain knowledge as a basis for political interventions.

Foucault likens this governmentality that caused citizens to process their own bodies for the sake of society with bio-power.[320] Bio-power is maintained through the mass production of certain knowledge and the withholding of others. The consequences of such governmentality are clear. Since we live under very different social conditions, it is the privileged who influence the non-privileged. The most vulnerable are controlled by the least vulnerable. The relationship between those who act and those to be acted upon is unequal, with the former having the power to deeply influence the thoughts, feelings, and behaviors of the latter.[321] Governance is sometimes referred to as support or care. But if what was done to fat people was really support and care, all the focus would be on protecting people's fundamental value as full members of

---

[319] Foucault 1981
[320] Foucault 2007, p. 1
[321] Hall & Roter 2011

society. The current institutional stigmatization would be unthinkable.

Social attitudes can change most quickly when those in power either act as role models or face negative consequences for their bad behavior. The most effective and ethical approach, therefore, is to focus critical attention on the actions and attitudes of those in power and institutions that perpetuate stigma rather than on those who are subjected to it.[322] We need to hear more about superhuman guides, beliefs, and actions simply because what they did to fat people was so damaging.

In his research on parents of autistic children and the stigma associated with it, sociologist David Farrugia showed that the stigma itself is extremely difficult to resist. Too little attention, he argues, is paid to how stigma emerges and grows out of the social structure's political devaluation of certain deviations. It does not arise by itself. Not all deviations are stigmatized. The parents of the autistic children learned through their shared experiences that in order to achieve dignity, dealing with their own stigma was not the most important thing. The most important thing was to interfere with the applied stigma. They gained knowledge about stigmatization and thus gained the power to address it at a political level.[323]

---

[322] Pearl 2018
[323] Farrugia 2009

If It Is Not Knowledge, It Cannot Be Used as Knowledge

In my understanding of how knowledge is created through struggle, there is a thesis that has made a deep impression on me. I have already mentioned AIDS in the section on how fat people are considered immoral and costly. The thesis is Stephen Epstein's Impure Science: AIDS, Activism, and the Politics of Knowledge. Epstein tells the dizzying story of how, after years of rising death rates, stigmatization, and contempt from societal institutions, AIDS sufferers lost faith in the research done on their condition. Instead, they began to ask a whole new set of questions that slowly forced science to follow up on those questions. From being seen as a behavioral disease - choosing to be homosexual - the sufferers themselves asked the questions needed to force science to come up with the curative drugs that exist today. The ones that save lives. Those that focus on blood contamination and not on behavior. A grassroots movement thus created applicable and ethical knowledge.

The title of Epstein's dissertation - *Impure Science*[324] – is taken from sociologist Eliot Freidson's groundbreaking analysis of the medical profession. In it, Freidson argues that doctors are actually an impure social form - a profession that is designed to help ordinary people, but

---
[324] Epstein 1996

which at the same time counts as the scientific discipline of medicine even though they are not scientists. This unholy alliance leads to doctors being able to interpret scientific findings in a completely idiosyncratic way in their powerful relationship with their patients in a way that was never intended by biomedical science.[325] This means, in turn, that the actual knowledge can be blocked, distorted, and hidden behind the self-imposed task of the health care system to moralize, control, govern, and convey cultural values in the encounter with patients they believe have done wrong.

If we return to the fat individuals, in their encounter with this impure form of medicine, they cannot question the knowledge in what they say - because it is not knowledge that is being discussed. It is morality, control, governance, values, and a certain view of humanity. A genuine negotiation between patient and doctor would, of course, mean a broadening of knowledge for healthcare. But all the fat people I have spoken to testify that the healthcare system does not want to take part in their experiences. Since life and death are not at stake for most fat people, as it was for AIDS patients, they do not resist this ignorance. The AIDS sufferers could not wait because their friends actually died in the prevailing ignorance. They simply had to take up the fight. Most fat people, unfortunately, are better off just turning away from the infantile advice they

---

[325] Freidson 1988

receive in the ignorance of fatness. And so the ignorance is not challenged but allowed to continue.

Because so many people today feel so alienated from their own bodies, says Marilyn Wann, there is hardly any room to revolt against the overall value system. "If we don't even feel at home in our own bodies, where do we go?" Well, outwards, I answer. We should turn outwards. We must demand useful knowledge, and if researchers cannot find it, we must demand other types of researchers who do. Other types of doctors, and so on.

The first step is to dare to trust your own biopsychosocial vulnerability, which has been loudly signaling for many years that they are hurting you. Something is wrong when the outside world gives you a shameful self-image. Now I'm talking about serious shame. The kind where the doctor's basic negative attitude towards fat people shines through the entire conversation, filling you to the brim with a total sense of abandonment.

Almost everything the medical profession and our authorities have done so far has been wrong, ignorant, and discriminatory and has put fat people in a situation where life itself has been put on conditional hold. We must have the courage to see that both science and so-called knowledge are sometimes extremely primitive, sometimes practically useless for many human variations, and, at worst, devastating for the people who are subject to them.[326]

Correlation Research Has Exhausted Itself

In 2013 and 2014, I conducted a search for all medical-epidemiological meta-studies on obesity published in Medline (PubMed in the web version). A meta-study is a compilation of lots of existing research. I found 596 such metastudies. They could be divided into four themes: correlation research, treatment and prevention research, biomedical research, and critical studies. The breakdown between them is shown below.

Topics from 596 meta-studies on the obesity epidemic published in Medicine in 2013-2014.

---

[326] Wann 2009, p. xv

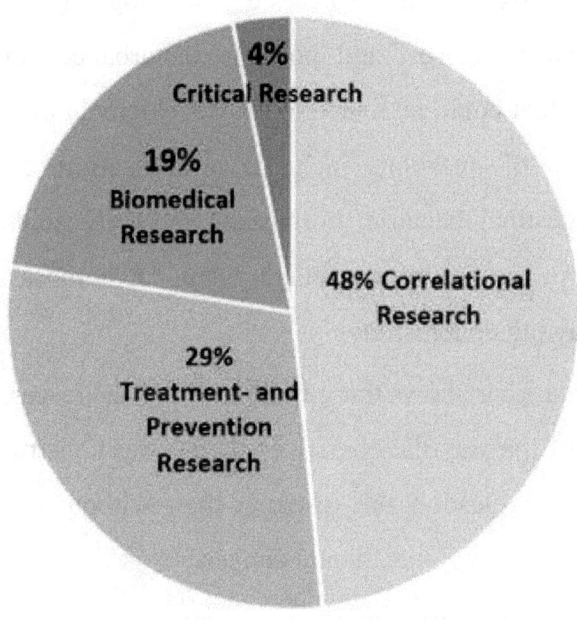

Almost half (48.3%) of all medical studies were devoted to correlation research. These were mainly in three areas: complications of obesity, contributing factors to obesity, and the relationship of obesity to other diseases. No study established a causal relationship, only an association.

Just under a third of the research was devoted to treatment and/or prevention (29.2%). This theme also fell into three main areas: effects of obesity treatment, obesity treatment methods and techniques, and interventions targeting fat children. None of the studies showed a successful intervention.

One-fifth of the studies were biomedically oriented (19%), looking for so-called pathological markers, biological processes, and possible disturbances in body function that could be linked to the development of obesity. Examples of questions included inflammation, genetics, gastrointestinal bacteria, hormones, and fatty acids. This was all in the preliminary stage, testing hypotheses rather than drawing conclusions.

The last bar shows that just over 3% of the research was critical of the way the obesity epidemic was constructed. It called into question the research that, without evidence, linked fatness to ill health and danger.

Let me address the issue of correlation research in particular. Sometimes, research funders are interested in correlations, sometimes not. Correlations are unusable in themselves because they are theoretically undeveloped data. They are the precursor to even beginning a search for useful and solid knowledge. It is absolutely teeming with connections. Everywhere and all the time. It is how we then use relationships and why certain relationships interest us that determines their importance. Every meta-study on the relationship of obesity to other negative factors concludes that if we see the relationships, we see the solutions to the obesity epidemic. But this is obviously not true. For example, the link between obesity and diabetes may actually mean that both develop from the same thing, not that one causes the other. It could be that disturbances in our evolutionary insulin system, in response to today's ultra-processed food, are the root cause of both diabetes and obesity.

The fat ones find themselves at a hot intersection between market forces, health ideologies, well-meaning advice, and, unfortunately, often their own self-loathing. A thousand correlations swirl between a thousand different ideas about knowledge from a thousand different actors. Everyone can pull out a study showing a link between thinness and spinach, a berry, an exercise, a measurement technique, or a lifestyle change they themselves advocate. And all of these connections are presented as a key to solving the obesity epidemic. At the same time, each of the links can be immediately questioned, challenged, denied, reinforced, or refuted by other studies.

In the case of COVID-19, for example, researchers have found a link between obesity and being more contagious. That's because, they say, fat people exhale more air based on the larger volume they have. But nothing is said in that study about how much air a thin, running person exhales, how much an athletic person exhales, or, for that matter, how much a laughing or singing person exhales. Or how much air playing children exhale. There are many reasons why people breathe out more air, but only the link to fatness was highlighted. Countless correlations about the disadvantages of fatness are highlighted, while studies that refute them or even demonstrate the benefits of fatness are never mentioned. In my opinion, correlation research has, therefore, morally exhausted itself to the point of being meaningless.

Regarding the other research categories in the Fig, I would just like to mention the following. Treatment and prevention research thus investigates how obesity can be cured. It is not about whether being fat is dangerous or not, but about how we can find ways to get rid of it, now and in the future. Biomedical research is searching high and low for a biological understanding of obesity. It would be interesting if it weren't for the fact that the vast majority of these studies are aimed at developing new drugs. Again, how to quickly find ways to get rid of obesity? The small pile of critical research actually asks the main ethical and human-oriented question: How dangerous is obesity really, and how justified is the attention given to trying to eradicate it?

It Is Not Enough to Not Stigmatize

Actively seeking ways to ensure that measures do not stigmatize an already despised human variety has proved impossible. This is not just about fatness but a much broader problem in dealing with all forms of so-called deviant citizens. A meta-analysis of one thousand (1,000) failed campaigns to remove prejudice against homosexuals, blacks, and various religious groups showed that there are inherent difficulties in addressing, through specifically designed methods, social prejudice regardless of the group concerned.[327] Prejudice is much deeper than that. The sociologist Charles Tilly, in his research on inequality, has shown that exploitation based on incorporated opposite categories has for millennia produced inequality expressed as differences in ability or corporate sameness (Tilly 2004). The categories fat and thin are only one of many such pairs.

The same people who, through ignorance, moralism, and hubris, have damaged the self-image of fat people are today looking for ways not to stigmatize them. At the same time, they continue the counterproductive counseling and degradation. This is not possible. In the battle for knowledge, we need to understand that the strongest forces of stigmatization are neither the words nor the method. The stigmatization lies in the cultural systems and beliefs that allow and facilitate thin people to continue moralizing about thicker people. Today, superhumans have learned that fat people have been hurt. But they are not going to stop dealing with them anyway. Instead of recognizing the mistakes made and ending them, they now try to present the same contempt for fatness in a more careful way.

Since the contempt for fatness is now embedded in the form of basic moral values about people, it is difficult for

---

[327] Forhan & Ramos 2013

conscious fat people to miss such values. The health ideology is within them, too. They feel what people think about them, and they see themselves through the evaluative eyes of others. In one study, nurses in an intensive care unit were interviewed about their thoughts and actions towards fat intensive care patients. The study found no overt contempt but a hidden one in the nurses' innermost thoughts. The nurses preferred thin patients to fat ones, they said, because they considered fat ones to be 'worse,' 'lazier,' and 'have less willpower than thin ones.'[328] The fat ones feel all this clearly.

Instead of trying to embed anti-stigmatizing techniques in the same old approach, the whole basis of stigmatization must be dismantled. Public health planners and practitioners need a wealth of new knowledge in this regard. Canadian public health researcher Lynne Maclean and her colleagues list that these people need to

- evaluate the stigmatizing effects of the methods.
- be aware of the danger of singling out overweight/obese people for targeted interventions.
- provide training for all professionals on how stereotypes are formed and look like.
- provide education about fatness and fat people.

---

[328] Robstad et al. 2019

- scan mass communication of public health messages for stereotyping, blaming, and disinformation.
- build self-examination mechanisms to prevent stigmatization into all interventions.
- reinforce fat people's coping strategies against social contempt.[329]

Taken together, these points suggest that we need to start looking at and treating even fat people ethically, based on principles of universal dignity and individual uniqueness. And it can also be a way out of the senseless handling of fat people. Many of the interventions automatically become impossible to implement if based on ethical principles. Today, we know that fat people deal with cultural body contempt on a daily basis, both from others and from themselves. With this knowledge behind them, those who still want to change the fat people should proceed very carefully. And if there is no scientific evidence whatsoever that the help offered has worked, it should not be offered. If the help is also proven to be downright harmful, it is actually a legal issue.

If you have a deeply embedded contempt for fat people, anti-stigmatizing knowledge does not matter at all. Fat people know what you think, and if you don't like fat people, you are not the right person to help them. Because then you are doing more harm than good, no matter what

---
[329] Maclean et al. 2009

you say. Therefore, I think a purely existential dimension should be added to the above list. Perhaps there should be licensed open-mindedness in those healthcare centers (there are in Canada) that want to keep their fat patients. Above all, the points make it abundantly clear that if it is the health care system that needs new knowledge, perhaps the health care system was never the right arena for managing fat people in the first place. Read the points again. They clearly show the ongoing reality that fat people face every day - the reality that needs to change. They show that healthcare has failed to evaluate, failed to pay attention, lacked proper education, acted on prejudice, lacked self-criticism, and increased social contempt for fat people.

New Ways of Thinking Are Needed

Some researchers want to stop focusing on discrimination and stigmatization as what extinguishes our well-being. Instead, they want to focus on the opposite, i.e., how dignity (status, feeling welcome, etc.) develops well-being. In particular, they argue that the direct practical mediation of health by institutions and interventions should have the client's dignity as a goal.[330] I fully agree with them. But at the same time, dignity as a foundation is already formally inscribed in human treatment systems. The UN, WHO, national social policies and health professions are subject to codes of ethics and human rights.

---

[330] Hall & Lamont 2009

The point is that as long as doctors, health professionals, family members, and the general public still fundamentally believe and think that fat people are incompetent, lazy, and sluggish, ideas of dignity as a goal in the treatment of fat people remain just words. Therefore, I believe that we need to go deeper than that and look for new ways of thinking from the ground up.

The multi-philosopher Gregory Bateson was convinced that the fundamental problem of humanity is our tragic blindness to the fact that we lack systemic wisdom. The problem is not our lack of systemic wisdom but that we are not even aware that we have such a lack. Bateson formulated a communication model that explains why most actions with clearly defined goals have, therefore, been doomed not only to fail but also to produce unexpected and uncontrollable results.[331] Because those who create the actions are not even aware of the knowledge they lack in order to have a chance to succeed.

Anti-fat policies have both failed and been counterproductive. Trying to beat the obesity epidemic by targeting the morality and character of fat people has resulted in stigmatization. And the benevolent superhumans seem to have no idea how they themselves have contributed to this stigmatization. They don't know that they lack systemic wisdom. It sounds like a theoretical

---

[331] Bateson 1972

gobbledygook, but the chapter is about new ways of thinking. New ways of thinking can explain why we have acted so ignorantly in dealing with fat people. And then, we can also shape the keys to real change.

There is a huge difference between lacking a certain knowledge and not knowing that you lack it. You can be much more reckless in the latter case. If your friend has a stroke and you know that you lack surgical knowledge, you will be careful to do something yourself about your friend's stroke. If you don't know that you lack that knowledge, you might start drilling holes in your friend's head with a drill. When superhumans constantly point out fat people's need for change and can't understand why the fat people don't obey, the superhumans don't think it's themselves who lack knowledge. They do not even know that they lack this knowledge. They think that they have knowledge. That it is the fat people who lack knowledge. Despite all the failures and all the stigmatization, and despite the fact that fat people are getting fatter, superhumans still imagine that they have knowledge. It's horrible.

We need to reflect on what is going on and how it has, for so long, prevented us from moving towards a more humane reality.[332] Health action cannot continue to be based on epidemiological data because the collection of this data has nothing to do with the vulnerabilities of the

---

[332] Grossberg 2010

individual. We, therefore, need to change the basic approach to what data we should even ask for in order to achieve a more humane world. The measures against the obesity epidemic have failed because they were the wrong way to go in the first place.[333] The failures are the proof. There has been a lack of knowledge, which they never realized they lacked. There has been a lack of systemic wisdom.

Researchers David Ludwig and Kelly Brownell have been struck by the way normally wise and sound scientists have helped push obesity measures based on unfounded over-interpretation of data. When such scientists are challenged, their response is that the epidemic is such a serious threat to both individuals and society that they cannot wait for accurate data.[334] But we have to be careful. When we face or magnify a new threat or a new area for intervention, we must also ask ourselves what we want to discover and why.[335] And what we want to do with that information.

Behind us are decades of primitive handling of fatness, repeating rituals that never worked as if they were based on knowledge. At a time when we as individuals have become increasingly self-critical, sociologist Patrick Baert makes the necessary demand that it is now science itself that needs

---

[333] Shugart 2016, p. 150
[334] Ludwig & Brownell 2009
[335] Todes 2001

to develop a deeper self-awareness. A science that is primarily humble in the face of people's immense biopsychosocial vulnerability need not be therapeutic. But it can at least avoid reinforcing the loss of meaning that those singled out risk suffering.[336] We are drawn to different types of knowledge depending on our inherent view of humanity.[337] If we want to produce knowledge that liberates and creates a basis for justice, it is our moralizing view of humanity that must be challenged. Particularly our view of the people who are singled out for study and action.

There Is a Need for Non-Distinguishing Knowledge

"Knowledge is for me that which must function as a protection of individual existence and as a comprehension of the exterior world. I think that's it. Knowledge as a means of surviving by understanding."[338]

Over the years, I have listened to hundreds of stories about how health services do not listen to what fat people say. This creates major wounds in the relationship between those who are supposed to be society's experts and those they are supposed to help. Unusually, when fat people have been asked about how they are treated, research shows a clear dissatisfaction with health experts. The fat people

---

[336] Baert 2005
[337] Rathbun 2012
[338] Foucault, 1997, p. 7

consider the professionals to be ignorant and simplistic and that the information they receive about dieting is accompanied by very negative attitudes toward fatness.[339] Such a distinction between people can never be knowledgeable - only distinguishing.

Several studies on attitudes towards fat people have shown that the more the public learns that fatness has biological, hormonal, or biomedical causes, the more positive they are about fat people in general.[340] The more they believed that fatness is about deviant and abnormal behavior, the more negative they were about fat people. Correlation research has focused almost exclusively on behavior and character. By suggesting that fatness depends on things like proximity to fast food and distance to walking paths, the research suggests that fat people cannot cope with their environment as well as thin people.

The epidemiological counting, I believe, is completely devoid of self-reflection. "They're just counting," they say, not understanding that market forces have decided what to count and why. But criticizing them for not being neutral has proven to be very provocative. Epidemiologist Katherine Flegal received a very strong, if not outright hostile, response from other epidemiologists when her statistical analyses, contrary to traditional epidemiology,

---

[339] Carr et al. 2008
[340] Ebneter et al. 2011

showed that so-called overweight was less linked to mortality than normal weight. Today, most people agree.

But not then. Flegal herself was surprised by the aggressive response: "Why is this so outrageous? Why does it provoke such hostility?" For my part, I believe that Flegal and her colleagues touched on a dissolution of the comfortable distinction that obesity researchers have made when studying the problematically fat as a different type of person from themselves. Some other researchers suggest that the answer to Flegal's questions lies in the increasingly blurred line between the scientific and socio-political significance of fatness.[341]

In the scientific description, fatness has taken on an invented but precise meaning - so-called obesity occurs at a BMI above 30. The social description of fatness is more complex, a problem that has grown as a historical disdain for fatness has blended with newly emerging public health models. Researchers Stacy Carter and Helen Walls describe the fat body as a new battleground where strong emotions are stirred up as people's professional identities are called to account when someone questions the link between fatness and ill health. The discovery that fatness may not kill you becomes a threat to all the forces that have been built up around the very idea that fatness kills.[342] Stanley

---

[341] Carter & Walls 2013
[342] Ibid.

Cohen calls this part of moral panic hostility - the moral outrage not only at those who embody the threat but also at those who defuse the same threat, thereby allowing fatness to continue to exist.[343]

Knowledge about Knowledge

An important area of knowledge is the link between medicalization and stigmatization. A number of researchers interpret this link to mean that contempt, shaming, and stigmatization have become a necessary part of public health policies against fatness. They argue that stigmatization is not only a result of public health policy but also its very precondition. In particular, they believe that so-called fat activists who speak "well" about fatness and fat people undermine the goal of reducing fatness by spreading the idea that it is okay to be fat. Lawyer Adam Pulver, for example, believes that the social stigmatization of being fat is actively perpetuated so that people are not encouraged to be fat in the first place.[344] The reason it is taking so long to get a discrimination law that protects fat people is probably because it would be in direct conflict with many of the public health measures that have been launched over the decades. Many of the interventions implemented would simply not be able to pass such a

---

[343] Cohen 2002
[344] Pulver 2008

law.[345] I think this discussion is very relevant. While research has found that medicalization does not protect against stigma,[346] I want to go one step further. When it comes to the management of fat people, stigma is not only a precondition for medicalizing fatness. In its blaming of people, medicalization is also what allows stigmatization to continue.

Another important area of knowledge in our understanding of the so-called obesity epidemic is statistics. Statistics do not exist independently of people. Statistics are not knowledge. To understand statistical data, you need to know who counted what, why they even started counting a certain phenomenon, and how they counted. People do not start by uncovering a piece of statistical information and then try to understand what they should think about that information. Rather, it starts with an interest that leads them to collect specific statistical information. When the statistics then support what the individual already believed - or hoped or feared - it is easy to acknowledge the statistics, to overlook their limitations.[347] The threat of an obesity epidemic set in motion enormous processes where all the collection of statistics was done with an underlying rhetoric of war rather than the open curiosity of researchers for possible social change.

---

[345] Ware 2013
[346] Kvaale et al. 2013
[347] Best 2004

A further area of knowledge that needs to be questioned is why the biological feedback mechanisms of the human body have been completely ignored in obesity interventions. When welfare analyst Katherine Hafekost and colleagues investigated several interventions, they discovered that no experts in physiology and metabolism were involved. Instead, the notion of "eat less and move more" was the basic knowledge used to create the interventions.[348] In this context, I would like to mention the ignorant equation between fatness and overeating. Fatness is not a behavior. Overeating, however, whatever it is, could at least be classified as a behavior. Professionals need to know more about the difference in order to change the way they express themselves about fat people. You can't look at a fat person and see how they eat. She can be gaining weight, she can be stable, she can be losing weight, and it all depends on a lot of things. Genes, biology, previous starvation attempts, stress, and slow metabolism are some of the factors that mean that fat people don't lose weight just by eating normally and exercising normally.

Many ignorant people I have spoken to over the years believe that the fat person is constantly overeating and sedentary. These same people, therefore, believe that the only thing required for the fat person to lose weight is to change their behavior and start eating 'normally.' However,

---

[348] Hafekost et al. 2013

being fat does not mean that you are gaining weight due to mindless gluttony. You can be fat for 20 years without gaining a gram. For a fat person to reduce their weight at all, they have to eat less than normal - not normal. If we are to continue to manage the ability of fat people to become thin, more sophisticated knowledge needs to be developed.

It is the nature of our curiosity that determines what knowledge our research will produce.[349] We should remember that the basis for eugenics science, for the lobotomization and sterilization of people considered different, and for the diagnosis of homosexuality as a mental illness was called knowledge. Here, I have tried to show that the word knowledge in itself is not a reliable tool if we want a fair and humane society. We must also be sensible and level-headed. We need to sort and reflect on whether certain knowledge is the right knowledge. We have to ask ourselves whether certain knowledge is even applicable, ethical, humane, or free from oppressive side effects.

Knowledge on Stupidity

Critical researchers say that the simplistic advice given to fat people does not take into account social and cultural issues, ethics, inequalities, conditions, and the reality of fat people and their experience of living in a judgmental

---

[349] Bateson 2007

society.[350] Other researchers believe that the failure of these measures points to a lack of knowledge on the part of the professionals, together with the fact that the individual is led to believe in the lack of knowledge himself.[351] In any case, widespread ignorance is an important element that has allowed the moralism directed at fat people to continue.

In Australia, the Fast Track to Health project has received millions of dollars to put teenagers on a starvation diet for a year - to starve them thin. First, the children will eat 800 kcal per day for a month and then 600-700 kcal three days a week for a year. The children will thus receive half as much nutrition as the healthy adult men in the now seventy-five-year-old *Key's Minnesota Starvation Study* for six months. That experiment resulted in compulsive behaviors, overeating, depression, apathy, uncontrollable hunger, and severe mood swings.[352] But it's more amazing than that. The results of the pilot study done before the Fast Track to Health experiment were clear. Of the children who participated in the pilot study, the vast majority lost very little weight. A large number dropped out of the project, and two years later, all the children had gained all the weight they had lost.

Australian psychologist Louise Adams, who wrote about the Fast Track to Health, is a fierce critic of child

---

[350] Raphael & Bryant 2002
[351] Forhan & Ramos 2013
[352] Tucker 2006

dieting. She argues that all the devastating consequences of starvation will go under the radar because they will arise after the results are hastily presented. Adams is also highly critical of those who orchestrated the interventions claiming to reduce the stigmatization of obesity. Their logic is as follows: because they are 'nice' to the fat kids, they are not prejudiced against fat bodies. They simply don't realize that they are looking at children through weight-centric lenses," says Adams. This can be compared to the conversion therapy of the past, where coercive measures against homosexuality were practiced using "welcoming and respectful language."

In the 1990s, a three-year study of eating disorders in 2,000 teenagers was conducted. The study found that dieting was the single most important risk for future eating disorders.[353] Another study of 17,000 children aged seven to fourteen found the same results.[354] In addition, the study showed that the risk of binge eating increased with the number of dieting attempts. Children who dieted frequently were up to 12 times more likely to binge eat than children who did not diet. The researchers summarized the study by saying that dieting for teenagers is not only ineffective but a pathway to weight gain. Another study that followed over

---

[353] Patton et al. 1999
[354] Field et al. 2003

2,000 adolescents for 10 years found that both dieting and eating disorders continue into adulthood.[355]

So, we have known for a long time that starvation never works in the long run. It leads to nutritional deficiencies, lowered metabolism, depression, weight gain, binge eating, and self-starvation - one of the most intractable mental conditions known to man. Yet the same mistakes are made over and over again. We need to ask ourselves what knowledge is, what it means, how we use it, who produced it, what its purpose is, and how pure stupidity can be allowed to continue.

Knowledge is not neutral. Sometimes, a strong political desire to do something drives the questions to be asked. Many people really wanted to do something about the so-called obesity epidemic. So, they looked for the knowledge they wanted. As I said, the whole management of fat people is based on the fifth rule of the fear hypothesis: "Anything we do is better than nothing." In order to do 'everything they can' about fat people, actions must be based on research where the desired answers are built into the question itself. Furthermore, some suggest that the changes in technical definitions of desirable body dimensions and associated measurement methods have had more to do with experts' attempts to establish and defend their specific

---

[355] Neumark-Sztainer et al. 2011

social role than with the search for "true knowledge."[356] I have been face-to-face with doctors who use the concept of BMI as if it were nuclear physics requiring specific expertise to interpret.

Obesity researcher Jeffrey Friedman points to the widespread ignorance of obesity statistics themselves. Contrary to what the public has been led to believe, the data does not actually show that everyone is getting fatter. He argues that before we call it an epidemic, we need to understand what the numbers say and what they don't say.[357] While the already fat have gotten fatter, thin people have not, he continues. Also, the already fat people have gained the most weight in those countries where income inequality has increased the most, making the lower class more vulnerable to cultural forces than ever before.[358] To open our eyes to such social power structures, the concept of knowledge that hides them most powerfully must be challenged in earnest. I am talking about the concept of health.

---

[356] Smith & Horrocks 2013, p. 90
[357] Friedman, In Kolata 2004
[358] Hacker et al. 2010

The Health Ideology Must Be Challenged

Unfortunately, health does not always mean health. The concept of health has gone so far afield that it can be described as a new religion. If we do not want to have a society that distinguishes people and thus destroys people's opportunities for quality of life, ideas about health as a super value and elevated morality must be questioned. Health has never really had a uniform meaning. A few decades ago, Jennie Medin and Kristina Alexanderson conducted a literature study of the concept of health and presented the following ten existing theories about what health is:

- The body is a machine programmed to function (biological approach).

- Health is being normal (biostatic approach).

- Health can be equated with the absence of disease (psychosomatic approach).

- Those who are satisfied with their own behavior have health (behavioristic approach).

- Health is the biological balance between the body and environment (homeostatic approach).

- Health is an expression of the individual's mental and physical existence in her environment (ecological approach)

- Health measures the ability to act (holistic approach).
- The ability to achieve set goals is health (mental health approach).
- A healthy person lives in a symbiosis between mind, body, and spirit (teleological approach).
- Health emerges when the individual achieves a strong sense of coherence (salutogenic approach).[359]

Every society creates its own dominant ideas of what health is. However, very few frame what should be included in the concept of health. This is done in conjunction with the prevailing ideologies and power relations. Body functions, normality, well-being, ability to act, balance - everything that is "good" can be included in the concept of health. However, we can look critically at this wide range of definitions if we imagine meeting a person who meets all of them. What kind of person is it who achieves set goals, who is in harmony with their inner self, who is normal? Is this a desirable ideal type at all? Can we achieve a constant state of health 24 hours a day without becoming insignificant to others? Is it not rather small moments of harmony that make life livable? Life offers constant resistance. The less resources, the more resistance you have. Viruses intrude. We hurt ourselves, we

---

[359] Medin & Alexandersson 2000

get older, and we lose various functions. Other people intrude, demand things from us, and interfere with our own free choices. Constantly facing resistance makes us alive. In living life, we will experience ill health. Some a little, others a lot. Some will have mild complaints. Others will have serious problems. Today, when society's idea of health is once again linked to ideologies of the perfect human being, it is more important than ever to relate the ideology of health to dignity, identity, and citizenship. The fact that today, we allow health to be linked to bodily perfection makes many people sick. When perfection is the goal, there is too much that we are not.

So, how does the idea of the perfect human being affect the rights and liberating possibilities of large groups? We have seen what such ideologies of perfection and purity have led to in the past. The stigmatization that has followed in the wake of singling out fat people is just another example of a group of people being harmed by people who have taken the right to do so. As a tool of power, health ideology has helped shape fatness as something to be despised, rejected, fought against, and controlled. The loss of meaning that this has caused among fat individuals, who, for one reason or another, continue to be fat or become even fatter, is unimaginable.

The health that represents self-production for the privileged has become an oppression for the non-privileged. The health ideology has also led many to believe that fat people should not even be able to claim health. Jonathan Metzl, a professor of psychiatry and sociology, and gender professor Anna Kirkland said over a decade ago that it is not only possible but timely that we criticize the prevailing idea of health.[360] In Against Health: Resisting the Invisible Morality, researchers question the status of health as a universal and self-evident good. Especially since 'illness' seems so closely related to lower social and economic status in our society. Being against health does not mean being against people's sincere attempts to reduce their potential suffering. Rather, the researchers argue that our pursuit of health is hampered by the ideology of health. I agree, and I suggest that we turn to a more humane definition of health - one that is non-judgmental and more concerned with how we are welcomed into the world.

The Best Definition of Health So Far?

After interviewing sober alcoholics, exercisers, individuals being rehabilitated from illness, healthy employees, individuals with physical, mental, and social disabilities and illnesses, and individuals who are dying, Margaretha Strandmark, a professor of public health sciences, came up with what she calls the essential meaning

---

[360] Metzl & Kirkland 2010

of health.[361] With a humanistic approach, health, she argues, can be seen as a resource, an experience, and a process. In my opinion, this is one of the most appealing and wise ideas about health that has been scientifically formulated. There are not really any new elements presented, but it is a specific combination of elements that gives the definition of health an applicable, ethical, and dignified dimension.

As a resource, health is the social, economic, and personal development and action created in everyday life, such as learning, work, play, and love. The individual's environment consists of both external (physical, social, and cultural) and internal (senses, energy, mobility, and intellect) factors. Health as a resource would optimally mean that the individual has what she needs to meet the demands of both her external and internal environment.

As an experience, health is about experiencing meaning. It is to feel vitality, harmony, balance, wholeness, fulfillment, control, and satisfying change. Optimally, health as an experience means that the individual can feel a sense of well-being independent of traditional pathological diagnoses of ill health.

As a process, health is about what Aaron Antonovsky once called a Sense of Coherence.[362] Having a strong sense

---

[361] Strandmark 2006
[362] Antonovsky 1987

of coherence means that the more comprehensible you perceive yourself and your place in the world, the more manageable the world is, and the more meaningful your existence in the same world is, the more health you have. Health as a process would then optimally be those moments when we experience a total sense of coherence. It is about feeling welcome in the world and having the resources and ability to act to overcome any obstacles that arise.

For health to be experienced at all by the widely differing individuals with whom Strandmark spoke, one central component appeared to be crucial - and that was vital force. Strandmark interpreted vital force as a balance between a zest for life, a self-image of worthiness and the ability to overcome obstacles. Having a self-image of worthiness is about being proud of and having respect for oneself. One's self-image is influenced by social norms and other people's attitudes towards oneself and, therefore, also by the feeling of being important to other people. The ability to face obstacles develops through conscious choices, the management of emotions, and by achieving insight. This is very much about wanting to make choices that make you feel good. When something doesn't feel right, you should dare to change, rethink, and choose a different path. For many of the people Strandmark interviewed, it was, for example, a matter of accepting their "sickness-judgment" for the first time through reflection and knowledge. Zest for life was about how the relationships you find yourself in are motivating and relieving instead of inhibiting and worrying. See my simplified model of Strandmark's model below.

Vital Force (simplified model from Strandmark 2006)

The above Vital force model can be used to understand how the management of fatness has impaired the health of fat people. I also believe that the model has a composition that bears traces of systemic wisdom. Not only because human lives as diverse as exercisers, dying people, and recovering alcoholics contributed to the understanding of the essence of health. In addition, self-reliance, social relations, and motivation are included, while traditional pathological ideas about disease are made redundant. It is a humanistic definition of health, as Strandmark herself points out. The model itself is about what gives vital force. But I am using it analytically, backward, to see what hinders people's development of vital force. Let me show what I mean by breaking down the model into its components and then explain how fat people are deprived of vital force – or health. It's about how their self-reliance, motivation, and relationships have been eroded by the staging of a looming obesity epidemic.

Self-Reliance – A Combination of a Self-Image of Worthiness and the Ability to Overcome Obstacles

Self-reliance emerges from a combination of a self-image of worthiness and the ability to overcome obstacles.[363] What prevents the emergence of self-reliance, then, is an unworthy self-image and an inability to overcome obstacles. The stigmatization of fat people is, as I have described, a moralistic stamping of an unacceptable identity. Moreover, since contempt for fat people has been shown to be more common among health and care professionals than among the general public, there is no one who strengthens fat people's self-reliance through, for example, professional care. Instead, fat people are constantly told that they are undesirable both by experts and by lay people. Such discrimination obviously

---

[363] Strandmark 2006

undermines one's entire self-image as a fully functioning human being.[364]

Fat people are considered to have caused their attributed ill health themselves due to irresponsibility and laziness. The attitudes place a social debt on fat individuals, a debt they can only repair by becoming thin. Or at least by trying to become thin. Since most fat people do not become thin, the guilt is absorbed as shame in the fat people's self-image, reducing their ability to overcome other obstacles in life. The handling of fat people has thus weakened fat people's self-reliance.

Motivation – A Combination of Zest for Life and the Ability to Overcome Obstacles

Numerous studies have shown that attempts to motivate fat Individuals to lose weight are ineffective. Thus, they are ultimately detrimental to the zest for life that comes from overcoming obstacles in life. Nurses and dieticians believe that they are motivating children to lose weight if they weigh them, point out their weight, and give them leaflets about staying slim. Such actions, which clearly show that children are 'wrong,' tend to evoke what we social scientists consider to be an obvious defensive response in vulnerable people and no motivation at all.

---

[364] Shafer & Ferraro 2011

Motivation cannot be given to anyone. It emerges, if we are lucky, from a favorable environment. Above all, motivation cannot be created in a power relationship between a superhuman and someone who has absorbed the contempt for fatness into their self-image. Being judged as "wrong" in comparison to others can never contribute to a zest for life but can only take it away. In a narrow-minded world, those who "need to lose weight" are turned into deviants, and as a deviant, you lose both your zest for life and the ability to overcome obstacles in the world from which you have been excluded. Motivation as a method actually succeeds in relationships where the person to be motivated feels equal, valued, and treated with respect by the motivator.

Relationships – A Combination of Zest for Life and a Self-Image of Worthiness

Many fat people today have to fight for a worthy self-image. The fat stigmatized individual grows into relationships where not only does everyone want to control or help them, but above all, to change them fundamentally. When expertise is given the right to say how the fat person should change, and a media market releases this expertise, then public attitudes are shaped, and the pressure on the fat individual increases. In order to have a chance of achieving a worthy self-image, fat individuals who do not become thin are eventually forced to engage in therapeutic self-healing, which in one way or another affects and is affected by their social relationships.

In various ways, degraded people have to avoid arenas where their bodies are discussed, such as healthcare.[365] But research also shows that fat people are inhibited in close relationships, where they may feel they have to protect their bodies from moral scrutiny. Stigmatization, therefore, closes off the social space for fat people, even in their closest relationships. Freedom is curtailed when their chronic experience of being unwelcome is established in a self-image of worthlessness. In this situation, creating mutually respectful relationships becomes impossible for those who no longer even respect themselves.

If Health Is Vital Force, Then Ill Health Is Everything That Extinguishes It

Sociologist Zoë Meleo-Erwin asks, like me, how our bodies and our desires are regulated by the current health ideology and whether our pursuit of some kind of health masks a new kind of morality. She has many questions. Why does my health matter to so many others? Who are the 'people' in 'public health'? What do people do to you when they claim to care about your health? When we pursue health, is it about how our bodies feel or how we look to others? What are the radical possibilities in the idea of accepting the imperfection of our bodies? What if pleasure

---
[365] Walls et al. 2011

is health? What if health is something that only the individual can know about, and it is not in the body?[366] Such a more detached view of personal health would take into account all the social, psychological, biological, and cultural resistances that the human project encounters every day.

Most importantly, such a view would make us more confident in our own body, regardless of its appearance and functions. We would not have to think of health as a requirement for constant improvement. Rather, we would be freed to resist the ideas and actions that extinguish our health/vital force. It is about living and shaping your life in peace. Taking back your vital force from an excluding health ideological culture is not easy. Fat activists that try to do this are met with a rage that even surpasses the very fat-phobia that drove them to become activists in the first place. The superhumans need fat people to plead guilty to the moral crime of "letting themselves go". Otherwise, the health ideological tower from which they looked down on the fat individuals will collapse into the abyss of the deviants they separated themselves from. It is a belief system as primitive as any other distinguishing cult.

The Responsibility of Science - Part I

I believe in the potential of science to improve people's lives. Like Foucault, I believe that this is the very meaning

---

[366] Meleo-Erwin 2012

of knowledge. But we can no longer ignore the fact that science can affect people in ways that may not have been intended. Sometimes, science can reach far into fragile self-image processes that we have not yet seriously reflected on. Our knowledge about ourselves also becomes stories about ourselves, giving us different ideas in our existential search for meaning. By extension, scientific findings can tell us which qualities are desirable and which are reprehensible, which behaviors are right and which are wrong. To avoid such moralism, a different approach to research ethics is needed. Research ethics has usually been about not harming the people involved in the study. I am talking about the need for ethics in which research is ultimately not allowed to harm the groups being researched.

Science, knowledge, and practices are about communication. No facts, results, or theories can be presented without communicating something to someone.[367] I once explained the subtle link between science and its sometimes negative impact on people to an epidemiologist. I said that we should be careful about what questions are asked, how the answers are put into practice, and what we then communicate to fat people. Even more important what we communicate to the public about fat people. She replied that if we hadn't asked such questions, we might not have come so far in cancer research, for

---

[367] Krippendorff 1994

example. She continued: "And no one is offended by cancer research, right?" No, of course not. The war on cancer and the war on obesity are not the same kind of war at all. Fat cells are not cancer cells. Fat people are blamed, people with cancer are not. There are no TV galas raising money for the victims of obesity. All the fight is against the fat people themselves - not for them.

Not only does the image of fatness itself differ from the image of cancer. Knowledge and practice also face very different challenges regarding these two phenomena. Fatness is exposed at many more levels of society than cancer. For example, if breast cancer was managed as fatness is managed, the following scenarios could emerge. Cancer patients could then be seen not only as sick but also as consuming citizens who caused the disease themselves by not listening to good advice. In every newspaper, on every television, in advertising, at work, in every shop, and from every acquaintance, products, methods, and tips to cure breast cancer would be sold under the pretext of being scientifically proven. Doctors would prescribe laughter, and a concerted neoliberal ideology of self-production would constantly remind us how both the origin and the solution to the problem lie in the inability and lack of motivation of the cancer patient. Moreover, human dignity and moral capacity would be directly related to how much cancer the individual in question can keep away. The person who doesn't keep the cancer away may have been making two to six wrong choices an hour, and as a consequence of those choices, costing the rest of us huge amounts of money.

Comparing breast cancer to fatness may seem like a stretch. And that is exactly my point. It is not possible. For example, there is no uncertainty about the lethality of the cancer. You don't have "under-cancer" or "over-cancer" in the same way that people are assumed to be "underweight" or "overweight."

Immediate action is being taken to eradicate cancer, and everyone is on board. It is about saving lives. Fatness, on the other hand, is an area of enormous scientific uncertainty regarding both health and mortality. Fat cells, unlike cancer cells, are healthy parts of our bodies.

'Nobody is offended by cancer research,' said the epidemiologist. Therefore, fat people should not be offended by epidemiological research on fatness, she said. "We just want to be good". What I claim, and what I have shown in my thesis, is that fat people are not 'offended' at all. Fat people are subject to stigmatization and oppression.[368] Cancer epidemiology does not distinguish between different human body variations. It separates the cancer from the human being. People are not their cancer. They suffer from cancer. Fat people cannot be separated from their fatness. They are fat people.

---

[368] Brandheim 2017

There are so many competing voices about fat people that science has become increasingly entangled with morals, myths, emotions, and judgmental attitudes. At a time when the fat body is so despised that it is comparable to racism, homophobia, and funkophobia, it is not easy to continue an objective search for correlations that could help us eradicate fatness. Critical scholars are increasingly questioning not only how we can use correlation research but, above all, its moral overtones and unethical consequences. Fatness is not a disease - like cancer - but rather a human variation. It is a variation that medical science has unfortunately been tasked with treating as a curable disease despite the fact that its dangerousness or curability has never been proven. All this moralism, all these myths, emotions, and judgmental attitudes surrounding the treatment of fat people matter. It may well be the very consequence of calling something that is not a disease a disease.

A more reflexive science must put its ear to the ground and listen instead of filling up data banks with statistics and facts. Simply collecting data without reflecting on the ideas behind the collection is primitive. The human world is not - and we should know this by now - a rule- or law-bound place that can be controlled and dominated by means of conventional data collection.[369] The problem, however, is more profound than insight. Since there is a lot of money at stake, as the pharmaceutical companies themselves finance large parts of the correlation research that is carried out, there is no willingness to be self-critical.

More Free, Independent, Critical Research Is Needed

"Research is a value-laden activity, from the choice of research subject and the questions to investigate through to the interpretations and publication of the results."[370]

The silencing of the research that has consistently criticized the image of fatness is serious. It gives rise to an obesity science without self-criticism, a self-criticism that is one of the most important tools for obtaining the best possible knowledge. The lack of an open critical approach allows researchers to continue to claim that their facts are objective when they are not. This is like saying that the science involved in Sami skull measurement was 'pure' science and that it was the political use of that science that was ideological. This is wrong. There would not have been head measurement as a science if there had not first been an ideology that demanded scientific research into the differences between peoples and the Sami.

---

[369] Pickering 2004
[370] Muncie 2006

If we reflect on the outcome of three decades of obesity research on fat people, we have to say stop. The negative answer is unequivocal. Not only are fat people still fat or even fatter. They have more anxiety, fewer life opportunities, and reduced vital force. They live under the chronic stress of carrying a full-blown stigma. They don't get fair healthcare. They starve themselves, and fat children are bullied at school, not only by peers but by the school nurse. Grown-up people wait to live until they are able to become thin. Everything is encouraged in a way that makes it impossible for them to escape the pressure. For the sake of health, everyone wants to help motivate, train, inform, weigh, entice, tip, threaten, and pressure the fat to become thin.

In this deluge towards the same goal, I believe that collaborative science has a responsibility to criticize ideologies that harm a huge group of people. If this responsibility is not taken, research risks losing its self-critical intrinsic value and becoming part of the ideology. Unfortunately, this seems to have already happened in the case of fatness, given how the main questions of research largely avoid questioning and just go along with the launch of an epidemic.

When I raise my eyes to analyze a system that promotes a thin/health ideology, I see only primitive, ideological rituals that do not move forward. They stand still. I see an unbelievable system of measures, thought processes, billions of investments, and violations that have completely failed to achieve the incomprehensible idea of making people thin through information. At the same time, science has participated in the damage because the fat people never managed to realize the scientifically supported government goals.

The unwillingness to see the failure shows that it is faith rather than critical science that continues to shape our perceptions of fat people. Unfortunately, it is more about what politicians and journalists have been convinced to believe than about knowledge itself.[371] The authorities and social institutions that have requested knowledge about fatness also want knowledge that supports their organization - not knowledge that speaks against it. This has meant that the cultural beliefs that surround fatness have not been pushed aside by critical science but rather incorporated into it.[372] The threat image I have described is so strong that the questioning of the danger of fatness, the benefits of interventions, and the moral beliefs behind them is received with pure aggression by those who are waging the war against fatness the hardest. There is, therefore, neither enough critical research nor even sufficiently

---

[371] Gard 2011
[372] Boero 2013

critical and free media that could highlight the critical research that does exist.

Media Simplifies Science and Makes It Worse

In 2017, a study was published claiming that four million people died as a result of high BMI. I got curious, downloaded the entire study, and started going through it carefully. With 154 authors, data from 195 countries, and statistics on 68.5 million people between 1990 and 2015, this is a seemingly huge study on the obesity epidemic. Perhaps the largest ever undertaken. The findings - that 4 million people died from being fat - have been widely quoted by researchers and in the media all over the world since its publication. But what I found was that the study didn't even come up with that result itself.

The study Health Effects of Overweight and Obesity in 195 Countries over 25 Years[373] does not show that fat has killed four million people in twenty-five years. The bulk of the study, like most obesity publications, is about how many people are fat in the world and that something must be done to slow down this trend. The method they used is not about counting how many people have died from being fat. There is no such data at all. Instead, they have made an estimate of how many people could be said to have died of obesity because they were fat when they died. Believe me, this is a huge difference.

---

[373] GBD Obesity Collaborators, the 2017

The study first showed that 56 million people died over 25 years from cardiovascular disease, diabetes, and cancer. It then determined that 4 millions of these deaths were related to higher BMI. So what they calculated was that 4 million of the 56 million who died from these selected diseases were fat. They used a measurement tool called Comparative Risk-Assessment. In simple terms, they compared two different types of data and drew conclusions from them. The data showed how much obesity has increased, and other data showed how many of the people who died from these selected diseases were fat. The authors found, they say, convincing or plausible evidence that a high BMI is associated with ill health. But when the results were presented in the media, the image was that obesity had killed four million people.

Not even the authors themselves write that fatness kills, but they think they have seen enough evidence to support a causal link between high BMI and certain cancers. This shows, in my opinion, how scientific results, through media reporting, can slip into more inflated results under the influence of a health ideology that despises fatness. I remind you that this study is one of the most widely reported in the entire Western world, and it has been constantly promoted as showing that four million people died from obesity between 1990 and 2015. But it is simply not scientifically correct. The difference between dying from fatness and dying with fatness, although only a few letters apart, is simply fundamental.

Katherine Flegal and colleagues, in a review of similar studies on the mortality of fatness, found that obesity and so-called mild fatness protected against premature death as the subjects got older.[374] The same research team found in a further study that fatness was associated with cardiovascular disease, while thinness was associated with certain lung diseases and infections.[375] Here, we can, therefore, say that both thinness and fatness are associated with mortality. But we only report on the association of fatness. This is extremely serious because those who deal with fat people are supported in their abuse by this kind of evidence. Fatness has gained such a superior status that we formulate research questions based on the firm belief that fatness kills. But so far, I have not found any study that shows that fatness kills. The majority of people die from body collapse due to cardiovascular disease, diabetes, kidney failure, and cancer. That seven percent were fat when they died has created the macabre notion that when thin people die of heart attacks, they die of heart attacks, while when fat people die of heart attacks, they die of fatness.

---

[374] Flegal et al. 2005
[375] Ibid.

The news about the dangers of obesity leading to health issues has unfortunately led some parents to resort to extreme measures, including restricting their children's diets. In some cases, school nurses may also play a role by weighing students and attempting to encourage healthier habits. It is such news that might lead a nurse in Australia to say that her patient died from obesity and not from lack of care for his severe diabetes, high blood pressure, asthma, chronic pain, and depression. It is the media reporting of epidemiological measurements of a deadly obesity epidemic that has worsened the psychological, social, and biological conditions and life chances of fat people. We cannot let them continue.

Resistance and Liberating Issues

Those who want to cure fat people are currently trying to learn non-stigmatizing methods. They know they have to.

The limit of what they can do to fat people has been reached. At the same time, they are still struggling to generate science to show that fatness - or obesity in medicalized terms here is a severe chronic disease in need of medical knowledge. Since healthcare got this so-called epidemic in their lap, they now have to perform triple flips to turn fatness into a disease. Because if it's not a curable disease, what would they have been doing all these years? Could it rather have been the repression of an undesirable body variation guided by an ideology of perfect people?

Nor does the market want to give up trying to turn fatness into a disease. The failure to cure fatness is the very idea of the business. The hard-dieting individuals are anxious and constantly ready for new products. And many fat people still hope for the miracle drug. They still hope that healthcare will help them feel normal. But three decades into this so-called epidemic, we now know they don't have that knowledge. Well, except for continued starvation. Either through surgery for chronic starvation or through the new appetite suppressants that cause nausea.

It is not the fat ones who have failed. It is those who launched, engineered, and organized the global war on fatness who have failed. What once started with a PowerPoint presentation on the spread of fatness has had consequences that can be described as unprecedented, to say the least. It was a value-laden activity from the start. The man with the presentation thought that we had not taken the increasing waist size of the population seriously enough. And he made sure we did. In the attempt to build a world with only thin people in the name of health, fat people have been dehumanized and made second-class citizens. The dignity stripped from fat people in the process has left them struggling to heal themselves. Unfortunately, this has led them to continue to turn for help to the very people who perpetuate the stigma. They believe that there is no other option. But there is. Liberation through knowledge of the system we are stuck in.

Being fat is not really that special. But to be deprived of your sense of normality, to have your vital force extinguished, to not be welcomed because you are fat, that is special. In the systemic stigmatization, fat people are used as walking symbols for everything we as humans should not be. It is the pressure from our strongest powers to achieve perfection in the form of thinness that must go away for good. It is the relentless pressure that has caused fat people to gain even more weight when they have tried so hard to be thin. It is the singling out that has dehumanized them. It is the moralizing attitude that fat people have a different character than thin people that have made so many people sick. The biopsychosocial vulnerability people carry has responded to the treatment! They have become fatter and more stigmatized. They have such deeply damaged self-images that they are ready to try new deceptive market drugs or to remove parts of their digestive system in order to cope with the full-scale humiliation.

But fat people are perfectly normal, living, working people. Waving a norm and then convincing people that they do not conform to that norm is psychological and deeply unethical manipulation. Treating a so-called disease through counseling at the level of a five-year-old is socially destructive for those who receive this counseling. The societal pressure to conform to a specific body image, one that emphasizes thinness, can lead to a panic-induced obsession with what one is not. This 'obese body' narrative perpetuates harmful ideologies, making it crucial to challenge and reevaluate our perspectives on body image. In this moralizing drive towards thinness, the line between care and oppression has been blurred.

We must resist moralism. We must, in order to see what is really knowledge and what is really not. The threat image must be challenged, nuanced, and dismantled. The limit of the threat image's function has been reached, as the stigmatization of people far exceeds the benefits of the threat image. The fat people have really been told what bad people they are in this scheme. They have been told that they are not welcome. This is moral oppression. So, we have to make moral resistance using knowledge. And science should become part of that new knowledge.

The Responsibility of Science Part II

As I said, I am a believer in science. In fact, I believe that a funded search for knowledge can help us to have better lives. At the same time, we should not forget that science about people also becomes stories about humanity. These stories give us different ideas in our existential search for meaning together with others. We, therefore, need to decide what kind of science can solve important problems and what kind of science cannot.

I've gone pretty hard on epidemiology and public health science. There is nothing wrong with these branches per se. But they are not applicable at the individual level. They have methods for collecting data at the population level. Yet these two institutions have played key roles in the media's coverage of fatness as an individual behavioral issue. They are, therefore, along with certain branches of medical science and health care, responsible for what has happened so far in the lives of fat people. They have maintained the stigmatization of fat people by only saying

'A' and never 'B.' What I mean by that is that they have never themselves gone out and explained to the public and to the media that their knowledge has a limit that ends long before the fat individual. They do not know how fat individuals live their lives. They do not know how fat people can be cured. Despite this, epidemiology and public health sciences are invoked when medicine tries to deal with the character and thought processes of fat people. Very little science has been done on the personal experiences of fat people about their lives.[376]

In my opinion, science has a responsibility to approach the issue of fatness from an ethical and inclusive perspective at the individual level. Despite all the stated political visions of inclusion and integration, we are far from producing inclusive social systems. This is especially true for the place of fat people in the health system. With a cold conviction, they have measured and compared people's bodies. They have distinguished the thin body from the fat one. In doing so, they have reproduced a system of distinction. Today's one-way obesity research shows a disregard for fundamental questions about how people create meaning and gain vital force.

Through the science that the media likes to present, people today are massively informed about who we should be. As a consequence, we are increasingly busy reflecting

---
[376] Boero 2012

on everything we are not. A critically oriented science must turn against the moralizing knowledge itself and ask why certain knowledge has been allowed to reproduce structural relations of exclusion and oppression. Two specific intentions of such questions would be to

- highlight systems of power that harm people, and
- find ways to both dismantle narratives that support such systems of power and emphasize that the protection of human vulnerability should be the main goal of a humanist society.

Let's not forget that both the health services and their fat patients believed that fat people should diet to get healthy. They dieted themselves sick - physically, mentally, and socially - when they gained all the pounds back. The body's own defense mechanisms against starvation are enormously powerful because it is a matter of pure survival for the biological organism. Trust in the science of obesity is therefore justifiably shaken, and a whole new attitude and transparency from the scientific community is needed to regain that trust.

The responsibility of science must be to explain more clearly the basis for the new questions to be asked. Are the questions in line with fat people's right to vital force, a sense of inclusion, and respect as dignified citizens? Are the questions ethically sound? Instead, if the questions are to continue as usual, mostly repeating the answers already given, thorough distinctions must be made by responsible science. Such distinctions should clarify which thickness is dangerous and which thickness is simply uninteresting from a societal perspective and only of interest to the individual.

The widespread stigmatization of fat people means that science must now step in with greater humility, openness, and self-criticism. The experiences of fat people must be taken into account in the new questions. These experiences must also be taken into account regarding which questions should not be asked. The question of whether being fat is a disease must be challenged. We are talking about two billion people who allegedly suffer from a serious chronic disease, even though there is nothing wrong with most of them.

Fat cells are our own biological building blocks, and we must be careful not to medicalize the parts of ourselves that actually have life-supporting functions.

Obesity research has entered sensitive territory in the war against an obesity epidemic. People have starved themselves to death or disease. Children have been scarred for life. The mental health of fat young people has risen in tandem with the ideological presentation of the perfect body. People are systemically stigmatized and have agreed to surgical procedures that put them in a lifelong state of chronic starvation. And many of them regret the procedure.

The contempt that health fanatics have for fat people echoes openly in all media channels. Parents have anxiety about their young children's bodies. Fat people believe that life is not for them. They feel that they are not welcome. Therefore, they avoid arenas where they risk experiencing all this most strongly. Is that how it was meant to be? Why is there no self-critical reflection on such results among science journalists, in healthcare, in the media, and in public health policy? And why has there never been a cure for fatness?

Yes, why was there never a working medicine for fatness?

If it was so important to so many people if so many billions and resources were spent on getting rid of fatness, why was there never a medicine to slow down the body's ability to store fat? Why don't we have drugs today that release stored fat that the body can either use as energy or remove as waste?

Although I am not a biomedical scientist, it is relatively easy to understand that biological organisms are living, responding systems. These systems do not idly receive chemical substances and activities designed to drain them of stored energy. The biological system of the fat people has actively stored the fat and will actively defend it. Previous attempts to release the fat with central stimulants, now classified as dangerous drugs, have been banned on the market. These include amphetamines, adrenaline, ephedrine, and other appetite suppressants that create eating disorders and overactivity by stimulating the body's metabolism. The substances led to a higher heart rate, increased blood pressure, dilated airways, and increased oxygen turnover in the body. Many people lost weight, but the side effects were too severe, with heart disease, sleep problems, tremors, worry, anxiety, and even death. It is simply not possible to disrupt biological systems in this way without consequences.

Drugs have been developed to reduce appetite, reduce the absorption of fat in food, reduce the absorption of carbohydrates in food, and none of these drugs have worked. The fat body is in biological balance. The storage of fat is the body's way of balancing something else. And it always has to do with survival. Disrupting that balance has consequences, which is exactly why dieting doesn't work for fat people until they cut out large parts of the food-digesting system. And even then, it doesn't work for many.

The latest drugs are being launched as injectable, hormone-influencing agents that will "facilitate weight loss by suppressing feelings of hunger and increasing feelings of satiety, thereby helping people to eat less and reduce their calorie intake." The injections are to be taken as a complement to the usual dieting regime of eating less food and exercising more. Many fat people queue up to get the drug prescribed under high-cost cover. Most cannot wait for such approval and instead pay for the injections themselves. It is a matter of several thousand dollars a month to lose their appetite. In a few years, we will see how things have gone. Or rather, we who follow these experiments analytically will see it. The public will not see it because soon, the next "improved" medicine will be on the market.

Hope will be rekindled for those fat people who were unable to lose weight on the last drug, the one that disappointed them so much. With two billion people in the world classified as too fat, the pharmaceutical industry has indeed found a goldmine to dig into.

... perhaps because fatness is not a disease?

Perhaps the biggest reason why there has never been a medicine for fatness is that there has never been any medical evidence that fatness should be considered a disease. In a review of twenty-five meta-analyses and thirteen cohort studies, the results led to a sharp questioning of whether weight status can be equated with health status, even in the case of obesity.[377] There is no causal relationship between weight and disease. No research has shown that a certain weight status leads to a certain health status.[378]

---

[377] Padwal et al. 2012
[378] Mehta & Chang 2011; Merry & Voigt 2014

To be sure, some authorities, such as the American Medical Association (AMA) and our own National Board of Health and Welfare, have determined that obesity is a disease.[379] But other sources are much more cautious, with some arguing that obesity has certain features that could fit into the category of disease,[380] while others argue that the disease label really only suggests that fatness appears to be associated with certain diseases.[381]

It is also noteworthy that the World Health Organization (WHO) has been constantly changing its definition of fat people for almost 25 years. From referring to fatness (obesity in their vocabulary) first as a disease and then as a cause of many other diseases, in 2017, they described it as "an abnormal or excessive accumulation of fat that can impair health."[382] However, since the WHO does not explain what they mean by "abnormal," "excessive," or "impairment of health," they make it seem as if there is some kind of natural link between fatness of all kinds and poor health.[383]

It makes a huge difference whether human variations should be called a disease or not. This has enormous consequences. Disease does not really exist until society

---

[379] Mehta & Chang 2011; Merry & Voigt 2014
[380] BBC News 2013; Socialstyrelsen 2014
[381] Takahashi & Mori 2013
[382] WHO 2017
[383] Guthman 2013

agrees to try to cure it.³⁸⁴ It is, so to speak, society's response to a human variation that gives life to the idea of disease. In the case of fatness, this has developed into an absurd paradox. The cure for the disease has been to tell fat people to go home and cure themselves (dieting, or "eating more balanced"). But since dieting usually doesn't work for fat people, this means that today, it is a completely ineffective medicine that keeps the idea of fatness as a disease alive.

Historian Sander Gilman is clearly against calling fatness a disease. He argues that it is rather an obsession with body and citizenship control and the pursuit of an idea of universal health that has long shaped our culture.³⁸⁵ Several scholars, including myself, have come to similar conclusions.³⁸⁶

As I mentioned earlier, research has shown that many doctors don't really think fatness belongs in medical care.³⁸⁷ This attitude obviously plays a role when fat people encounter health care. If it is this attitude that causes the doctor to give patronizing advice to go home and do something about their fatness themselves, both the profession and the fat people are let down. This means that

---

³⁸⁴ Rosenberg & Golden 1997, p. xiii
³⁸⁵ Gilman 2010, 2008
³⁸⁶ Beausoleil & Ward 2009; Cobb 2007; Evans & Colls 2009; Oliver 2006; Rail et al. 2010
³⁸⁷ Ogden & Flanagan 2008

there is neither medicine nor a widespread desire to treat it as a disease. In this frustration, fat people are treated with deeply moralizing overtones. They become a problem for the health service, who simply don't have the knowledge to cure the disease that the National Board of Health and Welfare has placed in the health service's lap. This is why the health service has been clamoring for national guidelines for the treatment of fat people. They want to know what to say to fat people because they themselves have no idea. Instead of removing fatness from primary care, every effort is now being made to adapt words, texts, guidelines, and treatment ideas to make it a disease.

The system of classifying individuals by weight (BMI) was never designed for individual medical treatment but was an epidemiological tool intended to monitor trends at the population level.[388] As the media, public health authorities, and health care providers constantly refer to epidemiological studies, these have slowly been turned into a medicalization of the individual fat bodies.[389] Added to this were cultural explanations of fatness, as everything from individual, moral, medical, biological, evolutionary, socioeconomic, and emotional causes of fatness flooded the media landscape.[390] In this way, the disease label was fed by extending the meaning of being fat to other human

---

[388] Nicholls 2013
[389] Rail et al. 2010
[390] Shugart 2011

deficiencies. The affair between medicine and culture, especially in the media, has meant that those who hate fat bodies and consider fat people stupid and unattractive can always cite illness as a reason to keep hating. Even the opposite has occurred, as more and more bariatric surgeons cite the societal stigma associated with being overweight as one of the main reasons for performing surgeries on individuals struggling with ascribed obesity.

There Are Other, More Dignified Questions to Ask

The new questions must build on the answers we have already received from the management of the obesity epidemic itself. It is the overall impact of the measures that is the answer. They have not worked. They failed. On top of that, they lowered the health and dignity of fat people and made them sick. These are deeply existential violations. The ferocity of the organizing around fatness is remarkable. What are we as a society really doing to people? Aren't there other ways to live together? Shouldn't we be looking for a new dignity that removes such aberrations from our own systems? There are lives to be lived.

Rather than placing people in a category that our institutions lack applicable knowledge about, the new questions must challenge the narratives of fatness, the epidemic, and fat people at their core. From a radical humanist perspective, obesity science's self-image of objectivity must be seen as a problem in itself. That self-image is a problem because it has ultimately harmed the very people it claims to want to cure. We need to see that.

With this book, I have argued that the health-political, moralizing image of fatness has been senseless. Those who want to cure fat people have acted from tunnel vision: fatness is dangerous, and fatness should be removed.

This tunnel vision has shut down deeper, more dignified attitudes to people's right to live in peace. The tunnel vision has guided the research questions, the medicalization, the campaigns, the actions, the market, the public's attitudes, and the individuals themselves.

- Young, healthy people with a few kilos of so-called overweight have been blamed as individuals at risk of disease and treated with simplistic advice and moralizing sermons. It has normalized that whole generations live their lives chronically dieting. Even though the dangers of fatness have never been made clear.

- Very fat people, where fatness is an actual disability, do not receive equitable care when they seek treatment for illness because the focus is on behavioral changes and not on any illnesses in need of healing.

- Thin people have become thinner and more interested in staying thin, and thinness as a top priority has led to new forms of exercise- and eating disorders - even in children. Mental health problems among young people today are rooted in the search for identity. The identity they grow into is now poisoned by thoughts about everything they are not.

- A self-proclaimed superhuman has been constructed. Thin people imagine that they have abilities that fat people lack. They have also found ways to exploit fat people in an unholy collaboration with the health sector.

- An apartheid system based on body weight has left visible structural imprints where life chances and perceived opportunities have clearly deteriorated for fat people. An imagined stereotype of the fat individual has colonized our caring institutions where self-proclaimed superhumans simply cannot grasp why, on earth, the fat ones don't follow their advice. The stereotype of the mindless and unintelligible fat person is so penetrating that healthcare professionals find it difficult to listen to what their fat patients really tell them about their lives.

- The global failure is never blamed on the interventions, allowing them to continue. Fat people participate in the failure by waging war on their own bodies and lives rather than on the self-proclaimed superhumans' ignorance, exploitation, and threat images.

Those of us interested in social justice must be critical of the unwanted effects of interventions on vulnerable people. Not only because it has harmed people and been a waste of financial, political, and human resources but also because it fundamentally shakes the trust we have invested in our systems. The dignity of both those who managed and those who were managed must be protected by ensuring that the failure is owned by those who caused those failures. They must honestly and openly stop what they are doing, put it in reverse, and admit that it was the wrong way to go. That they have hurt people, that they made mistakes, that they allowed a large group of people to be stigmatized and regarded as idiots by parts of the public.

The Loss of Meaning Inflicted on Fat People is Deeply Existential

The management of human fatness has had an ideological rigor in which they have actually weighed and measured people and made decisions based on what the scales and tape measure showed. Such measurements have been allowed to determine how sick they are, even though no research has yet shown any link between body weight and health, except for the very fattest. This way of evaluating and trying to correct the individual has had devastating consequences. We have dieting toddlers and eating-disordered adolescents who continue to fear eating for the rest of their lives. We have an increase in mental illness, as the restriction of life opportunities has created profound feelings of not being welcome, not being enough, and not being able to live a full life. I have spoken to 60-year-old anorexic women who have struggled with eating all their lives and who never eat with others. They can't casually enjoy a piece of food without having severe anxiety about being disgusting. The philosopher Jean Baudrillard has extensively described the inhumane consequences of our modern culture:

> *"A battle would seem to be raging within us between the aspiration of an entire culture towards individual freedom and repugnance for individuality and freedom stemming from something deep in the species. The inhumanity of the undertaking can be seen in the abolition of everything within us that is human, all too human: our desires, our deficiencies, our neuroses, our dreams, our disabilities, our viruses, our lunacies, our unconscious and even our sexuality – all the features which make us specific living beings – are now being ruled out of court. And this contradictory movement finds expression in irresistible remorse, in deep resentment towards the world as it is, and in even more intense self-hatred."*[391]

This harsh evaluation of ourselves has no positive end result. Our contempt for humanity's vulnerability now requires resistance. Baudrillard, in the quote above, did not mention fatness in his view of where society has gone. He is describing something we have all started to feel more and

---

[391] Baudrillard 2001, p. 34-45

more. That there is actually something indescribably wrong with the whole thing. We are losing meaning.

So we run, diet, overeat, starve and vomit. We count calories, drug away all our innermost desires, cut ourselves, and, in far too many cases, take our own lives. I say, like the poet Bob Hansson: "Can't we be nice now, because then we actually die." A new radical humanism with a focus on meaning, ethics, and social justice is needed to address not only the disdain for fatness but all degrading treatment of people. As Joel Best points out, constructions of social problems have consequences in that public attitudes and social policy responses depend on precisely how the problem is defined.[392] Public attitudes and government responses have been clear. People should be induced (encouraged, motivated, shamed) to weigh less. Because they have a "disease". Because "we can't have a bunch of fat people walking around on the sidewalks." The ultimate spearhead of hardness, and the question we must now ask ourselves, is whether those who want to fix fat people want fat people to experience meaninglessness in their bodies. Do they not want fat people to feel good about themselves? This is an unimaginable idea to me, but it seems increasingly possible. If the self-proclaimed superhumans have such thoughts, it is not only their treatment but their own dignity that must be questioned.

---

[392] Best 2015

For hundreds of years, many thinkers have written about the unique biopsychosocial sensitivity of human beings. Sven-Eric Liedman makes an important distinction between reason and rationality. An action towards a carefully defined goal can be rational. But if the same action can damage nature, society, and ethical and aesthetic assets and values, it is not reason. Reason requires an overall evaluation. Liedman sees the ethical debate as the inevitable reaction to a social science that avoided the fundamental questions of value and instead devoted itself to making every problem empirically manageable - that is, possible to measure.[393]

It is through prevailing social narratives and ideologies that we humans discover our position, our importance, and our existential value. The day we started measuring and weighing people, we simultaneously created a narrative of value along a scale between purity and danger. And many were defined as pure, while others were defined as chronic danger. And thus, also managed as such.

Resistance as a Carrier of Vital Force and Thus of Health

Nancy Fraser, an American professor of philosophy, argues that people who are degraded must disarm the institutions that actively prevent them from participating in society on the same terms as others. To be discriminated

---
[393] Liedman 1999

against, she says, is to be denied participation in social life.[394] Others, speaking explicitly about fatness, speak in similar terms. They say that any real change requires us to turn against what oppresses us instead of trying to upgrade ourselves to fit the pattern.[395]

Life itself offers constant resistance. Resistance, or rather, being able to face resistance, provides vital force, and that vital force, in turn, enables us to face more resistance. Let me give an example from the biological immune system. The immune system is not complete in humans at birth but is built in relation to what the human body encounters over time. It is slowly built up in defense of constantly invading forces. The body is thus equipped to meet new invasions of things that the body neither needs nor wants. People who lack an immune system are fatally vulnerable.

Vital force can be likened to the development of a psychosocial immune system through learning, work, play, and relationships. If the development is favorable, we can experience meaning and feel strong, and resistances in life can be made understandable and manageable. At times, we can then feel a zest for life and pride in who we are. Much can be achieved by daring to think for ourselves and choosing new paths that do not harm us. The handling of

---

[394] Fraser 2005
[395] Shugart 2016

fat people is particularly invasive because it identifies people as deviants. People who are treated as deviants have lower self-reliance, less motivation, and more damaged relationships. This extinguishes the very basis for experiencing, having, and developing vital force - or health.

In order to dissolve the senseless threat image of fat people, fat people have to start resisting directly in degrading relations. On the one hand, the stigmatizing system must be resisted so that its processes are made more difficult, and on the other hand, the stigmatized, in themselves, must respond to the applied stigma in order to strengthen their own dignity. But those of us who study human beings and their surrounding social institutions know that most people are unable to argue in an unwelcoming environment. We all slowly grow into the identities that are most heavily promoted by those who have had the most room to speak. Eventually, we may be so convinced of the rejection of our identity that we no longer protest. We believe them, we let them continue, and we even participate in the degradation of ourselves. The more extensive the stigmatizing system is, the more it thinks for us, but it is kept alive by us as long as we do not question it. The price is paid only by the stigmatized themselves.

Because of the delusions that have blocked the minds of the self-proclaimed superhumans, being fat stirs up frustrated feelings in those you meet. You will stir up even more emotions when you start resisting. In their eyes, you then become not only a carrier of a terrible epidemic but a carrier in full denial. Resistance will be met with powerful resistance. As a superhuman, it is upsetting to have your self-image as "the one who knows and has knowledge" called to account. Especially from those who embody the whole problem! But then remember that they never had knowledge. All their attempts to fight the fat epidemic by invoking the weakness of the character of fat people have failed. It's not because a billion people can't follow instructions at the level of a five-year-old. It's because the self-proclaimed superhumans' understanding of fatness has been utterly useless.

Research clearly shows how stigma-induced stress both reinforces and creates illness.[396] The vulnerable person cannot escape unscathed from full-scale systemic biopsychosocial devaluation. Unless she actively refuses to accept it and decides to resist. As I stated earlier, the human need to be included and to be counted can become so overwhelming that individuals admit to crimes they never committed.[397] And, as I also pointed out, so far, most fat people have admitted their "crime." Either they have confessed by showing that they both want and try to lose weight. Or through silence and social escape.

---

[396] Puhl & Heuer 2010
[397] Braithwaite 1989, p. 162

Unfortunately, it becomes unsustainable for the fat people themselves to keep admitting that they are wrong and guilty. It only benefits those who do not like to see fat people, those who still claim that there is something fundamentally wrong with fat people's thinking and lives, and those who dehumanize people by body shape.

Resistance does not have to be violent or an attack on another person. Resistance can be like armor, like an extra skin, like a social immune system that simply stops the stigmatization attempt there and then. The more often you succeed with resistance, and the more people who succeed with the same resistance, the more powerful it becomes. Both for those trying to deal with you and for yourself.

There are probably psychologists who will think that this armoring of people who have been hurt is a bad coping mechanism for their psychosocial health. But then they usually talk about a wall that has been built defensively and almost unconsciously around a wounded person, a wall of pure survival that ultimately does not let anything in, neither bad nor good. But that is where we are now, we who are fat. We have already built such a wall. Otherwise, we would not have survived. With my nine keys of resistance, I am talking about tearing down the wall and building ourselves up actively and consciously. This is not self-therapy but outward resistance. This, in turn, will strengthen our own dignity but, above all, begin to disrupt the stigmatizing system. Bit by bit.

Nine Keys to Resistance

"Without a second thought, obese people passively agree with the major construction of obesity as their own fault because that is how they have been inculcated socially. They rarely publicly challenge the social construction that weight is the result of personal weakness and that their obesity is the product of self-gratification and moral failure." [398]

The research interest of Mary Rogge, in the quote above, is the pathophysiology of fatness. It is about understanding how physiological factors and not behavior lead to people becoming fat. And she is absolutely right. Fat people rarely challenge the narrative of their weakness of character. They do not resist. I hope that through the book, I have provided some explanations as to why. It's nothing new in history that singled-out groups in society are portrayed as weak in character. But fatness has developed into a new type of deviation. In the eyes of the general public, fat people are not only singled out. They are, according to many, sick! In the midst of a health ideology that unscientifically equated the thin body with health, fatness was decided to be a problem for medicine.

The nonsensical idea that medicine could cure fat people has hidden the fact that, in the failed medicalization,

---
[398] Rogge et al. 2004, p. 312

fat people have been stigmatized as deviants. It has been hidden even from the fat people themselves.

There are other human variations that have been medicalized without actual disease. But the massive build-up of various power bases is, in the war against the fat body, something very special. I argue that no other human variation involving so many people has received the same massive negative attention from the institutions of power as the fat body. No other management of an engineered disease has failed so catastrophically in its interventions as the management of the fat body. No other human body variation has met with more pronounced contempt. No other welfare management has harmed so many and helped so few.

In the next figure, I show which heavy power foundations have together pushed the stigmatization of fat people. The stigmatization is transmitted by individuals moving within and between the different foundations.

THE HEALTH IDEOLOGY
The "pure"

THE OBESITY EPIDEMIC
The threat image of "danger"

THE MEDICALIZATION
The practice of power

THE EXPLOITATION
The market

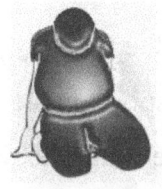

The strongest foundation of power is ideology. Ideology can be simply explained as the strong ideas about 'purity' that we collectively carry within us in different societies and times. Health ideology shines brightly in the privileged parts of the world. This does not mean that everyone is concerned with health and thinness. It just means that everyone knows that this is where purity lies.

In the protection of the pure, there is the dark threat - the 'danger.' In the large-scale launch of an obesity epidemic as the greatest health challenge of our time, the message went out to every citizen. It was clear that the threat resided in all those individuals who were not yet pure or thin.

To cure this epidemic, the most large-scale medicalization of people's bodies ever was staged. Medicine was tasked with eliminating the threat. Thickness was medicalized. Medicine already had access to the blaming of the individual. Healthcare professionals could point out the importance of addressing weight in every patient encounter. It was put into practice. Fatness was called a disease, but the only medicine was admonitions against unwanted behaviors.

This increased the legitimacy of exploiting the fat body in all areas of society. Fatness could now be despised in the name of health. A weight loss market could ride roughshod over people's feelings of guilt in the ideology of health and the identification of disease. The media had a new favorite threat to spread. Together, the market and the media formed the spearhead that drilled the message into the self-image of fat people. The fear of becoming or being fat has, at times, been so insane that it has penetrated the thinnest of people and even children.

Collectively, these foundations boil down to stigmatization, as individuals within these foundations constantly devalue the fat body. Most fat people, despite the enormous pressure, never lose weight. And therefore continue to be stigmatized. That most fat people, according to Mary Rogge, never challenge the idea that they have a particular personal weakness is not surprising. Where would they even start in these heavy foundations?

I Have Proposals for a Start

I have come to the conclusion that the first step to resistance lies at the social level, in the encounter with individuals who are dedicated to these foundations, in the encounter with those individuals within the foundations who, consciously or unconsciously, communicate chronic stigmatization of fat people. On the one hand, fat people must try to dissolve the dominant image of them, and on the other, they must hold those who perpetuate the stigma accountable. So, resistance starts on a small scale. I have formulated nine keys that can open up new avenues for even more organized resistance later on. Once the nine keys are established as self-evident, they can be scaled up and politically push away the toxic treatment of fat people.

The nine keys are not nine consecutive steps but rather strategies and little tricks that go in and out of each other. They are variously easy and difficult to adopt, but together, they can, over time, dismantle the senseless treatment of fat people that has characterized our health ideology. Everything they have thought and done against fat people is at a dead end. We cannot let them continue. Living a fulfilling life requires a strong self-image and self-confidence. When you are constantly told to be ashamed, to hide, or to remake yourself, your basic vital force is blocked. Resistance can slowly but surely remove that blockage. To use the words of philosopher Jean Baudrillard, with radical humanism, we can push the human back into the playing field.

1. Rethink

The philosopher Gregory Bateson, if he were alive today, would probably say that because of all the damage caused by the idea of fatness as a disease, we need to find new ways of thinking. He would ask us to think systemically. Systemic wisdom is about seriously starting to see that repeated patterns that are clearly hurting people are important information. In order to change society. And improve lives.

As a fat person, this means that you have to start by considering what has been done to you as oppression. It has been carried out with moralizing, marketing, and health ideological images. It has actively made you not feel at home in your own body. Look at the structure of the threat image, feel the power of health ideology, and dare to trust that the violence you experienced as a fat person actually existed. What you felt is important information. They said that fatness hit the earth like a meteor. It didn't. Fatness was singled out. It was advanced by an unholy alliance of public health policy, market forces, and a resurgent idea of the difference between a good citizen and a bad one. You did not cause chaos with your body. Your body was always just yours.

Think about what the media report about fatness and what they don't report. That's where ideology and moralism can be exposed. It is only when it is exposed that it can be challenged. Consider what hurts you as completely unacceptable, especially when the harm comes from so-called experts, doctors, and authorities. Don't let them keep repeating their simple and deeply patronizing rhymes about you not being complete. They make you sick. No one can live like that in the long run.

Keep in mind that the person attacking you is ideologically overwhelmed. You both have magnified the importance of the fat body. While they gain from it, you have only lost. The build-up of the fat threat has been enormous. No one has escaped it. It is primitive and makes our feelings and thoughts primitive. Many elaborate and persistent processes have slowly, ever reinforcing each other, succeeded in making fat people believe that they are walking around in one of the most dangerous and ugly bodies in the evolution of mankind.

This is no small and innocent claim. It is horrifying. And, in fact, downright idiotic.

Next time you are treated like an idiot, try to study the speaker and be impressed that ideology can speak through people. An ideology is not just something put on top of people and their thoughts. The ideology becomes their thoughts and feelings. Many people imagine that they are exercising care when they tell you that you are not desirable. Tell them that they are not. If you start pointing at the superhumans instead of letting them point at you, you can start shifting the guilt they put on you to them. This doesn't mean that you have to give up your idea of being thin. It's about understanding which ones can't help you at all and which ones only hurt you, which you need to free yourself from.

2. Resist

Speak up, question, and challenge the proclaimed knowledge about fat people that is thrown in your face every day. Do not obey. Don't be silent. Stop dieting. Today. Dieting is starvation, which is violence to the body. You have competence and readiness. No other bodily variation has been subject to the same constant pressure in modern times. That constant pressure means that even before any encounter or relationship, fat people are pumped up, ready to try to make it out in one piece. Use that readiness in yourself and resist the image of you that they will try to show.

Stop denying yourself things like meaning, good relationships, and interesting social contexts. You need to protect yourself by denying the suggestions about who you are that are created in social life." The most important part of human development in an oppressive environment takes place through an active ignoring and neutralization of most of the social suggestions a person is exposed to in everyday life."[399] Sharply question the social relationships and contexts in which you continue to be offended by your appearance. All research has shown for over sixty years that dieting does not work for fat people. Question what people say to you about you. Build on your dignity. Try to catch your dignity in the middle of the communication and win it back.

What you should resist are the attempts to differentiate. Actually, it is not the fat body that is highlighted in the threat image. It is the idea of a difference between fat people and thin people, a difference between your character and that of the self-proclaimed superhuman - an apartheid system. It is the difference between thin and fat that is maintained, dramatized, and magnified. To bring about change in distinguishing relationships, the image of difference must, therefore, be dissolved. This is difficult. It may take a while to even believe in that dissolution yourself. You will be overwhelmed by the instinct not to resist. Meanwhile, saying stop, slowly develops into a social resource as you demonstrate to yourself that you

---

[399] Valsiner 1998, p. 393

have what it takes to protect yourself in a threatening and degrading environment.

3. Dare to Testify

In your imagination, slip out of yourself and stand to the side and witness the communication that takes place between you and the self-proclaimed superhuman. Create a third person of yourself - the defender, the lawyer. Consider the encounter you have with the superhuman as in a movie. The trick to seeing it from the outside, like a movie, is that it is easier to stand up for others than for yourself. Dare to speak for all the fat people in the meeting. Dare to bear witness to the prejudiced, ignorant, and contemptuous treatment of fat people. You know that the fat person in the movie has experiences that superhumans lack. It's about the life experience of being told you're not good enough. Stand up for the fat person in the movie - yourself.

Dare to testify that the treatment has been unacceptable. Demand better health centers, better doctors, certified free from prejudice and moralism in their basic task of healing people who seek help. Write to doctors, politicians, and health centers and testify. Create documents. Tell them that you do not feel there is anything wrong with you but that it is the fault of those who claim such a thing. Show that you know that it's about fat phobia that can hide behind claims of science and care. Dare to say that fat people don't experience any care, that the campaigns against fat people have rather been tools for humiliation and primitive shaming in a less knowledgeable system.

Think of all the headless fat bodies shown for decades when the fatness epidemic was portrayed in various media channels. Put the head back on that body by testifying. Go against the spontaneous flight reaction that occurs when people try to shame you. Represent. In this witnessing process - yes, it is a witnessing process - your vital force develops as society changes. The more you represent the fat people, the more understanding you become of yourself, the more manageable the world becomes, and the more meaningful your encounters become. No matter how the other party in the meeting reacts. Self-esteem and social change come from how you react to people who hurt you. Don't let them hurt you. Tell them to stop hurting you.

4. Question the Threat Image

Question those who claim to know about fat people but have only hurt you. They have the burden of proof. Ask questions and listen if they really have a nuanced knowledge or if they are just blinded by the ideological threat. Remember, they have no medicine for your, according to them, dangerous condition. Therefore, they make disparaging assumptions about your lifestyle. They, therefore, know neither how to cure fatness nor how to stop stigmatizing. You need to recognize that sometimes experts are completely wrong. The threat has been massively exaggerated and needs to be challenged, nuanced, and resolved. The limit of the threat of dangerous fatness has been reached, as the offense to people far outweighs any possible benefit of the threat. And if they keep repeating the same old myths and beliefs about fat people, you don't have to listen to it anymore.

The alarmist threat has not been displaced by science but incorporated into it. Expect that the threat is so strongly established that questioning it will be received with pure aggression by those who are pushing the war on fatness the hardest. What superhumans see in your body is a living threat, and they think their job is to react to that threat. But because the threat is not true, it must be seriously challenged.

Remember that the fat threat has been built for more than 40 years, and it is not based on knowledge. In the management of the so-called obesity epidemic, accumulated knowledge has been neglected to provide a basis for policy interventions. The accumulated knowledge tells us that interventions against fat people do not work, that the link between body weight and health is fictitious, and that fat people do not have difficulties understanding guidelines. In the absence of knowledge, the management of fat people has been entirely dependent on the dramatic threat images. Therefore, when dealing with self-proclaimed superhumans, we need to address the threat images they carry. Ask them how and why they were formed. Ask what knowledge they have behind them. If they pull the "health card", i.e., "everyone knows that being fat is bad for your health," ask how they can know that. Penetrate deeper. You will feel motivated when you hear that they have no real references, that they don't really have any knowledge, but just let the constructed threat image speak through them. Question the insane proportions of the threat. Compare with real threats to our shared world.

5. Require Knowledge

What kind of knowledge and research do you want? We can actually choose. The answers provided by traditional obesity research so far depend on the questions asked by researchers. Believe me, research is never value-free. What values do you think should guide the issues that affect us all? Over a million scientific publications have been produced on the danger of obesity without any evidence of danger. This is, to put it kindly, a bit amazing. It happens partly because you don't make demands. You have believed that scientists know more than you do - that they always find important things. That that's what they do. Unfortunately, that's not true. I'm sorry to write that. It is not true.

New research questions, new distinctions, new evidence, and hypotheses are needed to give fat people the right to exist as they are. Question the knowledge of health care providers and how they got that knowledge. Search for, collect, and cultivate knowledge. Seek more information on why all measures against the obesity epidemic have failed worldwide. Listen carefully and reflect on the answer. If you see news about successful interventions, look up those interventions, find out how the results were determined, and what they mean by "successful." In addition, look at the same results a few years later to include the re-obesity that fat dieters are at risk of suffering in the assessment. If you don't know how to look up such data, someone else can do it.

Ask the doctors if there is any internal scientific reflection on all the failed interventions against fat people. Ask for scientific evidence for what they say and for what the studies actually found. Listen if they say anything about the biological causes of fatness, if they continue to give sub-intelligent dieting advice, talk about immoral behavior, or if they emphasize the cursed threat.

Today, after decades of dieting advice, health professionals will agree that dieting is wrong. They will motivate you to eat a balanced diet instead. Or some other new concept. They've learned some things, and right now, they're going to avoid the concepts of dieting and obesity. Because they've realized they don't work. But their agenda is still to reduce the fatness they see. Therefore, fat people must continue to be portrayed as problems in themselves. Therefore, the doctor's job is still to make you feel bad in your own body. But saying that people are problems is not knowledge. It is a value judgment. Therefore, question what they present as knowledge. Be difficult. Having a dignified self-image is about being proud of and having respect for yourself and about feeling important to other people. Wanting knowledge is not being in denial. It is standing up for your dignified self-image as the superhumans themselves would stand up for theirs.

6. Own the Story

Earlier, I described how, after years of rising death rates and stigmatization, AIDS sufferers lost faith in both the healthcare system and the research done on them. They began to ask new questions, forcing science to move away from the idea of a behavioral disease and focus instead on a blood infection. The sufferers thus changed the narrative themselves in order to gain the applicable knowledge that would actually save their lives. Narratives matter because, in some narratives, moral and cultural values block pathways to new knowledge.

After all, fat people do not carry a deadly virus. The example of the AIDS sufferers only shows the necessity of occasionally challenging the prevailing narrative that exists – the one that both science and health care carry and constantly reproduce. As long as we do not do everything we can to own our own narrative, they can continue to apply their imagined notions of fat people. And in health care, for example, their image of fat people's abilities and characteristics is not a flattering one. Hidden microphones in healthcare lunchrooms would reveal quite a lot.

James Charlton, who wrote about the oppression of disabled people, drew conclusions that are perhaps closer to the fat people than the deadly disease AIDS. Charlton said that oppression can only be resolved by the group itself clarifying its own history and asserting its fundamental rights to self-determination. Right now, the history of fatness has been absorbed by movements already calling for a new order based on gender, sexuality, and freedom of expression. This is a good thing. But I believe that fatness needs its own narrative, its own story of oppression. Because it is unique. There has been an open, global, powerful, authoritative devaluation of the fat body, completely without a safety net. I would even say that the contempt has been so accepted that we have not yet understood that fat people must now be protected in their basic human dignity. Before the oppression becomes even more severe, remember that history has shown that groups of people have always been capable of harming other groups that they considered disruptive.

Other people would never accept being portrayed the way fat people have been portrayed. Make sure that your own story is moving forward. Other people do not have access to your life and your story. Do not let them tell you who you are, how you live, and how you function. Argue against them, tell them when they are wrong. It is difficult. But I promise that a different kind of story will emerge if we just start dismantling theirs. Their story is filled with ideology, threats, their self-images as superhumans, their distinctions, their infantile advice, and their ignorance of the biopsychosocial human being in general and of fat people in particular. Their dreams of a slim world have blinded them to the fact that every single intervention against fatness has been misguided and, therefore, failed all over the world. But you can tell them that. If they reply that the failure is due to the failure of people like you to put simple information into practice, ask them if a billion people have lost all their judgment and what the superhuman thinks that is.

The opposite of vital force is being cast in stories that de-motivate and stifle one's inherent creativity, which makes one inhibited, anxious, and conditioned in one's daily life. There is another story, one that is about living peacefully as you are without being subjected to others' degrading thoughts about you. Dig up that story. Present it to those who have never heard it before. One small step at a time.

7. Separate Medicine from Culture

Sander Gilman, like many other critics, talks about the management of fatness as an obsession with the idea of universal health linked to body production.[400]

"Our understanding of the pathological is rooted in an awareness of the human organism's fragility – not simply its mortality, though that has always and everywhere inspired fear of the ultimate loss of control, but its susceptibility to disease, pollution, corruption, and alteration, things that we experience in our own bodies and observe in others. Every group has laws, taboos, and diagnoses distinguishing the "healthy" from the "sick." The very concept of pathology is a line drawn between the "good" and the "bad." [401]

The stigmatization of fat people has completely merged with the medicalization of fat people. It is unacceptable that people who hate to see fat people are allowed to hate openly by invoking a medical science that does not exist. Not wanting to see fat people on the streets has nothing to do with ideas about disease. Here, medicine must be required to be clear, rigorous, and make distinctions. We cannot allow medical research to be used to attack human variations they only find culturally unattractive. They have

---

[400] Gilman 2010, 2008
[401] Gilman 1985, p. 23

had many tricks to get around this critical issue. The danger of fatness has not yet been seriously questioned by science. When does thickness become dangerous? When is it completely harmless? Why don't medical drugs work? Why are people's digestive systems cut up for weight loss to even be possible? Is it because fatness is not a disease but just another body?

Mia Forrest showed convincingly how the BMI tool is used by those who deal with fat people. Numbers seem to make the disease real for those who already treat fatness as a disease. The numbers seem to prove to them that treating fat people scientifically is about medicine (health) and not about appearance (culture).[402] But they are still just numbers. Created by humans. This is an important reason why the treatment of fatness needs a separate historical review. Imagine that they could measure this "disease" with a tape measure and scales! It must have been medicine's wet dream to have measurement tools that could determine whether or not a sick person was sitting in front of them.

The omission of the research that has constantly criticized the moral basis of treatment is serious. It gives rise to a management of fatness that is completely lacking in self-criticism. That cultural moralism has long been associated with definitions of disease is well known to social scientists and philosophers. Historically, once the

---

[402] Forrest 2009

moral and cultural aspects of human selection were revealed, medicine was eventually forced to backtrack. Today, those who were forcibly sterilized or forcibly lobotomized have received compensation. Homosexuals and people with disabilities are now protected from discrimination (at least on paper) after fighting for the basic human rights that medicine undoubtedly violated. This has not yet happened in the case of fatness, perhaps because there are so many fat people that they don't even seem to exist as a vulnerable group.

If you ask those dealing with fatness whether they are dealing with medical health or cultural desirability, they will have to make a choice. In the unlikely event that they choose culture, the real oppression is revealed. That they simply don't like what they see. They actually have to deal with that problem therapeutically within themselves. If they choose medicine, the research is clear. There is no proven causal link between body weight and ill health. Moreover, all research shows that dieting is harmful to fat people. And that the stigma is heavier than pounds.

8. Challenging the Health Ideology

Few ideas are as sacred as the relatively new idea of what health should mean. Health is now equated with a thin body. Anyone who has been inundated by social media and traditional media in recent decades knows that the hatred of those who do not seem to be visibly working off their subcutaneous fat is inexhaustible. Health ideology prevents fat people from creating a position from which they can resist stigmatization because it is health that the haters refer to. It is health they cite as the main reason why they act contemptuously towards fat people. The positive charge of the concept of health is thus used for purely negative purposes, much like as the devil reads the Bible. It is a terribly dark invocation of health care. Because who can be against health?

I can. It is time that we criticize the prevailing idea of health. The only way to discern the contempt for fat people is to link health to wider issues of justice and human dignity. Then, it becomes clear how the ideology of health affects the ability of large groups to experience vital force. Being against health does not mean being against people's attempts to feel better. Rather, the efforts of fat people to feel good have been hindered by the oppressive and narrow nature of the prevailing health ideology.

Challenge the health ideology of self-proclaimed superhumans. Ask why they have problems with your health or ill health. What about their own? What is it that really bothers them? What is it that they find so difficult to deal with when it comes to fat people? Why this senselessness? The resistance here consists of denying and questioning their attribution of ill health rather than defending our own health. Let them do their risk calculations and measurements if they find it rewarding. But don't let them call you sick when you are not. And don't let them have the nerve to claim that the cure for this attributed ill health is being able to tell the difference between a bag of chips and a carrot. Attribution of ill health and infantile advice as medicine makes you sick, not healthy.

With a radical humanist view of health as a vital force, you should ask yourself which relationships give you value, which ones increase your ability to overcome obstacles, and which ones contribute to a zest for life. And above all, which relationships don't give you these opportunities? What if health is feeling safe, welcomed, respected, and protected? And never had anything to do with how many kilograms you weigh per square meter.

9. There Was Never Anything Wrong with You. They Were the Ones Who Had Problems

When the obesity epidemic was launched in the late 90s, excitement was in the air. The public health ideologues were onto something big. They had good, secure jobs and exciting positions with a view of society. They were tasked with improving public health. If fatness was now considered an epidemic, they could perhaps stage a completely unprecedented fight against a social enemy - obesity. It was a desktop product presented with powerful graphs and charts. Could this be the holy grail the new public health ideology needed? Could this be the optimal control over a society? An enemy incubated in every single person's body. All blame and solutions were to be placed on individuals to purify society. Weight loss was something "easy" that everyone could do in their daily lives and throughout their lives. Everyone could become healthy and fit (slim) citizens. And therefore, society could also become healthy and beautiful. Fatness was an enemy we could actually defeat, they thought. They called it a manageable disease. Today, we know the results of this large-scale experiment. They didn't understand how this global dieting experiment would affect fat people.

The problem they wanted to solve was not with the fat people. The threat of the obesity epidemic never came from fat people. It came from thin, privileged people's unworthy thoughts about people who are fat. The problem was formulated by health ideologists, who transformed the concept of health from the absence of disease to a project of self-actualization. Project slim body! It was their interests, their desires, their status markers, their bodies. They were superhumans who projected their own desires for a produced and disciplined body onto those who had neither the same lives nor the same bodies as them.

Focus on the people who extinguish your vital force. Turn your gaze on them, and point out those who are hurting, if not openly, then at least to yourself. Go back to the fundamentals that built their ideological and moralizing drama about the difference between fat and thin. Shake up the original ideas. Ask why fat people should become thin. Ask how they know that fat people are sick. Ask how they see their own role in the obesity epidemic. Ask if it could be that they were completely wrong from the start and what that would mean. Ask if it is possible for you as a fat person to live a rich life, get help from the health service if you become ill, and avoid a life where the obesity epidemic is imposed on you as soon as you slip into a health center. Ask if you can have the right to feel free from stigmatization, discrimination, and condescending advice, especially in relationships that are portrayed as caring. Ask them how they think it went with their projection of a middle-class value system. Ask yourself how you think it went. You now know how it went.

The Nine Keys Are Carriers of Vital Force

This is not a self-help book in the sense of self-improvement. It is a book of knowledge and resistance. It is a book that directs power toward those who destroy us. By the nine keys, I don't mean that we have to start loving our bodies from now on. Body activists have described this much better than me. Moreover, such words are used by the very market that keeps selling you diet crap. My basic idea is that the very resistance to the devaluations of others is itself a carrier of vital force. In the very act of resistance, you slowly create new conditions for feeling good and liking yourself while dissolving the image of fat people. There was never anything wrong with being fat. Fat people have been portrayed as epidemically ill. It was a bloody awful suggestion. Because the language of medical power gives the false impression that they were only responding to an emerging disease, we missed the social and systemic dimension of obesity - how the idea of fatness as a disease was constructed.

Eventually, the threat was so great that it grew over everyone's head. Those who continue to sound the alarm about an epidemic now have to turn themselves inside out to try to squeeze the fat people into the threat. They deny critical research. They try to shape new words. They twist and turn to hide the total lack of applicable knowledge. At the same time, a completely different knowledge is emerging outside the stagnant ideology. They were wrong. They did wrong. On an ethical level, the image of fat people was deeply problematic, and all actions taken in the wake of that image have failed and harmed people.

New knowledge emerges through resistance. Turn the critical eye and point a finger at those who hurt you. We are born with a core of life deep within us, an inner drive to move forward. The singling out of the fat body as unworthy has damaged that core. That's how vulnerable we are to social, chronic pressure. With a damaged life core, you turned to your own body to try to escape the judgmental gaze. You starved, you gained weight, you starved again, gained even more weight, and the chronic stress established itself, robbing you of your biological, psychological, and social vitality. The only knowledge you sought was new slimming methods, therefore simultaneously fueling the image of the fat person as a human being not yet complete. Not until she becomes thin. You did not challenge the social construct that your weight was the result of personal weakness. Instead, it was actually the launch of an obesity epidemic that made you weak.

Resistance is a core, provides a core, and builds a core in that the outward direction must draw from something deep within you. Inside, there is you. The one who has the right not to be degraded, not to be made sick, not to be seen as a sign of an evolution gone wrong. The right not to be conditioned by other people's undignified ideas about human variations. Whoever has the right to live in an environment where they don't have to hide in order to make self-proclaimed superhumans feel good.

It is not really about trying to come up with a new ideology. Rather, it is a dissolution of the opposites of health ideology - thin versus fat, good versus bad, purity versus danger. Moralism was allowed to penetrate the cracks left by ignorance of human vulnerability. It became a singling out of fat people, with devastating consequences for their ability to live at peace with themselves.

A process of resistance does not have to be seen as a war at all. It doesn't even have to be activism. It can start deep within each individual, in new ways of thinking about the world and your place in it. It can be seen as a cultural representation of a new image, one where singled-out people show the way to meaning for themselves. It becomes a process where morality and human dignity are negotiated, where the opposites of good and evil are turned upside down and backward and forward as the singled-outs begin to point. Where does good actually exist in a society, and where does evil arise? Where do our moral values lie? In the social drama of an obesity epidemic, they tried to both create a problem and point to its solutions. But they failed. The handling of fat people is the problem, and the solution is resistance to that management. They will be reluctant. There will be many traps along the way.

Traps on the Way to Knowledge

There are many traps on the way to the resolution of the senseless image of fatness. Moreover, I believe that more than a resolution is needed. The whole approach should be scrutinized and dealt with openly and publicly. Probably, this demand will be met with skepticism and even aggression. Have fat people really been portrayed and treated so appallingly badly? Aren't they just easily offended? Fat people have not been displaced, persecuted, or dehumanized like other ethnically, religiously, or racially categorized groups. This is not a mass murder, a displacement by armed force, or a rigged attempt at extermination. No, it is not. It has just been a handling in total absence of sense and reason. The fact that the negative image of fat people has been so large-scale and has affected the health of so many individuals makes a review all the more important. It is about finding out how extensive and pervasive a moral panic can still be, even though we live in a time that is supposedly characterized by science and knowledge rather than primitive beliefs.

We need to hear from those who orchestrated this senseless view of fatness and know how they were able to do it and how it happened. Where did it go so wrong? Science itself has a role to play in summarizing the research behind the management and the research that was ignored. The moralizing self-proclaimed superhumans are free to talk openly about their own self-image in the commercialization of an obesity epidemic. Those who have constantly reinforced the negative image of fat people - the National Board of Health and Welfare, the Public Health Agency, and the WHO - are also the ones who have had the power to apply the brakes. They must now explain why they accelerated instead. The pharmaceutical, health, and food companies that claim to have developed the miracle cure for obesity should be questioned by the best journalists in the mainstream media in prime time. Those who maintained the whole system through their direct practice in dealing with fat people - doctors, nurses, dieticians, psychologists, and health coaches - should be asked what they thought of fat people during this health ideology era. Such a survey could provide us with an enormous amount of knowledge about society's most primitive division of purity and danger. As I see it, there are six major overhanging traps on the road to liberation:

- that we do not see through the power of the market
- that we depoliticize the obesity epidemic

that we do not turn against our own desire to become superhuman

- that we stop believing in the liberating power of knowledge
- that we do not have the energy to participate in a real change

- that we continue to stigmatize without seeing where it comes from.

Trap 1: That We Do Not See Through the Power of the Market

Market forces are self-preserving. Their profit-driven entrepreneurs will turn the concepts inside out in order to continue selling exactly the same slimming products in new costumes. It is important to keep a cool head and see through the sales tricks. Not because people shouldn't be allowed to make money but because they participate in the stigmatization of fat people in this particular profit production. Their products have never been officially blamed for not working. That burden has been placed on all the fat people who failed to lose weight with them.

Weight Watchers have refocused their advertising in recent years from weight loss to wellness or well-being. Over the years, even they have had to recognize the difficulties for fat people to lose weight. The customer base disappeared after decades of dieting and subsequent weight gain. With the concept of wellness, they now intend to try to get these customers back. Their product is, therefore, marketed differently. It is about 'getting in shape,' 'finding balance,' and 'losing a bit of weight.' They play down the weight thing and pretend that they have never been a pure diet company making money from people gaining weight after losing it. But it's the same calorie counting as usual, and the joy of every pound lost is still the measure of success. They just have new marketing words.

Weight Club is currently the most advertised slimming club in Sweden. It has changed its name to Wellobe because "the old name focused too much on weight and too little on what works and gives our users a healthier life," said the acting manager of Wellobe. At the same time, they continue to exclusively promote weight loss in their advertisements by claiming that it is about simple actions such as starting to think. Today, Wellobe claims to strongly distance itself from the word 'dieting.' Instead, they advocate "a healthy and balanced diet". Dieting doesn't work, they write. Instead, it's about lifestyle change - eat everything but not always. Count calories. On the same page, you can fill in your height and weight and calculate how long it will take to reach your goal, which is thinness. "Now we know that the body resists starvation," they say. "We now know that fat bodies that have been starved will do anything to gain weight," they say. But at the same time, they continue to advertise people who have 'succeeded.' They have managed to become thin. "But, they say we should not diet. We should live wisely," they say. The slightly newer dieting company Noom says: "Stop dieting. Get lifelong results." But for the 45 million (!) people who have downloaded this app, it's the same old calorie counting as usual. And the same old restrictive eating and the same recipes as the last fifty years. Don't think, for the thousandth time, that this is something new.

They are taking new approaches. They are introducing new methods. They say they are on the side of fat people in a stigmatizing time. But the contempt that fat people face cannot be removed by introducing new words and methods. The stigma is now so deeply ingrained that even an anti-discrimination law would not succeed in removing it at the initial stage. The negative views and attitudes people hold in relation to fatness are now so subtle but elaborate that they would escape the radar of legislation.[403] Initially, I still believe that an anti-discrimination law protecting body shape and appearance must be established as soon as possible. It will be important in freeing us from the market's future grip on the fat body because believe me. They are coming. They have found a golden vein.

The evidence that dieting has never worked is piling up, and the market is extremely quick to adapt its rhetoric. Right now, for example, pharmaceutical companies are working hard to wash away the term obesity and replace it with the even more morbid-sounding term *obesitas*. The trap for fat people is that it may sound to them that the market has changed its attitude towards fatness, that they now understand them, respect them, and have more knowledge. But this is not the case. It's about big money. In

---

[403] Link 2001

order to get the fat people to agree to treatments in the future, they try to change the marketing without actually changing the products. If we don't see this, the market will continue to fuel the weight drive and, therefore, the contempt for the fat body.

Trap 2: That We Depoliticize the Obesity Epidemic

To depoliticize an essentially political phenomenon is to strip away the historical background and the powers that have actually created the phenomenon. The measures against fat people have symbolized an idealized middle-class lifestyle where body regulation is a routine that structures everyday life. It is the routines of the privileged that are imposed downwards on people with completely different realities. But the state and the authorities do not want to hear concepts like 'class differences.' They find the concept unpleasant and distasteful and not relevant to individualized behavioral interventions. In this depoliticization, we are tricked into believing that the world is populated by equal individuals with equal opportunities and bodies. Thus, depoliticization allows for judgmental attitudes and oppressive actions to be directed at those who do not seem to take their thinness-production responsibility despite these equal opportunities. I hope that by now, I have shown that it was not so much about science or equal individuals but about ideology. A middle-class ideology that distinguished between complete and incomplete people.

As I mentioned in the chapter on threat images, government agencies and other authorities cannot go as far as they like with a threat. There is a limit when the harm to people becomes more pervasive than the threat itself. At that point, human rights issues begin to be discussed. Human rights issues are political issues.

Therefore, opposition to the senseless treatment of fat people is a political issue. Let me remind you of Farrugia's research on parents of autistic children. He showed how difficult it was for parents to deal with the stigmatization they faced. To achieve dignity, the parents decided to become political instead. Instead of trying to live with the stigma, they turned against the applied stigmatization. By gaining knowledge about how stigmatization was formed, they also gained the power to respond to it politically.

An increased politicization of the view of fat people is about responding to an attributed position as a social pariah. The goal is that self-proclaimed superhumans must stop all the activities that degrade the lives of fat people. This is a political goal that should not be confused with identity politics. It is about the fundamental right to live free from daily prejudiced and ignorant oppression. An oppression that today is based on our own democratic institutions' prejudiced treatment of fat people. Not on knowledge. It is politically unacceptable.

The failed attempts to diet people mean something real. Children have been tempted to starve, and parents have encouraged them. The normalization of fatphobia has closed the doors to new research and criticism of those who created the stigma in the first place. This is a political problem not only in terms of citizenship, justice, equality, and human rights but also in terms of how we as a society choose to create and maintain distinctions between purity and danger. The management of fatness is about social injustice. We do not see it because the threat of fatness is considered to reflect the poor choices of the fat individual[404] and not an ideological drive.

When something has been so obviously ineffective, counterproductive, and harmful, we need to stop and think again. We need to do something politically different. We need to choose new issues and change our approach. If we don't do that, now that we know how the treatment of fat people has failed at every level, it means that we accept the segregation system. This means that we accept a system where we process, blame, and punish those who do not make visible attempts to adapt to the prevailing ideological trends. Unfortunately, I think many people want such a moral distinction. But hopefully, there are many more who

---

[404] McHugh & Kasardo 2012

do not. A society that makes distinctions between folks and folks historically has, time and time again, proved to be a bad society for most people.

The distinction benefits some and harms others, not only materially but psychologically, socially, culturally, and emotionally. We must, therefore, 'de-politicize' the management of fat people. This can be done by holding politicians, government officials, and various interest groups accountable for their intentions and beliefs about fat people. Anyone who wants to critically examine an ideology that harms people needs to pay as much attention to the ideologues' proponents as to the methods they use to achieve it.[405] Rouven Porz, a professor of medical ethics, and ethics researcher Christine Bally-Zenger argue for the need for a better understanding of entrepreneurs' personal values about fatness.[406] What values and views of humanity have they based their questions on? What has been their starting point, and why has their negative curiosity about fatness been kept alive at all costs?

In fact, all cultural phenomena are inherently political because they are about being able to see, open up, and realize new possibilities for people.[407] A curiosity about meaning, ethics and social justice must be developed in the critique of the idea of a rampant obesity epidemic. They

---

[405] Daigneault 2013
[406] Porz & Bally-Zenger 2013
[407] Grossberg 2010

cannot be allowed to continue to stigmatize people who have done nothing wrong.

Trap 3: That We Do Not Turn Against Our Own Desire to Become Superhuman.

Fat people also stigmatize fat people. They do. Among those who have "succeeded" in losing weight, many are quick to condemn the fat person they once were and celebrate the new thin person they have become. The newly slimmed people will tell you how tired, sad, and sick they looked in the pictures before salvation. How bad they felt. Unfortunately, they tend to forget and hide the pictures in which they were radiantly fat or suffered life's hardships as thin. The ideology is there, deep in our thoughts about ourselves. When we start thinking about whether we are happy or not.

I have described the self-proclaimed superhuman as an ideologue who sees fatness as an obstacle to the production of a dignified identity. Both in themselves and others. In order to comply with the ideology and strengthen the self-image, the superhuman, therefore, "chooses" to "stay" healthy and thin. Contempt for fat is most prevalent among those who have made slimming their life's work.[408] Contempt for fat is expressed by superhumans as benevolence and as the possession of knowledge, they are happy to share. I have met many people with the same

---
[408] Shugart 2016

attitude. Those who could never imagine becoming fat themselves and want to help everyone become thin.

However, I have also met many fat people who hate the talk of being as good enough as they are. They think it's bullshit. I have debated with aggressive fat people who despise themselves for their fatness and thus hate anyone who tries to claim that their fatness is okay. This whole book is provocative to fat people who actually think that they should suffer from being fat, that they should be pressured, and that they actually have no right to live full lives as they are. Here lies perhaps the most crucial superhuman in the resistance to stigmatization.

The bottom line is that most fat people don't want to be fat. Being fat is not like choosing to get a tattoo or choosing a spectacularly provocative identity. While there are many ways to choose to be a deviant, I have yet to meet anyone who has chosen to be fat. The contempt is too great, the ideology too strong, for anyone to make such a choice. As I have repeated, the contempt is institutionalized in health care, schools, workplaces, families, social arenas, media, globally and locally, and in daily practices and orders. To be fat is to be chronically dehumanized and de-normalized at the societal level. It is difficult, if not impossible, to enjoy life as a fat person, at least without fighting for that right. In fact, movements like fat activism and body positivism are all about this fight for the right to enjoy life regardless of size.

The trap, in this case, is not that fat people crave thinness. Of course, they can do that. Of course, they can strive for thinness if that is what they want to do. The trap here lies in the desire to become that ideological superhuman who is considered to have the *right* body and, therefore, the right dignity. Participating in the singling out of one's own body for everything it is not, and thus not giving oneself permission to live as an equal in the present, is extremely destructive. The desire to be superhuman, to be "worthy," is a mental and social prison maintained by superhumans. It is no coincidence that fat people who have become thin are quick to want to help other fat people over to the "right" side. This is how ideology survives: by people continuing to spread it. Fat people who stop being fat often join the band of self-proclaimed superhumans who actually believe they have achieved a higher wisdom. They believe that they have now acquired a knowledge and ability that those who are still fat lack and need. But it is not about knowledge if you feel that you are a superhuman. It is about a belief in salvation. Salvation means that you are allowed to feel liberated- by others.

And when we feel that we have achieved salvation - or purity - we want to save others. So that they don't have to live their lives in impurity, that's the superhuman in a nutshell. She has come into closer contact with God, or rather, with the sacred thin body of a distinguishing health ideology.

Trap 4: That We Stop Believing in The Liberating Power of Knowledge

Much of what we thought we knew is neither true, sustainable, nor desirable. In many cases, what we have believed is also deeply degrading to other people. The search for knowledge has gone so wrong in the case of fatness that we risk ceasing to believe in knowledge at all. I myself believe that the way forward is knowledge, after all. But to reach new knowledge, new questions are needed.

Sociologist Michael Gard argues that our beliefs are not only about why we believe what but also about what he calls the ethics of belief - that is, how we *should* believe. What is needed, he argues, is a clearer understanding of how moral, ideological, and theoretical motivations interact, intertwine, and blind us to the fact that they are beliefs.[409]

The public, through traditional obesity research, has come to believe things about fat people. By categorizing fatness not only as a disease but as an epidemic, we have all come to value fatness in a totalitarian negative way. The market, government, and science have also provided

---

[409] Gard 2011

techniques and methods to deal with fatness, both locally and globally, in everyday life. The ineffectiveness of these measures, the devaluation of fat people, and the flood of fantasies about the lives of fat people in every little health center have not stopped the management. This is because the accepted truth of a threatening obesity epidemic has been cast with a moral and cultural health ideology that has masked the underlying biomedical uncertainty about fatness.[410] The mere realization that it has been faith instead of knowledge is knowledge. Meanwhile, that is a knowledge that those who deal with fat people don't want. For fat people themselves, however, it is vital.

Despite the fact that medical science knew as early as 1958 that dieting does not work for 95% of fat people, and despite the fact that public health initiatives have not found a single cure for fatness, the same failed treatment of fat people is still being applied. We seem incapable of suspecting that the authorities could have made such gross errors. A relative once said: "Surely you understand that our authorities would not continue with something that is not good?" This view of our authorities is enviable in its naive confidence. Unfortunately, it also contributes to the continued senseless treatment of fat people.

A paradox is that a stronger biomedical knowledge focus on fatness could reduce weight-related

---

[410] Evans et al. 2008

stigmatization.[411] The stigma problem has been greatly amplified precisely because the biomedical research that really investigated metabolism, the immune system, hormone chains, and other body functions have been buried in the "fat talk" that focuses on fat people's lack of self-regulating behavior. The trap is that we risk missing the existing research that is already liberating if only it is highlighted.

Trap 5: That We Do Not Have the Energy to Participate in A Real Change

What if we don't really want to change the way things are but are comfortable with a distinguishing order? We want to separate right from wrong, bad from good, desirable behavior from less desirable behavior, right? A distinguishing order has many positive effects for many people. Otherwise, it would not continue. A society built on moralizing rituals, where we let our institutions think for us, is, in many ways, a comfortable society for many of us, especially for those who are never singled out for action. Both formal and informal rules and norms are made clear in everyday life, and conforming is immediately rewarded.

The inequality of a society creates a tension with enormous benefits for those on the 'right' side and for those hopefully striving towards it.

---

[411] Ebneter et al. 2011

People spend large parts of their lives adjusting and adapting their behavior and, at the same time, reproducing the specific social order that consists of norms and values.[412] Dieting has long been a positively charged interest for many. It is a bit of fun to do, hopeful, and encouraged by everyone. And it is creative to have goals up the hierarchy.

But singling out fat people is a very different kind of distinction than one we can use as a guide in everyday life for fat people. Fat people who openly try to lose weight get a certain amount of respect from those around them just for the effort. After all, it shows that they "know" what they should look like. But when over 95 percent gain all the weight again, plus some more, the distinction becomes more cemented. It becomes not a simple normative guideline but a weighty stigma. Therefore, it is the stigmatizing order that must be removed. But as I said, this is much more difficult than adapting to the prevailing system of discrimination.

People spend very little time trying to fundamentally change institutions. Far too much time is spent instead by the fat ones, fighting for their dignity within the distinguishing system.[413] The institutionalized management of fat people has become self-sustaining. It resists change

---

[412] Mik-Meyer 2010
[413] Brandheim 2012a

by constantly upgrading the rigid form it already has.[414] One example is how those who manage fat people today can use both health ideology and stigmatization to sell dieting to fat people. Fat people today are encouraged to lose weight both because of health and because of the stigma.

Mary Douglas has described self-sustaining systems as institutions that think for themselves.[415] She describes how members of society seem to believe that the institutions that exist there - the institutions of democracy, medicine, law, culture, and social life - are agreed on the basis of the best possible knowledge. But the truth is that the longer they have existed, the more they have become entrenched in rituals that no one feels at home with. While the human condition changes over time, institutions can be likened to slow, stagnant factories that carry on as usual. The trap here is that we just keep thinking we want it this way because that's how it is. And because there is something fundamentally good about society trying to heal problems that have arisen. No matter how and with what legitimacy, they do it. We must dare to question both medicine and other belief systems. We must even dare to question science. Otherwise, it, too, will become rigid.

---

[414] Coddington 2012
[415] Douglas 1987

Philosopher Zlavoj Zizek says we have misunderstood the real impact of ideologies on our lives. Many people believe that ideologies are superimposed on people's 'true' selves. But ideology is deeper than that, says Zizek. Ideology becomes a person's 'true self.' An ideology we have fully embraced prevents us from thinking of it as an ideology at all. It becomes the true thing. It lies beneath our emotions, behind our reason, and forms the very basis of how we live our lives.[416] Consider sociologist Jeffrey Alexander's words on power in the chapter on the threat image. He said that certain groups are singled out through appealing, rather than provocative, images.[417] The threat of an obesity epidemic is an appealing image for most people. What I have tried to show is that the construction and organization of it are not at all appealing.

Therefore, in order to change or leave an ideology, you have to turn yourself inside out and question your own innermost thoughts. This is where it lies, in the nagging thought that there must be something wrong with fat people. Because otherwise, our institutions wouldn't keep repeating that there is? It lies in the nagging thought that "it's good if doctors try to get fat people to lose weight." Then, we need to think again. We must remind ourselves that the greatest historical assaults on parts of humanity

---

[416] Zizek 1989
[417] Alexander & Smith 2003

have taken place through the ideological institutions of power.

Trap 6: That We Continue to Be Stigmatized Without Seeing Where It Comes From

When I started my thesis on how fat people are stigmatized, individuals from the health sector were unexpectedly interested in what I had to say. In my naivety, I first thought that they had realized that they were a big part of the problem and wanted to understand more. But this was not the case. They actually wanted to learn new methods to continue the war against fatness but in a less stigmatizing way. The question on the minds of healthcare professionals right now is how they can continue to emphasize the need for self-regulation among fat people in a kinder way. But they can't. They have misunderstood what full-blown systemic stigmatization is really about.

Singling out a group of people as carriers of an epidemic allegedly related to personal characteristics is always a cultural degradation. No matter if the naming is done in a 'nice' way.

When vulnerable groups are singled out in a sufficiently convincing way, the public no longer sees that someone has actively singled out the group. The identified group seems to have emerged on its own as a problem rather than being highlighted by ideological intentions. The measures aimed at fat people have been described as 'answers' to a problem that has suddenly appeared on the horizon. Yet the obesity epidemic was actually engineered by governments. It was launched as an invading virus that has darkened more and more parts of the world (by the number of fat people). The subsequent build-up of the threat has convinced people that what was identified was actually an invasive threat. They did not see that those who pointed the finger were responding to a newly awakened health ideology. An ideology that wanted to put more pressure on the individual to be pure and that saw fatness as the perfect enemy to defeat.

Ideological power is a foundation that pushes from above. It took hold in our operating institutions and eventually began to press directly on socially fragile people. The ideology, which sounded like a science, could then be used by the other layers. They could confidently exploit, agitate, hate, judge, and moralize by referring to the expertise that launched the very idea of an epidemic.

But fat people had not done anything. They had no subversive agenda. They were not contagious and were never as sick as they were portrayed. They were just fat. In fact, they just existed. In order to understand what I mean when I say that the handling of fat people has been senseless, this is central. There are many different ways of trying to improve public health. Clean water requirements, control of deadly diseases, more sanitary housing, better sewage systems and treatment facilities, good food policy, security, good elderly care, beautiful parks, a thriving culture, and global climate responsibility are just a few. These are historically important ideas that have been realized by society working together to create new living conditions for the population. Singling out fatness to justify thinness is a completely different, unethical, and inhumane dimension. Those who point out the obesity problem are not really doing anything. They are not building anything that improves people's living conditions in society. They are looking straight at the fat individuals, pointing them out as walking social problems and telling them to do something - to stop being fat.

In close relationships, it is considered violence when one partner intimidates, harms, and/or abuses the other in a way that impairs their ability to experience trust, security, and love. Today, no one can deny that fat people's life opportunities have deteriorated following the launch of an obesity epidemic. Even the old experts, health services, and pharmaceutical companies recognize or at least pretend to recognize this today. Millions of fat people today can testify to the stigmatization that has damaged their self-image reduced their social security and positioned them as failures simply because they did not have thin bodies. The trap is if fat people do not see that it is the ideologically cemented stigmatization, not their own bodies, that is the main enemy.

The Traps Are Set with Good Intentions

Scientific theorist Donna Haraway talks about "situated knowledge." It is a term that describes how the search for knowledge starts in each person's specific situation.[418] Traditional obesity researchers have had a privileged situation where they have been able to point out that knowledge about dieting is based on so-called scientific objectivity.

It's as if they don't "think" anything about fat people but look at the obesity epidemic with completely neutral eyes. However, according to Haraway and many others, there is no such objectivity. "Facts are theory-laden, and theories are value-laden."[419] Since it was privileged self-proclaimed superhumans who formed the knowledge that has been so damaging to fat people, new knowledge in the future must come from the situated experiences of the fat.

Fat people must question those who have identified them as problems. They need to counter the experts' autocratic position with knowledge based on their experience. Only when they see stigma as something actively created by other people can they challenge it. Research on the effects of racism, prejudice, and

---

[418] Haraway 1988
[419] Haraway 1984, p. 79

discrimination is clear. I repeat that stigma-induced stress both amplifies and creates illness.[420] A person does not emerge unscathed from full-scale systemic biopsychosocial devaluation. Unless she actively refuses to accept it and decides to resist. Unless she makes her body a matter of integrity rather than an arena for ideological and degrading propaganda.

The traps on the road to liberation from stigmatization are set with good intentions. The market is currently selling its slimming products through so-called empathic marketing. They say that fat people do not have it easy and that they have been treated badly. Our political authorities are scrambling to create guidelines to combat the obesity epidemic - guidelines that should not stigmatize fat people. Inside every person is the hope of being thin, super healthy, and beautiful. We are tired of the external and internal pressure to produce ourselves into something that is celebrated in the eyes of others. And so the stigmatization can continue.

Meanwhile, we are slowly but surely losing confidence in the existence of any knowledge that can make us feel good at the core.

Good intentions with bad results are a mockery. Good intentions provide those who do things to other people with moral confidence. They can imagine that any harmful

---

[420] Puhl & Heuer 2010

effects of their actions are acceptable on the path to the greater good. I am reminded of the debate where I called for schools to stop taking fat children out of their classrooms to weigh them. The response from the prominent obesity doctor was that we must do everything possible to help these children with this serious disease. Everything except listening to the harmful results of the fat kids, that is.

The morally constructed good intentions mean that those who violate, discriminate, and stigmatize fat people feel no need to listen to feedback that might change their course. They are already doing 'the right thing.' In this sense, those who deal with fatness today suffer from wisdom impotence. There is a huge hierarchy of power, with some people taking the right to do things to others without listening to their real reactions. In this power hierarchy, the subordinate is expected to adapt at the expense of their own social self-reliance. Even gratitude is expected.

Both the wisdom impotence of the self-proclaimed superhumans and the sacrifice of self-reliance by fat people are nourished by the good intentions that permeate the senseless handling of fatness. Resistance means both resisting the wisdom impotence and standing up for the self-reliance of fat people. By resisting and standing up, fat people can protect themselves from the degrading suggestions about who they are created by the idea of an obesity epidemic.

Concluding Thoughts

Unless they are broken, fat people do not need to be repaired by thin people. Thin people are no more whole than fat people. Fat people have been portrayed as broken. This has taken place via health policy, the market, the media, in-jokes and talk about fat people, and in the moralizing attempts of health care to motivate fat people to expel and reject the body's own tissue. These attempts have been fueled by selected medical science, a new public health ideology, and newly awakened eugenic attitudes towards humanity. And an unforgiving belief that fat people are stupid. It has been an abject failure from all points of view.

But there is really nothing wrong with failure. Everyone can fail. The mistake is not learning from the consequences of the management - acting with a total lack of self-criticism. The mistake is the self-righteous management of a launched obesity epidemic, where superhumans, without knowledge, made fat people feel bad about their bodies. The fault lies with all those who, with their actions, have repeated that there is something wrong with fat people. There isn't. You have the right to everything - good care, respectful treatment, relevant knowledge, a dignified self-image, the ability to face resistance and to experience a zest for life. No matter how many kilograms per square meter you weigh.

I have given my view of the driving forces behind the contempt for fat people. I have shown how they managed to keep fat people down - because they were considered wrong. I have shown how they have managed to make fat people sick - through a medically camouflaged moralism that has stigmatized rather than healed them. I have outlined how this vast system has kept fat people themselves out of the debate by dismissing them as a danger to society - as less worthy citizens. The handling of fat people has neither saved the world from the obesity epidemic nor helped sick people get well. Instead, a large-scale segregation system has made life much more difficult for fat people.

"It wasn't me," say those who have been most active in the fight against fat people. The contempt under which fat people live is increasingly visible, but no one claims to have been behind it. However, those of us who study social systems know how stigmatization can be perpetuated by people who slavishly follow an ideology. The primitive and harmful ideology of purity and danger, of thinness and fatness, is presented in small portions in everyday life. It flows through the people who incorporate it. We carry the ideology with us every day. In order not to become passive channels for the divisions of the ideology, a constantly activated self-reflection is required to even see that we carry it ourselves. Therefore, it may well be that they did not "know" what they were doing. But if they had bothered to look for knowledge about human vulnerability before they started fighting the fat people, they would have found it.

Back in 2009, as I've already told you, Canadian health researcher Lynne Maclean and colleagues called for those dealing with fat people to

- evaluate the stigmatizing effects of the methods
- be aware of the danger of singling out overweight/obese people for targeted interventions,
- provide training for all professionals on how stereotypes are formed and look like.
- provide education about fatness and about fat people
- scan mass communication of public health messages for stereotypes, blame, and disinformation.
- build self-examination mechanisms to prevent stigmatization in all interventions.
- reinforce fat people's coping strategies against social contempt.[421]

---

[421] Maclean et al. 2009

At the time of writing, thirteen years have passed since the above proposal. Although nothing has happened to the call, I added an eighth dimension: the existential one. Knowledge of the enormous sensitivity of the human being as a biological, psychological, and social organism must be developed in all organizations dealing with people.

Just one year after the obesity epidemic was launched internationally as the greatest threat to humanity after war and terrorism, a study showed the problem of focusing on weight in attempts to make fat people healthy. That was in 1998. Canadian psychology researcher Lynne Tanco had already learned that fat people can almost never reach and maintain so-called normal weight. Therefore, her research team thought that interventions aimed at increasing the well-being of fat people would be much more fruitful than focusing on weight loss. They conducted a study in which sixty-two fat women were randomly assigned to two different treatment programs. One program (CT) dealt with cognitive therapy, i.e., the women's thoughts. The second program was behavioral therapy (BT), which focused on women's behaviors. In both groups, the women lost an equivalent amount of weight. Furthermore, in the CT group, depression, anxiety, and eating disorders were significantly reduced, and self-esteem among the women increased significantly. There were no such results in the BT group. The conclusion was that the less they focused on weight loss, the better the fat people felt.[422] It has, at the time of writing, been twenty-four (24) years since the study was conducted. But I have not once heard that studies like this have been brought up in discussions about weight loss measures.

One study is a full thirteen years old, the other twenty-four. But there are even older ones. I previously reproduced psychology professor Albert Stunkard's discovery that: Most obese persons will not stay in treatment. Of those who will not stay in treatment, most will not lose weight, and of those who do lose weight, most will regain it.[423]

The above research is, at the time of writing, sixty-four (64) years old. And no study has ever refuted it. Same with the other two studies. No study has shown that stigmatization, blaming, and ignorance of stereotypes would work as a cure for fatness. No study has shown that a single-minded, rigid focus on fat people's behavior has led to any solution, either for the global obesity epidemic or for fat people. Instead, as the jurist Paul Campos rightly observed eighteen years ago, the only link so far established between health policies and fatness is that of counter-productivity, the burden placed on the shoulders of the fat.[424]

---

[422] Tanco et al. 1998
[423] Stunkard 1958
[424] Campos 2004

Government officials, new acquaintances, health ideologues, and at least one drunk at every party I've ever been to have taken the liberty of telling me I'm too fat and how to stop being so. Seriously ill people, heroin addicts, cancer patients, and dying 90-year-olds have expressed how sorry they are for me. They have seen the possibilities of my appearance, how beautiful I would be if I were thin, how many people would want to fuck me if I were thin. They have told me that I am worth being thin. They have presented themselves as my savior, my light in the darkness, as the ones who can deliver me into the world of real people. There have been many tips on recipes and different methods. And I have allowed them to continue.

They thought that, unlike them, I was emotionally obsessed, unrestrained, headless, and unsatisfied in relation to food. They told me I was sick when I was not. They told me I was sad when I was not. They told me they had the cure when they never did. They took their own thinness as a sign that they knew something I didn't. With threats and conditions disguised as motivation, they tried to make me human - thin. I also obeyed far too many times through countless periods of starvation. After each starvation period, I gained even more weight. They said it was because I probably ate even more after the starvation attempts; that I became even more emotionally obsessed with food. None of that was true. But no one believed me.

No one defended me. They were concerned about my health.

Final Words

"We cannot declare war on fatness without also declaring war on fat people. People live in these fat bodies. Therefore, the war affects them. Please stop. Please stop. Just stop." - Linda Bacon

I have witnessed fat people being humiliated and made ill. The sight of their fat bodies seems to have overshadowed all the human qualities that would otherwise be appreciated in a thin body. So much have fat people been dehumanized that, at times, they have gone into hiding, like monsters do.

When I turned my gaze outwards, rather than inwards, and started to look at what was being done to fat people, I saw the threats and the new compulsive health ideology. I saw the pathological self-image of the superhumans with which they looked down on people's vulnerabilities. At the same time, they remained unaware of their own problems. I saw how institutions put oppression into practice. They repeated ignorant and infantile advice on weight loss until people started to starve their bodies. The increasing desperation of the fat people led them to line up to surgically sew up their digestive organs and make normal eating impossible. This is the kind of thing that history books will write about.

I saw how science put the same threats in its questions and, therefore, in its answers.

And I saw how everything made fat people sick and devastated without anyone protecting them. It is still legal to discriminate against fat people. Scientists are still allowed to openly warn that the increase in "human biomass" due to "obesity" is equivalent to another 935 million people on earth.[425] Reducing fat people to a "biomass" is disgusting. If we want to do the math on the different impacts of humans on the commons, the burden of being fat would be far outweighed by the burden of over-consumption, inequality, poverty, deadly diseases, mental and physical abuse, crime, unnecessary production of goods, Big Pharma, war, chemical use, violence, aging, and the reckless exploitation of the Earth's resources. Just to name a few examples of the human impact on our planet. Again, if we are to count the human debt in the common good.

I saw how the fat got fatter, and the thin got thinner. The fat people were stressed by the distinguishing injunctions. The thin ones flowed in their proximity to the same distinguishing ideals. I listened to all the fat people who told me that they were not allowed to be healthy or sick in the same way as thin people. When they told health professionals that they felt healthy, they were told that they

---

[425] Walpole et al. 2012

were or would be sick. When they told healthcare professionals that they were sick, they were told that they were just fat. In this way, health care providers missed cancer, pneumonia, ruptured intestines, arthritis, and other serious conditions because they never even did a thorough examination of fat people's bodies. They couldn't see past the fat. Many doctors still find it difficult to touch fat people's bodies and hide their horror at the uncontrolled fat.

I saw how the lack of wisdom became chronic. Year after year, increasingly stupid proposals were made in the war on fatness. The sugar tax debate is still flourishing, raising the tax on sugar as a measure against the obesity epidemic. Of course, the so-called obesity epidemic is not because the sugar tax is too low. And, of course, a sugar tax cannot eradicate fatness.

The handling of fat people seems to have gone over everyone's head. There are now entire libraries of research on an epidemic that is said to be easy to fix. All that is needed is for fat people to stop being fat. Politicians are appointing consultants to target fat children in socio-economically disadvantaged areas. Medical centers request national guidelines on how to treat fat patients without having a single medicine for this disease. Pharmaceutical companies have built entire factory towns to keep pumping out new deceptive weight-loss drugs with unexpected side effects. And in about 6-year intervals, new "revolutionary" drugs will replace the former ones – that never worked in the long run. It seems incomprehensible that everything is allowed to continue, seemingly beyond all sense and reason.

Systems scientist Stafford Beer explained that the purpose of a system is what it does, not what it says it does.[426] I agree. Ethics researchers find over and over again that health care's focus on the behavior of fat people is not scientifically sound. It has powerfully affected people's identity, emotions, and self-image. However, none of these studies are ever highlighted as important findings.

The conclusion can only be that the system dealing with fatness wants to hurt fat people. They claimed to have good intentions, but the consequences of all the steps taken have been devastating. People's vital force, self-image, and self-reliance have been fundamentally disrupted as they are questioned as worthy citizens. The ideology of self - proclaimed superhumans, their epidemic, their medicalization, and their exploitation have ended in stigmatization and disease. As so many times before, the degradation of certain groups of people has had a fundamental systemic basis. And as I said, human beings have always been able to use ideology to harm other people. Therefore, it is not the open, purely imbecilic hatred of fat bodies expressed today on social media that

---

[426] Beer 2004

constitutes the real oppression. Those who hate do so on the basis of how fatness is treated by those in power. As a disease. As a danger. As a cost. As decay. As disgust. The fact that they claim to be doing this in the name of health, care, and good intentions does not remove an ounce of the stigma attached to fat people. Quite the contrary. The words have exacerbated the stigma. The labeling of the fat body has been dressed up in such fine words by such established institutions and on such a scale that fat people never had a chance to fight back.

Sources

Alabduljader K, Cliffe M, Sartor F, Papini G, Cox WM & Kubis H-P (2018) Ecological momentary assessment of food perceptions and eating behavior using a novel phone application in adults with or without obesity. Eating Behaviours 30: 35–41.

Albala K (2002) Eating right in the Renaissance. Berkeley: University of California Press.

Alexander JC, Eyerman R, Giesen B, Smelser NJ & Sztompka P (2004) Cultural Trauma and Collective Identity. The University of California Press.

Alexander JC & Smith P (2003) The strong program in cultural socio-logy: elements of structural hermeneutics. In J Alexander (Ed.), The Meanings of Social Life: A Cultural Sociology (11–26). New York: Oxford University Press.

Allison DB (2011) Evidence, discourse, and values in obesity-oriented policy: menu labeling as a conversation starter. International Journal of Obesity 35 (4): 464–471.

Angera O, Albertsson P, Karason K, Råmunddal T, Matejka G, James S, Lagerqvist B, Rosengren A & Omerovic E (2012) Evidence for obesity paradox in patients with acute coronary syndromes: a report from the Swedish Coronary Angiography and Angioplasty Registry. European Heart Journal, September 4.

Antonovsky A (1987) Unravelling the mystery of health: how people manage stress and stay well. San Francisco: Jossey-Bass, cop.

Arborelius E (2001) Varför gör dom inte som vi säger: teori och praktik om att påverka människors levnadsvanor. Partille Upjohn AB.

Ayo N (2012) Understanding health promotion in a neoliberal climate and the making of health-conscious citizens. Critical Public Health 22 (1): 99–105.

Bacon L & Aphramor L (2011) Weight Science: Evaluating the Evidence for a Paradigm Shift. Nutrition Journal 10 (9).

Baert P (2005) Towards a Pragmatist-Inspired Philosophy of Social Science. Acta Sociologica 48 (3): 191–203.

Ball SJ (2003) The teacher's soul and the terrors of performativity. Journal of Education Policy 18 (2): 215–228.

Barry CL, Brescoll VL, Brownell KD & Schlesinger M (2009) Obesity Metaphors: How Beliefs about the Causes of Obesity Affect Support for Public Policy. The Milbank Quarterly 87 (1): 7–47.

Bateson G (1972) Steps to an ecology of mind. New York: Ballantine Books.

Bateson N (2007) Slippery rigor. Kybernetes 36 (7/8): 1141–1142.

Baudrillard J (2001) Impossible Exchange. London: Verso Books.

BBC News (2013) Obesity is a disease in the US. Should it be? http:// www.bbc.co.uk/news/23011804 [2013-06-25]

Beausoleil N (2009) An impossible task? Preventing disordered eating in the context of the current obesity panic. In J Wright & V Harwood (Eds.), Biopolitics and the 'obesity epidemic': Governing bodies (93–107). London & New York: Routledge.

Beausoleil N & Ward P (2009) Fat panic in Canadian public health policy: obesity as different and unhealthy. Radical Psychology 8 (1).

Becker HS (1963) Outsiders: Studies in the Sociology of Deviance. New York, NY: Free Press.

Beer S (2004) World in Torment: A Time Whose Idea Must Come. Kybernetes 33 (3): 774–803.

Berg S & Grönvik L (2007) Crip Theory – en preliminär positionering. http://www.kvinfo.su.se/seminarieserier/CripTheory-enintroduktion. pdf [2011-12-01]

Best J (2004) More Damned lies and statistics: How numbers confuse public issues. Berkeley: University of California Press.

Best J (2015) Beyond Case Studies: Expanding the Constructionist Framework for Social Problems Research. Qualitative Sociology Review 11 (2): 18–33.

Biltekoff C (2007) The Terror Within Obesity in Post 9/11 U.S. Life. American Studies 48 (3): 29–48.

Bocquier A, Verger P, Basdevant A, Andreotti G, Baretge J, et al. (2005) Overweight and obesity: knowledge, attitudes, and practices of general practitioners in France. Obesity Research 13: 787–795.

Boero N (2012) Killer fat. New Jersey: Rutgers University Press.

Boero N (2013) Obesity in the media: social science weighs in. Critical Public Health 23 (3): 371–380.

Braithwaite J (1989) Crime, Shame, and Reintegration. New York: Cambridge University Press.

Brandheim S (2012a) The Misrecognition Mindset: A Trap in the Transformative Responsibility of Critical Weight Studies. Distinktion: Scandinavian Journal of Social Theory 13 (1): 93–108.

Brandheim S (2012b) Silence of a Savage: When a Trivial Health Machine Targets Overweight. Paper presented at NOOS (Nätverket i Offentlig Organisation och

Styrning) Conference: Sweden, Karlstad, Feb 9–10, 2012.

Brandheim S (2012c) Fetman pekar tillbaka: Från omforskat objekt till forskande subjekt. I K Piuva & L-B Karlsson (red.) Genusperspektiv i socialt arbete. Natur & Kultur.

Brandheim S (2012d) Psychological Distress at the Top of the Scale: The role of appreciative and condescending response. Paper presented at the International Association of Social Work Conference: Sweden, Stockholm, July 8-12, 2012.

Brandheim S, Rantakeisu U & Starrin B (2013) BMI and Psychological Distress in 68, 000 Swedish adults: A weak association when controlling for an age-gender combination. BMC Public Health 13 (68).

Brandheim S (2017) A Systemic Stigmatization of Fat People. Social Work Dissertation, Karlstad University Press.

Brandheim S (2018) Justifying Fatness Stigmatization by Animating a Self in Crisis. Critical Social Work 19 (1).

Brandheim S (2020) Den tjocka kvinnokroppens riskordningar. I J Hobbins, E Danielsson & A Sjöstedt (Red.), Genus, risk och kris (177–200). Lund Studentlitteratur.

Brown W (2006) Regulating aversion: Tolerance in the age of identity and Empire. Princeton, NJ: Princeton University Press.

Brown H (2015) Body of Truth: How Science, History, and Culture Drive Our Obsession with Weight – and What We Can Do About It. Philadelphia. PA: Da Capo Press.

Burrows L (2009) Pedagogizing families through obesity discourse. In J Wright & V Harwood (Eds.), Biopolitics and the 'obesity epidemic': Governing bodies (127–140). London and New York, NY: Routledge.

Callahan D (2013) Chasing an elusive epidemic. Hastings Centre Report 43 (1): 34–40.

Campos P (2004) The Obesity Myth: Why America's Obsession with Weight is Hazardous to your Health. New York: Gotham Press.

Campos P, Saguy A, Ernsberger P, Oliver E & Gaesser G (2006) The epidemiology of overweight and obesity: Public health crisis or moral panic. International Journal of Epidemiology 35 (1): 55–60.

Canguilhem G (1989) The normal and the pathological. New York, NY: Zone Books.

Cannella GS & Lincoln YS (2009) Deploying qualitative methods for critical social purposes. In NK Denzin & MD Giardina (Eds.), Qualitative Enquiry and Social Justice (53–80). CA, USA: Left Coast Press.

Carper JL, Orlet Fisher J & Birch LL (2000) Young girls' emerging dietary restraint and disinhibition are related to parental control in child feeding. Appetite 35 (2): 121–129.

Carr D, Jaffe KJ & Friedman MA (2008) Perceived Interpersonal Mistreatment Among Obese Americans: Do Race, Class, and Gender Matter? Obesity 16: 60–68.

Carter SM & Walls HL (2013) JAMA Forum: Separating the Science and Politics of" Obesity." By news@JAMAonFebruary14.

Casazza K, Fontaine KR, Astrup A, Birch LL, Brown AW, Bohan Brown MM, Durant N, et al. (2013) Myths, Presumptions and Facts about Obesity. New England Journal of Medicine 368: 446–454.

Cawley J (Ed.) (2011) The Oxford Handbook of the Social Science of Obesity. Oxford University Press.

Charlton JI (1998) Nothing about us without us. Disability oppression and empowerment. Berkeley: University of California Press.

Chen C, Ye Y, Zhang Y, Pan X-F & Pan A (2019) Weight change across adulthood in relation to all-cause and cause-specific mortality: prospective cohort study. BMJ 2019: 367: l5584.

Christie N (1986) 'Suitable enemy.' In H Bianchi H & R von Swaaningen (Eds.), Abolitionism: toward a non-repressive approach to crime. Amsterdam: Free University Press.

Cobb N (2007) Governance through publicity: Anti-social behavior orders, young people, and the problematization of the right to anonymity. Journal of Law and Society 34 (3): 342–373.

Coburn C (2003) Rethinking Scale: Moving Beyond Numbers to Deep and Lasting Change. Educational Research 32 (6): 3–12.

Cohen S (2002) Folk Devils and Moral Panics. The creation of the Mods and Rockers. New York, NY: Routledge.

Conrad P (2005) The Shifting Engines of Medicalization. Journal of Health and Social Behaviour 46 (1): 3–14.

Conrad P (2007) The medicalization of society. On the transformation of the human condition into treatable disorders. Baltimore: The John Hopkins University Press.

Cooper C (2007) 'Headless Fatties' [Online]. London. Available: http:// charlottecooper.net/fat/fat writing/headless-fatties-01-07.

Couldry N (2008) Reality TV or the secret theatre of neoliberalism. The Review of Education, Pedagogy, and Cultural Studies 30: 3–13.

Coveney J (2000) Food, Morals, and Meaning: The Pleasure and Anxiety of Eating. London: Routledge.

Crawford R (2004) Risk ritual and the management of control and anxiety in medical culture. Health: An Interdisciplinary Journal for the Social Study of Health, Illness and Medicine 8 (4) 505–528.

Crawford R (2006) Health as a meaningful social practice. Health 10 (4): 401–420.

Daigneault P-M (2013) Reassessing the concept of policy paradigm: aligning ontology and methodology in policy studies. Journal of European Public Policy 21 (3): 453–469.

Davis-Coelho K, Waltz J & Davis-Coelho B (2000) Awareness and prevention of bias against fat clients in psychotherapy. Professional Psychology: Research and Practice 31 (6): 682–684.

De Vogli R, Kouvonen A, Elovaino M & Marmot M (2014) Economic Globalization, Inequality and Body Mass Index: A Cross-National Analysis of 127 Countries. Critical Public Health 24 (1): 7–21.

Dew K (2012) The Cult and Science of Public Health: A Sociological Investigation. New York, NY: Berghahn Books.

Diprose R (2008) Biopolitical technologies of prevention. Health Sociology Review 17 (2): 141–150.

Dixon J & Winter C (2007) The environment of competing authorities: Saturated with choice. In J Dixon & DH Broom (Eds.), The Seven Deadly Sins of Obesity: How the Modern World Is Making Us Fat. Sydney: UNSW Press.

DN (Dagens Nyheter) (2013) http://www.dn.se/insidan/insidan–hem/varannan-kvinna-med-svar-fetma-har-kant-sig krankt [2013-03-02]

DN (Dagens Nyheter (2015) http://www.dn.se/nyheter/sverige/kommunalrad-vill-se-skarpta-krav-pa-feta/

Douglas M (1984) Purity and danger. Routledge.

Douglas M (1987) How institutions think. Syracuse University Press.

Douglas M (1992) Risk and blame: Essays in cultural theory. London and New York: Routledge.

Dutta MJ (2007) Health information processing from television: The role of health orientation. Health Communication 21: 1–9.

Ebneter DS, Latner JD & O'Brian KS (2011) Just world beliefs, causal beliefs, and acquaintance: Associations with stigma toward eating disorders and obesity. Personality and Individual Differences 51: 618–622.

Edwards P & Roberts I (2009) Population adiposity and climate change. International Journal of Epidemiology 38: 1137–1140.

Elbel B, Kersh R, Brescoll VL & Dixon LB (2009) Calorie labeling and food choices: A first look at the effects on low-income people in New York City. Health Affairs 28: 1110–1121.

Eller GM (2014) On Fat Oppression. Kennedy Institute of Ethics Journal 24 (3): 219–245.

Epstein S (1996) Impure Science: AIDS, Activism, and the Politics of Knowledge. Berkeley: University of California Press.

Erling A & Hwang CP (2004) Body-esteem in Swedish 10-year-old children. Perceptual and Motor Skills 99 (2): 437–444.

Europaparlamentet (2007) Vitbok om kost, övervikt och fetma. European Parliament's website: http://www.europarl.europa.eu

Evans J, Rich E, Davies B & Allwood R (2008) Education, Disordered Eating and Obesity Discourse: Fat Fabrications. New York, NY: Routledge.

Evans B & Colls R (2009) Measuring Fatness, Governing Bodies: The Spatialities of the Body Mass Index (BMI) in Anti-Obesity Politics. Antipode 41 (5): 1051–1083.

Fabricatore AN, Wadden TA & Foster GD (2005) Bias in health care settings. In RM Puhl et al. (Eds.), Weight Bias: Nature, Consequences, and Remedies (29–41). London: The Guildford Press.

Farrugia D (2009) Exploring stigma: medical knowledge and the stigmatization of parents of children diagnosed with an autism spectrum disorder. Sociology of Health & Illness 31 (7): 1011–1027.

Feyerabend P (1975) Against Method: Outline of an Anarchistic Theory of Knowledge. London: New Left Books.

Field AE, Austin S, Taylor C, Malspeis S, Rosner B, Rockett HR, et al. (2003) Relation between dieting and weight change among preadolescents and adolescents. Pediatrics 112: 900–906.

Fildes A, Charlton J, Rudisill C, Littlejohns P, Prevost T & Gulliford MC (2015) Probability of an Obese Person Attaining Normal Body Weight: Cohort Study Using Electronic Health Record. American Journal of Public Health 105 (9).

Flegal KM, Graubard DI, Williamson DF & Gail MH (2005) Excess Deaths Associated with Underweight, Overweight, and Obesity. JAMA 293 (15): 1861–1867.

Flegal KM, Graubard BI, Williamson DF & Gail M (2007) Cause-Specific Excess Deaths Associated with Underweight, Overweight, and Obesity. JAMA 298 (17): 2028–2037.

Flegal KM, Kit BK, Orpana H & Graubard BI (2013) Association of All-Cause Mortality with Overweight and Obesity Using Standard Body Mass Index Categories. A Systematic Review and Meta-analysis. JAMA 309 (1): 71–82.

Flegal KM, Panagiotou OA & Graubard BI (2015) Estimating population attributable fractions to quantify the health burden of obesity. Annals of Epidemiology 25: 201–207.

Forhan M & Ramos X (2013) Inequities in Healthcare: A Review of Bias and Discrimination in Obesity Treatment. Canadian Journal of Diabetes 37: 205–209.

Forrest M (2009) Swedish Obesity Specialists: Obesity and its Treatment at a Specialist Clinic in Stockholm. Masterexamensarbete i socialantropologi, Stockholms universitet.

Fothergill E, Guo J, Howard L, Kerns JC, Knuth ND, Brychta R, Chen KY, Skarullis MC, Walter M, Walter P & Hall K (2016) Persistent Metabolic Adaptation 6 Years After "The Biggest Loser" Competition. Obesity 24: 1612–1619.

Foucault M (1981) The History of Sexuality, Vol. 1 Harmondsworth: Penguin.

Foucault M (1988) Politics, philosophy, culture. London: Routledge.

Foucault M (1997) Ethics/subjectivity and truth. New York, NY: New Press.

Foucault M (2007) Security, Territory, Population: Lectures at The Collège de France 1977–78. Houndmills: Palgrave Macmillan.

Fraser N (2005) Reframing justice in a globalizing world. New Left Review 36: 69–88.

Freidson E (1988) Profession of Medicine: A Study of the Sociology of Applied Knowledge. University of Chicago Press.

Friedman KE, Ashmore JA & Applegate KL (2008) Recent experiences of weight-based stigmatization in a weight loss surgery population: psychological and behavioral correlates. Obesity (Silver Spring) 16 (Suppl. 2): 69–74.

Frye M (1983) The politics of reality: essays in feminist theories. Crossing Press.

Gard M (2011) Truth, Belief and the Cultural Politics of Obesity Scholarship and Public Health Policy. Critical Public Health 21 (1): 37–48. Obesity Studies (66-74). New York, NY: Routledge.

Gard M. (2022) Crisis revisited: historical notes on a modern "obesity epidemic." In M Gard, D Powell & J Tenorio: Routledge Handbook of Critical.

Gard M & Wright J (2005) The obesity epidemic: science, morality, and ideology. New York, NY: Routledge.

Garland-Thomson R (1997) Extraordinary Bodies: Figuring Physical Disability in American Culture and Literature. New York: Columbia University Press

GBD Obesity Collaborators, the (2017) Health Effects of Overweight and Obesity in 195 Countries over 25 Years. The New England Journal of Medicine, June 12.

Gibson O (2008) Now Jamie Oliver wants Britain on a wartime diet. The Guardian 29 March.

Gillison F (2018) Sending parents letters to fight childhood obesity does not work. The Conversation, Oct 10.

Gilman SL (1985) Difference and Pathology: stereotypes of sexuality, race, and madness. Ithaca, NY: Cornell University Press.

Gilman SL (2008) Fat: A Cultural History of Obesity. Cambridge: Polity Press.

Gilman SL (2010) Obesity: The Biography. Oxford University Press.

Goffman E (1963) Stigma: Notes on the Management of Spoiled Identity. New York, NY: Simon & Schuster.

Gracia-Arnaiz M (2010) Fat bodies and thin bodies. Cultural, biomedical, and market discourses on obesity. Appetite 55 (2): 219–225.

Greco M (2004) The Politics of Indeterminacy and the Right to Health. Theory, Culture & Society 21 (6): 1–22.

Greener J, Douglas F & van Teijlingen E (2010) More of the same? Conflicting perspectives of obesity causation and intervention amongst overweight people, health professionals, and policymakers. Social Science & Medicine 70: 1042–1049.

Greenhalgh S (2015) Fat-talk Nation: The Human Costs of America's War on Fat. Ithaca, NY: Cornell University Press.

Greenhalgh T & Wessely S (2004) 'Health for me': a sociocultural analysis of healthism in the middle classes. British Medical Bulletin 69: 197–213.

Grossberg L (2010) On the political responsibilities of cultural studies. Inter-Asia Cultural Studies 11(2): 241–247.

Guo F & Garvey T (2016) Cardiometabolic Disease Risk in Metabolically Healthy and Unhealthy Obesity: Stability of Metabolic Health Status in Adults. Obesity (Silver Spring) 24 (2): 516–525.

Guthman J (2007) Fat Ontologies? Towards a political ecology of obesity. The University of Berkeley. Presented to Berkeley Environmental Politics Colloquium, March 9.

Guthman J (2009) Teaching the politics of obesity: Insights into neoliberal embodiment and contemporary biopolitics. Antipode 41 (5): 1110–1133.

Guthman J (2013) Fatuous measures: the artefactual construction of the obesity epidemic. Critical Public Health 23 (3): 263–273.

Guthman J (2016) Opening Up the Black Box of the Body in Geographical Obesity Research: Toward a Critical, political Ecology of Fat. In M-P Kwan (Ed.), Geographies of Health, Disease, and Wellbeing (65–71) London and New York: Routledge.

Hacker JS, Huber GA, Rehm P, Schlesinger M & Valetta R (2010) Economic security at risk: Findings from the Economic Security Index. New York, NY: The Rockefeller Foundation.

Hacking I (2006) The curse of the Western world: a history of obesity. RearVision ABC Radio National. Http://www.abc.net.au/rn/rearvision/stories/2006/1765845.htm

Hafekost K, Lawrence D, Mitrou F, O'Sullivan TA & Zubrick SR (2013) Tackling overweight and obesity:

does the public health message match the science? BMC Medicine 11: 41.

Hall JA & Roter DL (2011) Physician-patient communication. In HS Friedman (Ed.), The Oxford Handbook of Health Psychology. Oxford: Oxford University Press.

Hall P & Lamont M (2009) Successful Societies. How Institutions and Culture Affect Health. Cambridge University Press.

Halse C (2009) Biocitizenship: Virtue discourses and the birth of the biocitizen. In J Wright & V Harwood (Eds.), Biopolitics and the 'obesity epidemic': Governing bodies (45–59), London, ENG: Routledge.

Haraway D (1984) Primatology is politics by other means. In R Bleier (Ed.), Feminist Approaches to Science. London: Pergamon.

Haraway D (1988) Situated Knowledges: The Science Question in Feminism and the Privilege of Partial Perspective. Feminist Studies 14 (3): 575–599.

Harrington M, Gibson S & Cottrell RC (2009) A review and meta-analysis of the effect of weight loss on all-cause mortality risk. Nutrition Research Reviews 22: 93–108.

Hartmann-Boyce J, Johns DJ, Jebb SA, Summerbell C & Aveyard P (2014) Behavioural weight management programs for adults assessed by trials conducted in everyday contexts: systematic review and meta-analysis. Obesity Reviews 15: 920–932.

Hatzenbuehler ML, Phelan JC & Link BG (2013) Stigma as a Fundamental Cause of Population Health Inequalities. American Journal of Public Health 103 (5): 813–821.

Hebl MR & Mannix LM (2003) The weight of obesity in evaluating others: a mere proximity effect. Personality and Social Psychology Bulletin 29 (1): 28–38.

Hebl MR, Ruggs EN, Singletary SL & Beal DJ (2008) Perceptions of obesity across the lifespan. Obesity (Silver Spring) 16 (2): 46–52.

Hellquist E (1922) Svensk etymologisk ordbok. Lund: CWK Gleerups förlag.

Herman CP & Polivy J (2011) The self-regulation of eating: Theoretical and practical problems. In KD Vohs & RF Baumeister (Eds.), Handbook of self-regulation: Research, theory, and applications (2nd Ed., 522–536). New York: Guilford.

Ikeda J, Lyons P, Schwartzman F & Mitchell R (2004) Self-Reported Dieting of Women with Body Mass Indexes of 30 or More. Journal of the American Dietetic Association 104: 972–974.

Jansen T, Chioncel N & Dekkers H (2006) Social cohesion and integration: Learning active citizenship. British Journal of Sociology of Education 27 (2): 189–205.

Jutel A (2009) Doctor's orders: Diagnosis, medical authority, and the exploitation of the fat body. In J Wright & V Harwood (Eds.), Biopolitics and the 'obesity epidemic': Governing bodies (60–77). London: Routledge.

Kavka M (2008) Reality Television, affect and intimacy: Reality matters. London: Palgrave Macmillan.

Keith SW, Redden DT, Katzmarzyk PT, Boggiano MM, Hanlon EC, Benca RM, et al. (2006) Putative contributors to the secular increase in obesity: exploring the roads less traveled. International Journal of Obesity 30: 1585–1594.

Kim DD & Basu A (2016) Estimating the Medical Care Costs of Obesity in the United States: systematic review, meta-analysis, and empirical analysis. Value in Health 19: 602–613.

Kira IA, Lewandowski L, Ashby JS, Templin T, Ramaswamy V & Mohanesh J (2014) The Traumatogenic Dynamics of Internalized Stigma of Mental Illness Among Arab American, Muslim, and Refugee Clients. Journal of the American Psychiatric Nurses Association 20 (4): 250–266.

Klawans HL (1989) Toscanini's Fumble and other Tales of Clinical Neurology. Bantam Books.

Komesaroff P & Thomas S (2007) Combating the obesity epidemic: Cultural problems demand cultural solutions. Internal Medicine Journal 37 (5): 287–289.

Kolata G (2004) The Fat Epidemic: He Says it is an Illusion. New York Times (Late Edition (East Coast)). New York: Jun 8, p. F.5

Krahnstoever Davidson K & Deane GD (2010) The consequence of encouraging girls to be active for weight loss. Social Science & Medicine 70: 518–525.

Krippendorff K (1994) A Recursive Theory of Communication. Departmental Papers (ASC), University of Pennsylvania.

Kuhn T (1970) The Structure of Scientific Revolutions, 2nd Ed. Chicago: University of Chicago Press.

Kvaale EP, Haslam N & Gottdiener WH (2013) The 'side effects' of medicalization: A meta-analytic review of how biogenetic explanations affect stigma. Clinical Psychology Review 33: 782–794.

Lawrence SA, Hazlett R & Abel EM (2012) Obesity-related Stigma as a Form of Oppression: Implications for Social Work Education. Social Work Education: The International Journal 31 (1): 63–74.

Leach Scully J (2004) What is a disease? Disease, disability, and their definitions. EMBO reports 5 (7): 650–653.

LeBesco K (2004) Revolting Bodies? The Struggle to Redefine Fat Identity. Amherst: University of Massachusetts.

LeBesco K (2010) Fat panic and the new morality. In J Metzl & A Kirkland (Eds.), Against Health: How Health Became the New Morality (72–82). New York University Press.

Lewis S, Thomas SL, Blood W, Castle D, Hydee J & Komesaroff PA (2011) How do obese individuals perceive and respond to the different types of obesity stigma that they encounter in their daily lives? A qualitative study. Social Science & Medicine 73: 1349–1356.

Lewis S, Thomas SL, Hyde J, Castle D, Blood RW & Komesaroff PA (2010) 'I don't eat a hamburger and large chips every day! 'A qualitative study of the impact of public health messages about obesity on obese adults. BMC Public Health 10: 309.

Liedman SE (1997) I skuggan av framtiden – modernitetens idéhistoria. Bonnier Alba.

Link BG & Phelan JC (2001) Conceptualizing stigma. Annual Review of Sociology 27: 363–385.

Lobstein T (2014) Prevalence and costs of obesity. Medicine 43 (2): 78–79.

Longhurst R (2001) Bodies: Exploring fluid boundaries. London & New York, NY: Routledge.

Loseke D (2007) The Study of Identity as Cultural, Institutional, Organizational, and Personal Narratives: Theoretical and Empirical Integrations. Sociological Quarterly 48 (4): 661–668.

Ludwig DS & Brownell KD (2009) Public health action amid scientific uncertainty: the case of restaurant calorie labeling regulations. JAMA 302 (4): 434–435.

Maclean L, Edwards N, Garrard M, Sims-Jones N, Clinton K & Ashley L (2009) Obesity, stigma, and public health planning. Health Promotion International 24 (1).

Maguire T & Haslam D (2010) The Obesity Epidemic and Its Management. London: Pharmaceutical Press.

Malhotra A, Noakes & Phinney S (2015) It's time to bust the myth of physical inactivity and obesity: You cannot outrun a bad diet. British Journal of Sports Medicine 49(15): 967–968.

Malterud K & Ulriksen K (2010) Norwegians fear fatness more than anything else – a qualitative study of normative newspaper messages on obesity and health. Patient Education and Counselling 81 (1): 47–52.

Maltz M (1960) Psycho-cybernetics. Englewood Cliffs, N.J: Prentice Hall Inc.

Mann T, Tomiyama AJ, Westling E, Lew AM, Samuels B & Chatman J (2007) Medicare's search for effective obesity treatments: diets are not the answer. American Psychologist 62: 220–233.

Maranta A, Guggenheim M, Gisler P & Pohl C (2003) The Reality of Experts and the Imagined Lay Person. Acta Sociologica 46: 150–165.

Martin CK, Das SK, Lindblad L, Racette SB, McCrory MA, Weiss EP, et al. (2011) Effect of calorie restriction on the free-living physical activity levels of nonobese humans: results of three randomized trials. Journal of Applied Physiology 110: 956–963.

McAllister EJ, Dhurandhar NV, Keith SW, Aronne LJ, Barger J, Baskin M., et al. (2009) Ten putative contributors to the obesity epidemic. Critical Reviews in Food Science and Nutrition 49: 868–913.

McClure KJ, Puhl RM & Heuer CA (2011) Obesity in the news: do photographic images of obese persons influence anti-fat attitudes? Journal of Health Communication 16: 359–371.

McHugh MC & Kasardo AE (2012) Anti-fat Prejudice: The Role of Psychology in Explication, Education, and Eradication. Sex Roles 66 (9): 617–27.

McKinnon RA, Orleans CT, Kumanyika SK, Haire-Joshu D, Krebs-Smith SM, Finkelstein EA, Brownell KD, Thompson JW & Ballard-Barbash R (2009) Considerations for an Obesity Policy Research Agenda. American Journal of Preventive Medicine 36 (4): 351–357.

McPhail D (2009) What to do with the "Tubby Hubby"? Obesity, the Crisis of Masculinity, and the Nuclear Family in Early Cold War Canada. Antipode 41 (5): 1021–1050.

Medin J & Alexanderson K (2000) Begreppen hälsa och hälsofrämjande – en litteraturstudie. Lund: Studentlitteratur.

Mehta NK and Chang VW (2011) Secular Declines in the Association Between Obesity and Mortality in the United States. Population and development review 37 (3): 435.

Meleo-Erwin Z (2012) Disrupting normal: Toward the 'ordinary and familiar' in fat politics. Feminism & Psychology 22: 388.

Merry MS & Voigt K (2014) Risk, harm, and intervention: the case of child obesity. Medical Health Care and Philosophy 17 (2): 191–200.

Metzl J & Kirkland A (2010) Against Health: Resisting the Invisible Morality. New York, NY: New York University Press.

Misheva V (2000) Shame and guilt: sociology as a poietic system. Uppsala University: sociological dissertation.

Monaghan LF (2008) Men, physical activity, and the obesity discourse: Critical understandings from a qualitative study. Sociology of Sport Journal 25 (1): 97–129.

Monaghan LF, Hollands R & Pritchard G (2010) Obesity Epidemic Entrepreneurs: Types, Practices, and Interests. Body & Society 16 (2).

Morgan DJR, Ho KM & Platell C (2019) Incidence and Determinants of Mental Health Service Use After Bariatric Surgery. JAMA Psychiatry, Sept. 25.

Morgan M, Shanahan J & Signorielli N (2009) Growing up with television: cultivation processes. In J Bryant & MB Oliver (Eds.), Media effects: Advances in theory and research (43–67). New York, NY: Routledge.

Morris GL, Chapman K, Nelson D, Cisler RA & Walker R (2014) Wisconsin physician survey on diagnosis and treatment of obesity. Journal of Patient-Centered Research and Reviews 1: 147–148.

Muncie J (2006) Critical Research. In V Jupp (Ed.), The SAGE Dictionary of Social Research Methods (52–53). London: SAGE Publications, Ltd.

Neumark-Sztainer D, Wall M, Larson NI, Eisenberg ME & Loth K (2011) Dieting and disordered eating behaviors from adolescence to young adulthood: findings from a 10-year longitudinal study. Journal of the American Dietetic Association 111 (7): 1004–11.

Nicholls S (2013) Standards and classification: A perspective on the obesity epidemic. Social Science and Medicine 87: 9–15.

Nixon S & Forman L (2008) Exploring synergies between human rights and public health ethics: A whole greater than the sum of its parts. BMC International Health & Human Rights 31 (8): 2.

Nordström P, Pedersen NL, Gustafson Y, Michaelsson K & Nordström A (2016) Risks of Myocardial Infarction, Death, and Diabetes in Identical Twin Pairs with Different Body Mass Indexes. JAMA International Medicine 176 (10): 1522–1529.

Ochner CN, Tsai AG, Kushner RF & Wadden TA (2015) Treating obesity seriously: when recommendations for lifestyle change confront biological adaptations. The Lancet. Diabetes & Endocrinology 3 (4): 232–234.

O'Dea J & Abraham S (2001) Knowledge, Beliefs, Attitudes, and Behaviours Related to Weight Control, Eating Disorders, and Body Image in Australian Trainee Home Economics and Physical Education Teachers. Journal of Nutrition Education 33: 332–340.

Ogden J & Flanagan Z (2008) Beliefs about the causes and solutions to obesity: A comparison of GPs and laypeople. Patient Education and Counselling 71 (1): 72–78.

O'Hara L & Gregg J (2012) Human Rights Casualties from the "War on Obesity": Why Focusing on Body Weight Is Inconsistent with a Human Rights Approach to Health. Fat Studies: An Interdisciplinary Journal of Body Weight and Society 1 (1): 32–46.

O'Hara L & Taylor J (2018) What's Wrong with the 'War on Obesity?' A Narrative Review of the Weight-Centered Health Paradigm and Development of the 3C Framework to Build Critical Competency for a Paradigm Shift. Sage Open: 1–28.

Oliver JE (2006) Fat Politics: The Real Story behind America's Obesity Epidemic. Oxford University Press.

Ouellette L & Hay J (2008) Makeover television, governmentality, and the good citizen. Continuum: Journal of Media & Cultural Studies 22 (4): 471–484.

Padwal RS, Wang X and Sharma AM (2012) The impact of severe obesity on post-acute rehabilitation efficiency, length of stay and hospital costs. Journal of Obesity 972365.

Patton GC, Selzer R, Coffey C, Carlin JB & Wolfe R (1999) Onset of adolescent eating disorders: population-based cohort study over 3 years. BMJ 318: 765–768.

Pearl RL (2018) Weight bias and stigma: public health implications and structural solutions. Soc Issues Policy Rev. 1(1): 146–182.

Peretti J (2013) Fat profits: how the food industry cashed in on obesity. The Guardian, Aug 7.

Peterhänsel C, Petroff D, Klinitzke G, Kersting A & Wagner B (2013) Risk of completed suicide after bariatric surgery: a systematic review. obesity Reviews 14 (369–382).

Phelan JC, Link BG & Dovidio JF (2008) Stigma and prejudice: One animal or two? Social Science and Medicine 67: 358–367.

Pickering A (2004) The science of the unknowable: Stafford Beer's cybernetic informatics. Kybernetes 33 (3/4): 499–521.

Pieterman Roel (2015) Obesity as Disease and Deviance: Risk and Morality in Early 21st Century. I Contributions from European Symbolic Interactionists: Reflections on Methods. Published online: 09 Mar 2015: 117–138.

Porz R & Bally-Zenger C (2013) The complexity of obesity – some ethical perspectives. Therapeutische Umschau 70 (2): 139–141

Puhl RM, Andreyeva T & Brownell KD (2008) Perceptions of weight discrimination: Prevalence and comparison to race and gender discrimination in America. International Journal of Obesity 32: 992–1000.

Puhl R & Brownell KD (2006) Confronting and coping with weight stigma: an investigation of overweight and obese adults. Obesity 14: 1802–1815.

Puhl RM & Heuer CA (2010) Obesity Stigma: Important Considerations for Public Health. American Journal of Public Health 100: 1019–1028.

Pulver AR (2008) An imperfect fit: Obesity, public health, and disability anti-discrimination law. Columbia Journal of Law and Social Problems 41 (3): 365–415.

Rail G & Beausoleil N (2003) Introduction: Health panic discourses and the commodification of women's health in Canada. Atlantis: A Women's Studies Journal 27 (2): 1–5.

Rail G, Holmes D & Murray SJ (2010) The politics of evidence on 'domestic terrorists': Obesity discourses and their effects. Social Theory and Health 8: 259–279.

Raphael D & Bryant T (2002) The limitations of population health as a model for a new public policy. Health Promotion International 17 (2): 189–199.

Rathbun B (2012) Politics and Paradigm Preferences: The Implicit Ideology of International Relations Scholars. International Studies Quarterly 56: 607–622.

Rice C (2007) Becoming the fat girl: Acquisition of an unfit identity. Women's Studies International 30: 158–174.

Richardson SA, Goodman N, Hastorf AH & Dornbusch SM (1961) Cultural uniformity in reaction to physical disabilities. American Sociological Review 26 (2): 241–247.

Roberto CA & Brownell KD (2011) The Imperative of Changing Public Policy to Address Obesity. In J Cawley (Ed.), The Oxford Handbook of the Social Science of Obesity (587–608). Oxford University Press.

Robstad N, Westergren T, Siebler F, Söderhamn U & Fegran L (2019) Intensive care nurses' implicit and explicit attitudes and their behavioral intentions towards obese intensive care patients. Journal of Advanced Nursing 75: 3631–3642.

Rogge MM, Greenwald M & Golden A (2004) Obesity, stigma, and civilized oppression. Advanced Nursing 27: 301–315.

Rose N (1999) Powers of Freedom: Reframing Political Thought. Cambridge University Press.

Rose N (2009) Normality and pathology in a biomedical age. The Sociological Review 57: 66–83.

Saguy AC & Riley KW (2005) Weighing both sides: morality, mortality, and framing contests over obesity.

Journal of Health Politics, Policy, and Law 30: 869–921.

Sandberg H (2004) Medier och fetma: en analys av vikt. Lund Studies in Media and Communication 8: Lund University.

Sandel M (1982) Liberalism and the Limits of Justice. New York: Cambridge University Press.

Scambler G (2006) Sociology, social structure, and health-related stigma. Psychology, Health & Medicine 11: 288–295.

Shafer MH & Ferraro KF (2011) The stigma of obesity. Social Psychology Quarterly 74 (1): 76–97.

Shildrick M (2002) Embodying the Monster. Encounters with the Vulnerable Self. London: Sage.

Shugart HA (2011) Shifting the Balance: The Contemporary Narrative of Obesity. Health Communication 26 (1): 37–47.

Shugart HA (2016) Heavy: the obesity crisis in cultural context. Oxford: Oxford University Press.

Singh K, Russell-Mayhew S, von Ranson K & Mclaren L (2018) Is there more to the equation? Weight bias and the costs of obesity. Canadian Journal of Public Health 1–4.

Smith D & Horrocks S (2013) Defining Perfect and NotSoPerfect Bodies. In J Sobal J & D Maurer (Eds.),

Weighty Issues: Fatness and Thinness as Social Problems (75–94) London: Aldine Transaction.

Smith MC (2009) Obesity as a social problem in the United States: application of the public arenas model. Policy, Politics, and Nursing Practice 10 (2): 134–142.

Socialstyrelsen (2010) Nationella riktlinjer för sjukdomsförebyggande metoder. Artikel nr. 2010-10-15. www.socialstyrelsen.se [2011-03-19]

Socialstyrelsen (2014) http://www.1177.se/Stockholm/Fakta-och rad/Sjukdomar/Fetma/ [2014-12-19]

Solheim IH (2013) Identitet, kropp og hverdagsliv i et folkelig perspektiv: og erfaringskunnskapens plass innen folkehelsetenkningen. Avhandling från Karlstad University Press.

Stice E & Van Ryzin MJ (2019) A prospective test of the temporal sequencing of risk factor emergence in the dual pathway model of eating disorders. Journal of Abnormal Psychology 128 (2): 119–128.

Stoner L, Gaffney K, Wadsworth DP & Page R (2014) Should obesity be considered a disease? Perspectives in Public Health 134 (6): 314-315.

Strandmark M (2006) Health means vital force – a phenomenological study on self-image, ability, and zest for life. Vård i Norden 79 (26): 42–47.

Stunkard A (1958) The Management of Obesity. NY State Journal of Medicine 58: 79–87.

Sukhan T (2012) Bootcamp, Brides, and BMI: Biopedagogical Narratives of Health and Belonging on Canadian Size-Transformation Television. Television & New Media 14 (3): 194–210.

Sumithran P, Prendergast LA, Delbridge E, Purcell K, Shulkes A, Kriketos A & Proietto J (2011) Long-term persistence of hormonal adaptations to weight loss. New England Journal of Medicine 365: 1597–1604.

Sutin AR, Stephan Y & Terracciano A (2015) Weight discrimination and risk of mortality. Psychological Science 26 (11): 1803–1811.

Takahashi H & Mori M (2013) Characteristics and significance of criteria for obesity disease in Japan 2011. Japanese Journal of Clinical Medicine 71 (2): 257–261.

Tanco S, Linden W & Earle T (1998) Well-Being and Morbid Obesity in Women: A Controlled Therapy Evaluation. International Journal of Eating Disorders 23: 325–339.

Tangney JP (1996) Conceptual and methodological issues in the assessment of shame and guilt. Behavior research therapy 34: 741–754.

Taubes G (2007) Do We Really Know What Makes Us Healthy? New York: New York Times Magazine.

Ten Have M, De Beaufort ID, Teixeira P, Machenbach J & Van der Heide A (2011) Ethics and prevention of overweight and obesity: An inventory. Obesity Reviews 12 (9): 669–679.

Thille P, Friedman M & Setchell J (2017) Weight-related stigma health policy. Canadian Medical Association Journal 189 (6): 223–224.

Tilly C (2004) Beständig ojämlikhet. Lund: Arkiv förlag.

Todes S (2001) Body and World. Cambridge, MA: MIT Press.

Townend L (2009) The moralizing of obesity: A new name for an old sin? Critical Social Policy 29: 171.

Tsenkova VK, Carr D, Schoeller DA & Ryff CD (2011) Perceived Weight Discrimination Amplifies the Link Between Central Adiposity and Nondiabetic Glycaemic Control (HbA1c). Annual Behavioural Medicine 41: 243–251.

Tucker T (2006) The Great Starvation Experiment. Ancel Keys and the Men Who Starved for Science. New York: Free Press.

Tylka TL, Annunziato RA, Burgard D et al. (2014) The Weight-Inclusive versus Weight-Normative Approach to Health: Evaluating the Evidence for Prioritizing

Wellbeing Over Weight loss. Journal of Obesity, Article ID 983495.

Ulrich W (2000) Reflective practice in civil society: the contribution of critically systemic thinking. Reflective Practice 1 (2): 247–268.

Valsiner J (1998) The guided mind. Cambridge, MA: Harvard University Press.

Vartanian LR & Smyth JM (2013) Primum Non-Nocere: Obesity Stigma and Public Health. Journal of Bioethical Inquiry 10 (1): 49–57.

Wacquant L (2009) Punishing the Poor: The neoliberal government of social insecurity. Duke University Press.

Wallace R & Wallace D (2003) Structured psychosocial stress and therapeutic failure. Columbia University. October 24.

Walls HL, Peeters A, Proietto J & McNeil JJ (2011) Public Health Campaigns and Obesity-A Critique. BMC Public Health 11: 136.

Walpole SC, Prieto-Merino D, Edwards P., et al. (2012) The weight of nations: an estimation of adult human biomass. BMC Public Health 12: 439.

Wann M (2009) Foreword. In E Rothblum & S Soloway (Eds.): The fat studies reader (ix–xxv). New York: New York University Press.

Ware D (2013) Against the weight of authority: Can courts solve the problem of size discrimination? Alabama Law Review 64 (5): 1175.

Warin M (2011) Foucault's progeny: Jamie Oliver and the art of governing obesity. Social Theory and Health 9 (1): 24–40.

Warin M (2022) The metabolic right between culture and liberalism in obesity interventions and policy. In M Gard, D Powell & J Tenorio: Routledge Handbook of Critical Obesity Studies (319-328). New York, NY: Routledge.

White FR (2013) "We're kind of devolving": visual tropes of evolution in obesity discourse. Critical Public Health 23 (3): 320–330.

WHO (2014) Controlling the Global Obesity Epidemic. http://www.who.int/nutrition/topics/obesity/en/ [2017-08-30]

WHO (2017) Overweight and Obesity. http://www.who.int/mediacentre/factsheets/fs311/en/index.html [2017-01-07]

Wiley LF (2013) Shame, Blame, and the Emerging Law of Obesity Control. The University of California, Davis [Vol. 47: 121]

Withrow D & Alter DA (2011) The economic burden of obesity worldwide: a systematic review of the direct costs of obesity. Obesity Reviews 12: 131–141.

Yeo G (2021) Why Calories Don't Count: How We Got the Science of Weight Loss Wrong. Pegasus.

Zizek S (1989) The Sublime Object of Ideology. London: Verso.

www.ingramcontent.com/pod-product-compliance
Lightning Source LLC
Chambersburg PA
CBHW051523020426
42333CB00016B/1746